THE INDEBTED WOMAN

CULTURE AND
ECONOMIC LIFE

THE INDEBTED WOMAN

Kinship, Sexuality, and Capitalism

ISABELLE GUÉRIN, SANTOSH KUMAR,
G. VENKATASUBRAMANIAN

STANFORD UNIVERSITY PRESS
Stanford, California

Stanford University Press
Stanford, California

Library of Congress Cataloging-in-Publication Data
Names: Guérin, Isabelle, author. | Santosh Kumar (Social worker), author. |
    Venkatasubramanian, G. (Govindan), author.
Title: The indebted woman : kinship, sexuality, and capitalism / Isabelle Guérin,
    Santosh Kumar, G. Venkatasubramanian.
Description: Stanford, California : Stanford University Press, 2023. |
    Includes bibliographical references and index.
Identifiers: LCCN 2023017517 (print) | LCCN 2023017518 (ebook) |
    ISBN 9781503636316 (cloth) | ISBN 9781503636903 (paperback) | ISBN 9781503636910 (ebook)
Subjects: LCSH: Poor women—India—Tamil Nadu—Social conditions. |
    Debt—India—Tamil Nadu. | Sex role—Economic aspects—India—Tamil Nadu. |
    Capitalism—Social aspects—India—Tamil Nadu.
Classification: LCC HQ1744.T3 G847 2023 (print) | LCC HQ1744.T3 (ebook) |
    DDC 305.48/442095482—dc23/eng/20230425
LC record available at https://lccn.loc.gov/2023017517
LC ebook record available at https://lccn.loc.gov/2023017518

Cover design: Gia Giasullo
Cover photographs: Shutterstock
Typeset by Newgen in Minion Pro 10/14

To all of our families and also to Hadrien Saiag, our anthropologist colleague and longtime friend, whose intellectual inspiration was crucial to this book. Hadrien, your absence leaves a huge void.

Contents

Tables and Figures

Tables

Figures

Authors' Note

To respect the anonymity and privacy of the women and men we talk about in this book, we have changed details of their personal lives and never mention the precise place names.

Acknowledgments

THIS BOOK HAS BEEN long in the making. We are indebted to many people, without whom this project would not have been possible.

This book is not the conclusion of a particular project but an outcome of a myriad of projects, of which we can only mention the most important. Our fieldwork was largely supported by the Institut de Recherche pour le Développement (IRD) and the French Institute of Pondicherry (IFP). Jean-Michel Servet unknowingly sowed the seeds of this book when he started his research on debt at IFP with Venkata in 2001. The Rural Microfinance and Employment (RUME) project, funded by the Agence Nationale de la Recherche (ANR, France), was a further step forward. A first survey was conducted in 2010 thanks to the invaluable commitment of Marc Roesch and Sébastien Michiels. The Observatory of Inequalities and Rural Dynamics in South India at IFP, codirected by Isabelle, Venkata, and Christophe Jalil Nordman, enabled our subsequent quantitative data collection. Our interviewers' professionalism and skill were crucial in collecting quantitative data while building personal relationships with the inhabitants, ensuring the quality not only of data but of the project's ethics. Besides Santosh and Venkata, who were involved in the data collection themselves, our thanks go to Andavan, Raja Annamalai, V. Chithra, Kumaresan, Mayan, S. Malarvizhi, B. Parameshwari, Pazhanisamy, Antony Raj, S. Rajalakshmi, R. Radhika, Sithanantham, Venkatesan, and R. Vivekraja. With the support of Isabelle, Marc Roesch, and subsequently Christophe Jalil Nordman, data management and analysis was done mainly by Youna Lanos, Sébastien Michiels, Cécile Mouchel, Arnaud Natal, and Elena Reboul. They were always very responsive and helpful.

Our three authors all carried out the ethnography, but we are very grateful to Antony Raj for his crucial role in collecting the financial diaries and their ethnographic components.

Our financial diaries data collection was made possible by the Research Program (2016–17) grant support of the Indian Council for Social Science Research (ICSSR), New Delhi. Tara Nair of Gujarat Institute for Development Research (GIDR) in Ahmedabad coordinated the project Financialisation and Its impact on Domestic Economies: An Interdisciplinary Inquiry in the Context of Select Indian States. We sincerely thank ICSSR for this funding, GIDR for hosting the research study, and Tara Nair for her crucial coordination role.

The Institute for Money, Technology and Financial Inclusion (IMTFI) has awarded us two grants, and our exchanges with Bill Maurer and his team have been highly inspiring and stimulating.

Part of the argument about unpayable debt was published in *American Ethnologist* in 2020, but since then the argument has been considerably elaborated and extended.

Joint work on data gathered from a neighboring region with Isabelle Agier, Supriya Garikipati, and Ariane Szafarz enriched our reflections on the sexual division of debt and the role of dowry.

Further short-term fieldwork was carried out throughout these years in Brazil (Isabelle and Venkata, with support from Isabelle Hillenkamp and Genauto Carvalho de França Filho), Mexico (Isabelle and Venkata, with support from Magdalena Villarreal), Morocco (Isabelle, with Solène Morvant-Roux, Jean-Yves Moisseron, and Pepita Ould-Ahmed), and in the Dominican Republic (Isabelle, again with Solène Morvant-Roux). Although not used directly, our contact with this wide range of places certainly forged our ability to think beyond the Tamil case.

Our work gradually took shape thanks to countless conversations, debates, and presentations. We presented a very preliminary outline of the idea in Barcelona in 2018, at the invitation of Susana Narotzky for her European project, Grassroot Economics. Discussions with Niko Besnier, Frances Pine, Susana, and her postdoctoral team confirmed the interest of the topic. The same year, another presentation was held in London during the SASE conference, in a miniconference organized by Joe Deville, Jeanne Lazarus, Mariana Luzzi, and José Ossandón. Once again, constructive feedback from the organizers and participants encouraged us to continue.

At Madras Institute for Development Studies (MIDS) in Chennai, S. Anandhi and M. Vijayabaskar regularly hosted us for formal presentations of our ongoing findings or informal discussions. We also had the opportunity to present our work at the Institute of Indian Technology (Chennai), Jindal Global University (Sonipat), the Indian Institute of Management (Bengaluru), the Gujarat Institute of Development Research (Ahmedabad), and the Center for Policy Research (New Delhi), all thanks to Kalpana Karunakaran, Kaveri Haritas, Rajalaxmi Kamath, Tara Nair, and Partha Mukhopadhyay. In every case, comments and suggestions from our colleagues and their teams were always constructive and extremely helpful.

The seminar Financialization from Below: A Political and Moral Economy of Debt was held from 2016 to 2019 at EHESS Paris by Isabelle, Solène Morvant-Roux, Hadrien Saiag, and Emilia Schijman, with the continuous presence of Bruno Théret, and was a fantastic opportunity to make progress on the conceptualization of debt. The organization of a final workshop in Cévennes, thanks to Hadrien and Solène, with the presence of Deborah James, Nicolas Lainez, Timothée Narring, Quentin Ravelli, Bruno Théret, and Theodora Vetta, was the occasion for a first draft of our arguments.

At the Centre d'Études en Sciences Sociales sur les Mondes Africains, Américains et Asiatiques (CESSMA), Isabelle's research unit, the gender group and its core team, Pascale Absi, Isabelle Hillenkamp, and Monique Selim, has been a constant source of inspiration.

In 2019–20, Isabelle was hosted by Didier Fassin and Marion Fourcade at the Institute for Advanced Studies (IAS) in Princeton. Exceptional working conditions, punctuated with endless phone discussions with Venkata and Santosh, enabled the book to take shape.

In early 2020, the IAS Debt Reading Group read an extremely rough and unstructured first draft of the introduction. Their feedback significantly helped us to clarify our arguments. We are grateful to Arnaud Fossier, Marion Fourcade, Lena Lavinas, Benjamin Lemoine, Susana Narotzky, Federico Neiburg, Horacio Ortiz, Fareen Parvez, Sarah Quinn, and Chloe Thurston.

In early 2021, the Beyond IAS Reading Group read a second, somewhat clearer but still improvable, version. For this, we are grateful to Marion Fourcade, Kaveri Haritas, Deborah James, Nicolas Lainez, Jeanne Lazarus, Benjamin Lemoine, Mariana Luzzi, Marek Mikuš, Susana Narotzky, Federico Neiburg, Horacio Ortiz, Fareen Parvez, Jing Wang, and Ariel Wilkis.

Regular discussions with Isabelle's former PhD students working on debt in various parts of the world—Magdalena Isaurralde, Nithya Joseph, Timothée Narring, and Elena Reboul—were always stimulating and a source of new ideas. Our chapter on financial diaries is based on joint work with Elena Reboul.

Support and advice from Marion Fourcade, Joan Scott, and Viviana Zelizer were both encouraging and very useful. Occasional discussions with Stéphanie Dos Santos, Hélène Guétat-Bernard, Kaveri Haritas, Judith Heyer, Barbara Harriss-White, Kalpana Karunakaran, Karin Kapadia, Tara Nair, Jonathan Morduch, and Christine Verschuur also helped to clarify our ideas and concepts.

Ongoing conversations with and regular rereading of chapters by Catherine Baron, Isabelle Hillenkamp, Nicolas Lainez, Susana Narotzky, Timothée Narring, Federico Neiburg, Solène Morvant-Roux, Horacio Ortiz, Monique Selim, and Jean-Michel Servet were extremely useful. Deborah James and an anonymous reviewer read the entire manuscript, and their suggestions greatly improved the first draft. The advice of and rereading by David Picherit, who has been present alongside the three authors at the IFP for over twenty years, were invaluable.

Jane Weston, in charge of proofreading the text, has been consistently available and responsive. This was funded by la Cité du Genre, IdEx Université Paris Cité, ANR-18-IDEX-0001, and Fédération Sciences Sociales Sud with IRD.

In periods of intensive fieldwork or writing, the patience of our families, sometimes limitless, has been priceless.

The editorial team at Stanford University Press has been remarkable for its attentiveness and efficiency.

Finally, our greatest debt is to those who are not mentioned here but who will be quoted throughout the book and who welcomed us in the field, talked to us, listened to us, and sometimes challenged us. Our debt to these people is real, and to those who were especially open and sharing, the debt is immense. Although incommensurable, our debt is not unpayable, and we hope in the future to have the opportunity to repay it, in an infinite cycle of exchanges that form the essence of life.

Introduction

WOMEN PLAY ONLY A minor role in contemporary financialized capitalism according to prevailing wisdom, let alone poor women. Financial actors are usually thought of as educated, wealthy men in megacities like New York, London, and Shanghai. These men are at the top of the pyramid. We picture them at work as investment bankers, hedge fund managers, financial analysts, or brokers, spending long days calculating, forecasting, buying and selling, resorting to evermore complex algorithms and mathematics. We assume that their often colossal wages must reflect rare and sought-after skills, as well as aptitude for risk-taking and great responsibility.

But if we look at the bottom of the pyramid, at the masses of ordinary people who keep the financial machine running, the key player is radically different. It is not the financial analyst or hedge fund manager but the indebted woman who is an essential cog in the wheel of capitalist finance. The indebted woman is most often ignored as a central figure of contemporary financialized capitalism. Yet without her and her hard debt work, without the multiple skills debt work requires, and without her sense of ethics and guilt, forged in her inner self and in her flesh, financialized capitalism could not operate.

This book highlights the crucial yet invisible roles played by women in the creation and consolidation of debt and credit markets and, more broadly, in the workings of capitalist economies.

1

A hallmark of contemporary capitalism is that it does not primarily finance so-called productive investment in areas such as industry, real estate, services, or trade but household debt. Under financialization, the logic of debit, credit, finance, and speculative capital serves to condition the reproduction of societies and human groups—that is to say, what makes them exist and remain sustainable.[1] Faced with stagnant incomes, rising standards of living, and reduced or absent social protection, households have to take on debt to make ends meet, cope with life's hazards, and manage life-cycle events such as births, marriages, and deaths. Since the turn of the twentieth century, household indebtedness has steadily risen. In the Global North, the rise in household debt stabilized during the global financial crisis of 2008 but subsequently increased again. In the Global South, household debt exploded over the 2010–20 decade.[2] At the time of completing this book in fall 2022, the world was facing the consequences of both the COVID-19 pandemic and the Russian war on Ukraine. Amid the biggest economic crisis since the Great Recession, household debt has continued to grow.[3]

The rise in household debt has been a concern for researchers, experts, and policy makers alike. International organizations have publicly raised the alarm about growth being driven solely by debt, including household debt, which has become the engine of consumption in many countries.[4] In 2019, the United Nations Conference on Trade and Development called for the "loudest alarm bell" on the financial vulnerability of businesses and households (UNCTAD 2019b, 76). But women's debt has mostly remained a blind spot. Little is known about it because it is most often folded into household debt, treating female and male debt as part of an inseparable whole. Yet men and women often cannot access the same borrowing sources. They do not borrow for the same reasons; nor do they build up their creditworthiness or make repayments in the same way. With household debt on the rise across most of the world, the fabric, meanings, and implications of female debt can no longer be ignored.

While economics and statistics have little to say given a lack of gendered data, historical and ethnographic studies have shed light on how women have come to specialize in expensive, degrading, and predatory loans.[5] These include the traditional pawnbroking and street-lending practices of industrializing Europe, which are very much alive today in many parts of the world. It also includes contemporary practices such as consumer credit cards, microcredit, and subprime mortgages. Beyond accessing credit services, women often take care of debt management and repayment. If money is tight and cash is needed to make ends meet, women are the ones to regularly pawn goods, manage bill arrears, juggle credit cards, deal with bailiffs, answer calls from collection agencies, file for bankruptcy, beg for help from neighbors, and deal with disapproval, contempt, or even insults from lenders, bankers, debt collectors, and bailiffs. Beyond narrow fields of research, however, their situation has tended to go unnoticed.

Predatory lending also impinges on the female body. It can involve the severe bodily dispossession of prostitution—a practice dating back to antiquity—contemporary trafficking, and sex work to repay debt. Others include "sugar daddies" who help students to pay off their loans, or the surrogacy that poor women, frequently of color, resort to in order to pay off family debt. It might seem surprising to link up such diverse cases, but what they all have in common is the corporality of women's debt. They raise the question as to whether there are also more ordinary, everyday, but neglected forms of debt's grip on female bodies.

How can we explain this sexual division of debt? What are the relations between the sexed bodies of women and the way in which they specialize in degrading and predatory forms of debt? What are the relations between the sexed bodies of women and their repayment ethics? Is female debt a product of capitalism, patriarchy, or both? How far can the sexual division of debt help us understand capitalism and patriarchy?

Feminist research has not remained silent on these questions. Philosophers, anthropologists, geographers, and political economists have denounced the hold of debt and financialization on everyday phenomena that are the very essence of life, such as food, water, caregiving, healthcare, education, housing, and marriages—activities that women are mainly responsible for and that feminists call "social reproduction" (Federici 2018, 179; Adkins and Dever 2016; Greene and Morvant-Roux 2020; Montgomerie and Tepe-Belfrage 2017; A. Roberts 2015). They have denounced debt as "the instrument by which global financial institutions pressure states to slash social spending, enforce austerity, and generally collude with investors in extracting value from defenseless populations" (Fraser 2017, 32). They have highlighted the "feminization of finance" (Allon 2014, 13) and how the poor, and women in particular, have become a new form of speculative capital for the global financial industry, always on the lookout for the market niche (Elyachar 2006; Roy 2010; Soederberg 2014; Kar 2018; Schuster 2015). They have stressed the persistent stereotyping of women as "financially illiterate," "impulsive consumers," or "paralyzed non-investors," both in social policy and in the financial industry (M. Joseph 2014, 97; Bylander 2021, 31). In their advocacy for *A Feminist Reading of Debt*, social scientists Lucí Cavallero and Verónica Gago call female debt a form of exploitation and obedience based on "financial terror" (2021, 58). In Argentina, Belgium, Greece, Sri Lanka, Morocco, and several regions across India, feminist activists are rising up against the violence of debt and its excessive weight on women and are actively campaigning for debt cancellation.[6]

This book builds on and extends this body of knowledge. Echoing feminist criticism, it examines how emerging credit markets exploit women in the classic sense of value extraction. But this involves more than an appraisal of financial markets. There is something deeper, though overlooked by feminist critique, that intimately connects debt and the very fact of being a woman, experiencing womanhood, and having a female body. We will highlight the largely unexplored ways in which capitalism transforms womanhood through debt and how this in turn feeds financial capitalism. These transformations are both shaped by and constitutive of radical transformations in kinship and sexuality systems. Exploring the co-constitution of female debt, kinship, sexuality, and capitalism is not just about deepening the narrative on capitalism and patriarchy. It reveals a different story about present forms of accumulation and womanhood. The indebted woman is consubstantial with capitalism and patriarchy. She is also their backbone.

We have adopted a unique method to best capture these processes. We have spent over two decades observing the emergence and consolidation of a capitalist credit market targeting women in South Arcot, a region in east-central Tamil Nadu in southern India. Our observations of a market under construction offer unparalleled insight into the norms, values, and mediations that support the proper functioning of a capitalist market. As is the case elsewhere in the world, women are absent from the top tiers of financial capital, and very few own or manage private financial capital. But at the very bottom of the ladder, women are unquestionably the ones who build and keep financial markets running over, through intensive debt work. Such markets can only take shape through the financial obligations of these women, on the back of their demand for credit, of their creditworthiness, and their repayment ethics.

In their pioneering European history of women's work, historians Louise Tilly and Joan Scott describe women, work, and family as "inseparable categories, defining one another and creating relationships of interdependence," showing how employers both mobilized stereotypes of women and contributed to redefining womanhood in nineteenth-century Europe (1989, 3). In contemporary South Arcot, where capitalism is just emerging and women's paid employment is on the decline, the debt/credit "dyad" (Peebles 2010, 225) is redefining womanhood. Expanding credit markets are encouraging the emergence of a new, indebted woman, especially among Dalits (former "untouchables" in Hindu theology). She has become an essential cog in the monetarization and commodification of Tamil society and its transformation into a capitalist society. But she is not just the product of the capitalist system's aggressive credit policies, as many critical voices have argued. She reflects profound changes in kinship and sexuality systems, expressing women's deep concern to improve their children's prospects, to escape caste domination, and to exist as a subject, for better or worse.

Of course, debt does not spare men, including their bodies. To pay off debt, men frequently have to leave the village, engage in slavish forms of labor, and work to exhaustion. There is, however, something unique about female debt: female debt is consubstantial with women's bodies, their sexuality, and their assignation to a status of a dependent, inferior being. Female debt is also consubstantial with women's obligations as wives, mothers, grandmothers, and daughters to maintain life.

This book sits at the crossroads of anthropology and political economics while offering further insights from history. It brings together the work of three researchers from across various disciplines, cultures, and genders. A strictly economic approach to debt would focus on wealth and income. The fact that women, on average, are poorer than men may indeed help to explain why credit is more expensive for them. There is ample evidence that women earn less and owe less than men on average, including given equal property rights and inheritance laws.[7] But why do women often make less out of investment loans than men, even given equal income and wealth levels?[8] And why, when it comes to social reproduction survival debt, do women often take on more debt and specialize in repayment?[9] And what about the emotional, moral, and bodily costs of debt? Economists often struggle to understand the gender of debt, and indeed tend to see it as irrelevant, since they usually focus on household debt as a whole.[10] Capturing women's debt requires disaggregating data by gender and using specific survey protocols since the distinction between male and female debts is sometimes blurred. It also entails calculating differently, for example by measuring repayment responsibilities, which statistics have largely ignored. As we will see, debt repayment has become the prerogative of women in South Arcot. We adapted a very useful method, the financial diary, developed by economist Jonathan Morduch and colleagues (Collins et al. 2009; Morduch and Schneider 2017), to capture gender differences.

Although anthropology is often shy about quantification, it is valuable if one is to measure the full extent of financial exploitation and its impact on women. Going well beyond counting, however, this book explores the intimate meaning of the multiple debts the indebted woman juggles. It considers the intertwining of financial debt, in the sense of monetary sum to be repaid, and moral debt, in the sense of an obligation that must be honored. And as we will see throughout this book, financial and moral debts are inseparable. Anthropology, meanwhile, helps us to understand the morality and the ambivalent nature of debt. It shows that debt can dispossess and govern bodies and subjectivities, as well as create new forms of interdependence and solidarity.[11] Credit, which is the other side of debt, creates money "from nothing" (James 2015) and may feed hopes and desires for emancipation and integration, open up new potentialities, and make care, friendship, and kinship relations sustainable, even in oppressive or precarious contexts.[12]

Our fieldwork began in 2003 and has continued into 2022. It has brought together ethnography, statistical surveys, and accounting methods such as financial diaries to examine Tamil Dalit women's experiences and life trajectories while systematically examining the specificities of this social category, region, and period of history. In South Arcot, the suffering and dilemmas of the indebted woman express the contradictions and aberrations of contemporary Indian society. We encountered unbridled capitalism, rising social inequalities, and proliferating patriarchal conservatism, which has resulted in a tragic devaluation of women. Over recent decades, neoliberal policies and mafia-style capitalism have brought nothing but ruin and despair to the poor and other disadvantaged groups (Harriss-White and Michelutti 2019; Michelutti et al. 2018; A. Shah et al. 2018). At the same time, the ruling party's Hindutva ideology continues its bid to construct a national male identity by disseminating norms of female purity and devotion (Das 1995a; Purewal 2018), even to groups that were previously spared, such as Tamil Dalit (Anandhi and Kapadia 2017). The indebted woman reflects these intertwined trends, albeit not as a unique case. Moreover, to what extent does today's indebted Dalit woman in South Arcot share experiences with a woman in postcolonial India who is chiefly indebted to her high-caste master, or to gods and goddesses (Galey 1980; Ramberg 2013)?

We will move across spaces to consider many other figures of the indebted woman, including the late-nineteenth-century working-class woman in London who would line up outside pawnshops (Tebbutt 1983), or the single mother in a neoliberal post-Pinochet Chilean slum who lives out her life in debt (Han 2012). We will also touch on some more obviously unusual cases where poor women are primarily creditors, such as the Wolof saleswomen of contemporary Senegal who take advantage of the rule of "separate purses" (Guérin 2008, 62), or the women of premodern Italy who had permission to manage their own dowries (Shaw 2018). Far beyond Tamil specificities, the indebted woman is a recurring, if changing, figure of capitalism, intertwined with kinship and sexuality norms that engrave debt in women's bodies and flesh. Our unique combination of methods and data offers a hard-hitting look at the materiality and intimacy of women's debt, bringing three key insights to light.

First, the indebted woman actively contributes to the workings of capitalism through her debt work. Extending long-standing feminist claims about women's unpaid and invisibilized work, we argue that managing debt is a true form of work. It is needed for the reproduction not only of workers but also of debtors and, by extension, of financial capitalism. This book echoes feminist debates about the blurred boundaries between sex work, monetized love, and marital sex, exploring the embodiment of debt and the multiple sexual arrangements deployed to construct and maintain women's solvency.

Second, in a challenge to dominant narratives that only highlight the corrosive role of money, markets, and private capital, we argue that the indebted woman is not only indebted to capitalism but first and foremost to her kinship group. Revisiting anthropological debates about debt as a power relationship imbued with guilt and moral conflicts, which are often restricted to class, racial, or caste domination, we argue that debt is also shaped by and constitutive of patriarchy. While debt proves itself to be an ontological condition of womanhood, this has worsened with the emergence of capitalism, dependency on the market for a livelihood, and specific norms of kinship and sexuality that assign women to a status of dependency and passive sexuality.

Third, and running counter to dominant narratives that vilify debt, we argue that the problem is not debt but debt subordinated to private capital and kinship. The indebted woman is sometimes able to create debt and credit "circuits" (Zelizer 2013, 303–4) outside the capitalist market and her kinship group, with her friends and lovers. Revisiting debates in economic and feminist anthropology on the intermingling of materiality and intimacy, we highlight the decisive role these relationships play in allowing some women to exist. They exist not only as indebted mothers, wives, sisters, or brides but also as financial subjects capable of borrowing and lending, as subjects of desire and care, and as women defying the norms of capitalism and forced sexuality from the margins.

Debt Work

Broadening the definition of work has been a major achievement in feminist studies. Far beyond the productive work of producing goods and services that are sold on a market and sometimes self-consumed, reproductive work is crucial to the very existence and reproduction of life.[13] Societies can only survive through the daily, repeated, time-consuming tasks done by women, from cleaning, cooking, caregiving, loving, and having sex to praying. The content and nature of reproductive work have varied across time, space, and social groups. As capitalism spread across Europe and North America, monetarization and dependency on the market broadened domestic and reproductive tasks. In the working classes, where money was scarce and often women's responsibility, frugal consumption and skillful management of a tiny family budget became essential skills. Sociologist Viviana Zelizer has discussed in depth what gradually became a female "domestic expertise" in the United States in the early twentieth century. Observers of the time—decision makers, activists, journalists—considered these both a "social skill" and a "sacred duty" (1994, 41). In contemporary South Arcot, even if nobody but the women themselves admit it, debt management has become both a skill and a duty. Managing debt is a routine task, requiring specific skills and know-how. It is a fully fledged form of invisible, unpaid, and devalued work.

Debt puts the poor to work, including women, and it sometimes forces them into dire working conditions (Federici 2018; Adkins and Dever 2016). It thus plays a crucial role in the proletarianization of workers under financialized capitalism. But in the event that debt flows are equal or exceed revenue flows, as in South Arcot, it is equally crucial to acknowledge debt management as real work, as some feminist scholars have already argued (Allon 2014; Kar

2018, 123; Radhakrishnan 2022, chap. 4). Extending their insights, we explore and quantify the makeup, intensity, and productivity of this debt work.

Alongside much popular opinion, many experts have claimed that reproductive work does not contribute to production or economic growth. Yet feminist research has long shown that such "unproductiveness" is a trick of the eye stemming from a biased view of wealth and the economy: work done to produce people (domestic work, childcare, schooling, affective care, and care to elders) is just as fundamental to economic growth as work done to produce commodities.[14] Women's unpaid work ensures both the biological and sociological reproduction of the workforce, making it the "essence-category" of capitalism and its "animating force" (Bhattacharya 2017, 19).

In South Arcot, much of women's unpaid work is debt work and contributes to the capitalist economy in various ways. It keeps household finances afloat while compensating for the failures of private capital, as reflected in low and irregular wages. It also helps to offset state failure, such as inadequate social protection. The financial cost of debt entails a huge transfer of wealth from households to the financial industry and dominant classes. On average, according to our 2016–17 data, households repay the equivalent of 48 percent of their income every month. For every 100 rupees earned, 48 go to servicing debt, and 30 of that toward interest payments. The scale of financial exploitation is therefore massive.

One of debt work's essential qualities—its productivity—is to minimize that cost, which varies greatly between women and households. Depending on the price women can negotiate, debt productivity either ends up feeding into private capital via high-interest payments or into family finances if cheap prices are negotiated. Throughout this book, we discuss the multiple tactics indebted women deploy to minimize the cost of debt and maintain their creditworthiness. These include putting household members to work, which primarily means husbands but also young adults. It also entails creating their own circuits of debt and credit, within which they are both borrowers and lenders. Accessing and repaying credit also, crucially, entails using one's body. From smiling, being charming, or touching to sexual penetration, women frequently use their bodies to build and maintain their creditworthiness, which has become integral to their female identity and sense of personal worth.

It is one thing to observe that female debt work is useful to capitalism. But to quote anthropologist Gayle Rubin, to argue that this usefulness "explains the genesis of the oppression of women [and, in our case, the indebted woman] is quite another" (1975, 163). Reconsidering debates on debt as a power relationship while exploring the intertwining of capitalism, kinship, and sexuality can offer us a way forward.

Debt as Power

Critical anthropologists, philosophers, and political economists conceive of debt as a power relation on a range of scales, where financial debt and moral obligation combine. Debt forges domination through financial extraction (via interest payments) but also, and sometimes primarily, through a subjectivity of guilt. Such in-depth research has documented the various ways in which debt reveals and reinforces social differentiations of class, race, and ethnicity and the various forms of infinite debt that ensue.

One of this book's key arguments is that debt is primarily a patriarchal power relation that is bound up with the rules of kinship and sexuality. We discuss throughout this book the concrete manifestations this takes in South Arcot and elsewhere, focusing on what we already know about debt as a power relation and why it is imperative to include gender in the equation.

Anthropologist David Graeber (2011) argues in his popular essay on debt—indeed the biggest best-selling anthropology book written—that monetary debt is the essence of capitalism and class society. Whereas precapitalist societies were founded on a continuous exchange of goods and services, capitalism monetizes exchanges and develops a specific debt morality, according to which "one has to pay one's debts" (2011, 4). In real life, however, not all debts and debtors are equal, and some have to pay more than others. Throughout history, the obligation to pay one's debt has above all held true for the dominated classes, while the dominant ones—today, the banking and financial system—have no such obligation and are even regularly bailed out by the state (and taxpaying citizens) in a crisis. Debt thus makes it possible to justify class relations: the dominated is in debt and is therefore "the victim who's doing something wrong" (2011, 5).

In another famous essay, *The Making of the Indebted Man*, philosopher Maurizio Lazzarato (2012) also stresses the subjective role of guilt under contemporary financialized capitalism. Austerity policies inaugurate a morality of personal responsibility, where every individual is responsible for his or her own fate. Each poor person feels guilty for her plight in a manner that

separates her from all her counterparts. The feeling of guilt conditions attitudes to oneself, to time, and to the world while shaping a faultless ethic of
repayment. It is because they feel guilty that the poor agree to pay their debts.
Here again, debt and the creditor/debtor relation are seen as class relations,
condemning the poor to endless debt.

Graeber, like Lazarotto, argues that the monetarization of obligations is at
the root of their perversion. They endorse the idea of the "commodified nightmare" raised in many critical approaches to money and the market (Fourcade and Healy 2007, 291; Maurer 2006). Yet they neglect the violence of other
forms of obligation, and the way in which they relate to and intertwine with
monetary debts and class relations. And as anthropologist Laura Bear and her
colleagues argue in their *Feminist Manifesto for the Study of Capitalism*, "class
does not exist outside of its generation in gender, race, sexuality and kinship"
(Bear et al. 2015), and also, one might add, religious and cosmological beliefs.

Debt as a power relationship consisting of material exploitation and guilt
is the foundation of much religious morality. Christian morality can be in-
terpreted as the construction of humans into beings imbued with guilt in the
face of a debt they can never repay, which philosopher Friedrich Nietzsche
describes "as eternity, as torture without end, as hell, as immeasurable punishment and guilt" (2006, 64). Morality sets up human beings as "beings of
promise": to be respectable, in one's own eyes and in the eyes of others, implies honoring one's commitments, whatever the price, whether it is offering
up one's body, the body of a member of one's family, one's work, one's life; or
even losing what one does not possess, such as one's afterlife or the salvation
of one's soul (2006, 40).

Debt as a power relationship, predicated on a combination of material
exploitation and guilt, can also be seen as the foundation of racism. Political scientist Paula Chakravartty and anthropologist Denise da Silva (2012)
interpret debt as consubstantial with racism. Racism, they argue, is about
"placing blame" on people, groups, spaces, or nations that have in fact been
produced by racial knowledge and power, for lacking moral attributes such
as self-determination, productivity, and honesty (2012, 382). This can be observed from slavery to bankruptcy of many indebted states in the Global
South, or the subprime crisis. Subprime mortgages were overwhelmingly sold
to African Americans and Hispanics. By defaulting en masse, borrowers were
accused of ignorance and irresponsibility and of being "unsuitable economic

subjects" (2012, 365). Yet it was those very subprimes, tainted by opacity and fraud, that produced these same inadequate economic subjects.

The caste hierarchy associated with Hindu theology and ideology is another form of endless debt, through which religious precepts draw on an ontological divide between Dalit and non-Dalit.[15] The term "Dalit" refers to people historically considered by Hindu theology to be outside the caste system: inferior, impure, and thus untouchable. Despite the promises of modernization and inclusion in Indian policies, Dalits remain at the bottom of the social hierarchy.[16] Though the Dalit category includes a vast number of subgroups and internal differentiations, all have one thing in common: their dehumanization and inferiorization by non-Dalits. The Dalit/non-Dalit division is therefore "racelike," both because it is a birth status from which there is no escape and due to physical and moral stereotyping (N. Roberts 2016, 3). As we will see throughout this book, these stereotypes include dirtiness and laziness, as well as promiscuity and sexual hyperactivity, irresponsibility, frivolous spending, and the inability to pay off one's debt. By creating inferior and impure beings, Hindu theology produces an endless debt that non-Dalits have to keep paying and that is owed to gods, ancestors, and higher castes.[17] We will have ample opportunity to come back to this throughout our book, highlighting the multiple meanings of caste and "dalitness" (Mosse 2020, 1227)[18] and their constant intertwining with class and gender (Kapadia 1996; Anandhi and Kapadia 2017).

There is no doubt that debt is a power relationship that reveals and reinforces hierarchies of class, race, and caste at various scales. But we can scarcely ignore gender while looking at debt as a relationship of power and domination. Graeber's key argument—that the obligation to repay is highly unequal—applies remarkably well to the Indian case but most of all to poor and Dalit women. The history of the Indian financial industry has been punctuated by fraud, default, and debt write-off for large companies, agribusinesses, and for banks themselves.[19] The overindebtedness of peasants and its tragic consequences of pauperism and suicide have long been acknowledged as a public and political problem in India. It has frequently resulted in protest and sometimes in debt cancellation.[20] Yet women's indebtedness has been ignored, despite becoming widespread. And no matter how great the crisis, they have had to pay their debt back in spades. Over the past decade, the financial industry's bad debt ratio (often called nonperforming assets) has consistently been above 10 percent.[21] This ratio has rarely exceeded 1 percent for microcredit, except during the pandemic when it rose to about 4 percent.[22] The COVID-19 pandemic and its consequences are a tragic illustration of this. While there has been mass-scale debt forgiveness in the banking industry, no similar measure has ever been granted to microcredit clients, who are almost exclusively poor women. A key argument of this book is that there is a specific female subjectivity of social inferiority, moral obligation, dependency, and guilt that forges a specific female ethic of debt. Debt is not only a power relation based in class, race, or caste but a patriarchal power relation that debt theorists have largely overlooked or even ignored.

Patriarchy and Kinship Debt

Above capitalism, gods, or dominant groups, Tamil Dalit women are all indebted to their kinship group, in a form of primordial and infinite debt that produces a guilt-based subjectivity. Women are assigned to the role of family reproducers and caretakers while being considered inferior and dependent, and they constantly feel guilty for not being up to the task. As we will see throughout this book, it is because Dalit women feel constantly obligated and guilty that they endlessly get into debt and pay it back, whatever the cost. They do this also for the sake of their families, to try to break an infinite caste debt and to climb the social ladder. Women's debt is as such the price one pays for the hope of alleviating caste and class debt. While Dalit men, as fathers, uncles, brothers, or lovers, can also be crushed by obligations and debt, women often serve as what social scientist Fiona Allon calls "providers of last resort" (2014, 16).

This has not always been the case, however. Fascinatingly, over the past two decades in Tamil Nadu, the female credit market—that is, both the microcredit industry and many so-called informal lenders—has developed concomitantly with women's transformation into dependent, economically worthless housewives. This has involved increased control over their bodies and sexuality and a significant shift in patterns of marriage alliances and payments. Whereas Tamil Dalit women in South Arcot were historically considered assets, they have now become "liabilities."[23] A clear illustration of this has been the transformation of bride price into a dowry-like practice—namely, the transfer of assets and cash from the bride's parents to the future groom's parents.[24] This book sheds light on the co-construction of finance capitalism and transformed kinship and sexuality, and the resulting devaluation of women. These have various theoretical implications for the gender of debt in South Arcot and well beyond.

It is difficult to prove the idea of matriarchal societies with women leaders and rulers.[25] Time and again, womanhood seems to entail maternal devotion, sexual availability, and social inferiority. Womanhood is defined by an original state of obligation.[26] But rather than postulate an "essence" of patriarchal debt, it is more useful to look at its "endless variety" (Kabeer 2016).[27] Feminist anthropology has argued that womanhood and manhood emerge from exchange: of bodily substances, food, care, feelings, sex, pleasure, goods, and money. In her seminal book *The Gender of the Gift*, anthropologist Marilyn Strathern (1988) points out that personal identities, gender being one among many, are made and unmade according to people's positions in webs of exchange and interdependencies. Another renowned anthropologist, Annette Weiner (1976), revisits fields previously explored by male colleagues to highlight specific circuits of female wealth that her colleagues had ignored, blinded by their own ethno- and androcentric conceptions of value. Much of the status assigned to women and gender differentials stem from definitions of value: What is a source of value and who produces and exchanges that value? Should land and agriculture, trade, industrial labor, finance, or new technologies be given primacy, or should it be beauty, art, or the quality of social relations and care? History is riddled with endless debates over the nature of value and its origin, which in turn determine the value placed on those who work to create it.[28]

How can we explain transformations in forms of exchange and value, and in the masculinity and femininity associated with them? Univocal explanations such as culture, religion, capitalism, or even biology are of no use in explaining both change and diversity. In the light of our own intellectual exploration, the most compelling explanation we have found is to look at exchange flows as the outcome of specific sexual political economies. Adopting Gayle Rubin's (1975) framework, these refer to the ways in which modes of production and accumulation are both shaped by and constitutive of norms of kinship and sexuality, often with the complicity or active support of the state.[29] Modes of production and accumulation, kinship, sexuality, and the state mutually construct each other to forge a system that makes sense in specific historical circumstances (Narotzky 1995, 122). This brings about varying degrees of access and control over resources for men and women. These variations also depend on women's positions within their own groups and life cycles (Sacks

1979). Far from being passive, or even less so a homogeneous category, women actively contribute to shaping sexual political economies and their underlying norms, whether they inhabit them, endure them, transgress them, or reinforce them (Das 1995b; Mahmood 2005).

Western marriage—contracted between two heterosexual, monogamous individuals over a lifetime and with bilateral descent and inheritance—is often seen as the norm. But it has been an exception in the history of humanity, as anthropology has long shown. Marriages can represent a union between two groups. They can be contracted with gods or with people of the same sex, this long before contemporary same-sex marriage legislation. Marriages can be seasonal or temporary and of fixed duration. Residence units can be based around the conjugal family, the extended family, and the clan, or around the mother and her offspring. Descent and inheritance can be patrilineal or matrilineal. This entails a great diversity of property rights and resource usage among men and women, brothers and sisters, elder and younger—be it in matters of land, agricultural production, symbolic goods, or cash. It also results in a wide diversity of rules for remunerating time and effort devoted to caring for others. Kinship, far from being limited to ties of consanguinity and affinity, dictates property rights and the distribution and remuneration of work. This brings extraordinarily diverse norms of sexuality and boundaries between so-called normal and deviant sex in its wake. Marriages may be chaste or even encourage a dissociation between sexuality, sexual pleasure, and procreation. Crucially, sexual and financial freedom are closely linked. Sexual passivity norms prohibit or limit women's financial freedom, which becomes branded as a sign of impurity and a risk factor for deviant sexuality. Conversely, a lack of material resources may force women to use their bodies as currency. This makes women subject to contradictory imperatives, which they must navigate with a body that is seen sometimes as an asset and sometimes as a stigma.

There is as such no universal indebted woman. But our exploration reveals a combination of processes that fuel the spread of the phenomenon. The nineteenth-century rise of the male breadwinner/female homemaker family norm under capitalism, along with market dependency, was certainly a turning point. It constructed women as wives and mothers who were supposed to be devoted to reproductive work and conjugal sexuality. But this construction turned out to be a fiction for the working classes, as feminist historians have clearly shown (Tilly and Scott 1989; Federici 2009; Mies 1998). Faced with the instability of men's employment, working-class women had no choice but to piece together odd jobs while being denigrated for transgressing respectability norms. It also fell to women to help make ends meet by taking on debt, as this went against prevailing male self-sufficiency norms. The very idea of freedom and human dignity includes self-sufficiency and freedom from all forms of attachment. But this is only for men, while women are relegated to the status of dependents and debtors. Meanwhile, women's devaluation became objectified through statistics to measure their "inactivity" and "unproductivity," reinforcing their social inferiority and lack of self-worth (Folbre 1991, 464; Nelson 1993). Passive sexuality norms imposed on women equally limit their freedom of movement and, by extension, their opportunities for employment and access to credit and debt.

What we see in South Arcot is eerily reminiscent of historical observation during the Industrial Revolution in Europe. Feminists have widely documented how employers, and private capital as a whole, continue to take advantage of the housewife norm and women's supposed dependency to pay them low wages (Mies 1998). Lenders have meanwhile grasped that new expressions of womanhood such as self-sacrifice, maternal devotion, and limited mobility due to sexual passivity norms are formidable assets. They are indeed far more useful than material securities. Dalit women in South Arcot have no property titles, no steady income, and are paid far less than men for any paid work they may do, yet despite all this, they have become a priority target for many credit providers. In line with observations elsewhere, these women's best collateral is their social resources, meaning their ability to seek help from friends and family to pay off their debts (Schuster 2015). But their bodies and their sense of obligation and dedication, which entail an inextricable sense of inferiority, are what push them to keep paying off their loans, no matter the cost.

Writing on the 1940s French bourgeoisie, philosopher Simone de Beauvoir defined the condition of womanhood as "the other . . . , the negation of masculinity. Femininity is a mutilated existence, impregnated with fault and defilement. . . . It is wounded, ashamed, worried, guilty . . . that she moves towards the future" (1990, 85).[30] Within a radically different context, South Arcot's indebted woman expresses strikingly similar torments. As we see throughout this book, she is up against not only the world but herself, seeing herself as a bad mother, a bad wife, a bad girl, or a whore. Her feelings of inferiority and guilt are engrained in her inner self and her flesh. In response, she keeps getting into debt and paying it back, in an endless process that makes the debt unpayable.

Sexuality, Guilt, and Unpayable Debt

In South Arcot, the indebted woman is caught up in an unpayable debt. Although she keeps repaying her financial debts, her kinship debt is impossible to repay. She constantly makes repayments from other debts and obligations, but it can never be extinguished. This unpayable debt involves a mixture of family obligation (taking on debt to fulfill one's duties as a mother, wife, and daughter-in-law), religious obligation (taking on the role of the good wife), aspiration (demanding eligibility for credit as proof of one's economic value), financial debt (endlessly borrowing elsewhere to pay off old debts), and repayment ethics (repaying to protect one's reputation). Lastly, there is shame and guilt. The shame stems from a social feeling toward others for being too indebted and not honoring payments on time. The guilt stems from an inner feeling of not fitting in and transgressing norms. The indebted woman often engages in transgressive sexual activities to honor her debt and maintain her creditworthiness. The initial guilt of being a woman is compounded by the guilt of a deviant sexuality.

While some debts end once they are paid off, others can never be completely settled. This is often the case with for-profit providers, who offer new loans even before maturity of the old ones. It is also often the case with some informal lenders, who only ask for regular interest payments.[31] In both cases, the extraction of value through debt is akin to a rent-based system. A perpetual financial debt is maintained through regular monetary repayments, but the unpayable debt is more than that. Not only is this debt infinite and ultimately incommensurable—its obligations are endless—but nothing seems to be able to extinguish it since each debt gives rise to new debts and new obligations.

The ambivalence of debt further complicates any analysis of the figure of the indebted woman. Debt is not only a power relation, it is also credit. If we look at credit, the other side of debt, we can better understand the singularity of contemporary financialized capitalism and the contradictions the indebted woman must contend with. Aspirations and desires are bound up with credit, which we define here as the temporary provision of a resource.

Credit is primarily a sign of trust and worth, and a promise for a desirable future (Gregory 2012; Peebles 2010). The growing indebtedness of the Global South is not simply about making ends meet: as societies become more democratic, they also respond to strong aspirations for social mobility, as social scientists Jean-Michel Servet and Hadrien Saiag (2013) have argued. Anthropologist Deborah James (2015) has discussed this in detail in the context of postapartheid South Africa. The debt/credit dyad contains a double injunction. It consists both of hopeful desire for a better future thanks to credit and of guilt if the debtor struggles to pay back (Deleuze and Guattari 1983). This double injunction takes on diverse forms, depending on the context and the social group in question. For example, anthropologist Catlin Zaloom (2019) has demonstrated how increasingly rampant student debt in the United States is forging both middle-class identity and precarity. Middle-class parents are now facing a deep moral conflict, torn between the desire to offer the best to their children and the cultural expectations of fiscal prudence that financial advisors, policy makers, and even lenders seek to instill.

The double-faced debt/credit dyad and its tragic outcomes are certainly worse for disadvantaged groups. Not only do they need credit more to make ends meet than to invest, and have to pay more because they lack capital, but their need for credit as a symbol of recognition is also greater.[32] Access to credit contributes to ordinary conceptions of a "life worth living" (Narotzky and Besnier 2014, S5). This explains the credit boom that has been observed with the emerging Black middle class in postapartheid South Africa (James 2015), the working classes of contemporary Argentina and Chile (Saiag 2020b; Gonzalez 2015), and the Fuzhounese villagers of the post-Mao era in China (Chu 2010, 5). In all these examples, eligibility to modern forms of credit is a sign of recognition and is experienced as a challenge to social differentiation along such lines as race, class, or rural "backwardness."

Tamil class and caste ideologies certainly contribute to forging the ethical dilemmas of the indebted woman. The credit market is attractive as a promised means of escaping an unpayable caste debt and lower-class condition. It is also attractive as a means for women to regain value. As we will discuss in depth in chapter 2, female paid employment has been in steady decline since the 1980s, including among Dalits in South Arcot. Dalit women are aware of their vulnerability and marginalization within an increasingly male productive economy. They are the first to demand credit in order to be "useful," as they themselves put it. This desperate need for recognition strongly fuels the rise of the indebted woman.

At the first sign of a late payment, the indebted woman faces harassment and contempt from many credit providers. Although the slightest failure is deemed her personal responsibility, her ethical dilemma lies elsewhere. The greatest moral conflict concerns the use of her body. What constantly torments her, as she kept coming back to discuss with us, is her difficulty reconciling kinship obligations, financial debt, and norms of femininity. The sexual act may cause suffering and disgust since it sometimes resembles rape. The shame and guilt of transgressive sexuality also weighs heavily on her. Another essential debt work skill emerges here—namely, being capable of seduction while limiting the risks of forced sex and protecting one's reputation and self-esteem. To ease her shame, the indebted woman deploys a range of tactics to remain discreet. She feels tempted to take on even more kinship obligations, and as such more debts, to appease her guilt. The collateralization of her body allows her to pay off some debts yet generates new ones in an endless cycle. In South Arcot, the indebted woman ultimately reflects capitalism's inability to reproduce its workers, a deep contempt for women, and increasingly unbearable caste and class inequalities. Credit offers a hope of escape.

Human Debt

As we will see throughout this book, the indebted woman is not doomed to exist but is rather a product of history. But the idea of unpayable debt may evoke a certain determinism. Is the indebted woman trapped in an endless cycle? We will discuss the range of tactics women use to transgress, circumvent, and resist their unpayable debt. As anthropologist Lila Abu-Lughod (1990) has argued, far from making heroines out of these women, these acts of transgression above all express the weight of power structures and the process by which they are transformed. Here we refer to an increasingly commoditized and male-dominated economy and the growing prohibition of female sexuality. But the weight of such unpayable debt should not hide the interstices that exist, hinting at different potential futures and a more human debt.

South Arcot's indebted woman emerged at the same time as capitalist credit markets, which in turn were shaped by the rules of kinship and sexuality. But the indebted woman continues to juggle a myriad of other debts. The women who best manage to embody their unpayable debts are those who contrive to set up debt and credit circuits outside the capitalist market and their kinship group, with their friends and lovers. These circuits are based on a logic of reciprocity and sharing. Financial transactions, care and recognition, friendship, and sometimes love and sexual pleasure come together here. Far from being antinomic, intimacy and finance are intertwined, as argued by Zelizer (2005). The indebted woman is not cut off from the market or her relatives but juggles these circuits and derives "marginal gains" (Guyer 2004, 25) from them, whether in the form of cheap loans or a reappropriation of her bodily autonomy. She plays with ceremonial gifts and countergifts; she mobilizes ceremonial networks to establish solvency on the market, and vice versa; she plays with temporalities and her body. Such juggling also involves a range of relational and emotional work that allows her to better live with her ethical dilemmas.

We should certainly not romanticize these interpersonal relationships. Lovers and friends—including female friends—can turn out to be the worst enemies: cheaters, wrongdoers, or exploiters. As remarkably shown in feminist anthropology, love and friendship emerge out of and are limited by specific structural conditions (Bernstein 2007; Brennan 2004; Constable 2010, 2009). That the indebted woman in South Arcot falls in love with her lender is certainly not a coincidence. We must, however, pay attention to what lovers and friends contribute in terms of care, affection, and love. This is understood here in its broadest sense as any form of affective communion and attachment. Ultimately, the indebted woman actively strives to exist both as a financial and creditworthy subject, and as the subject of recognition and care. Exploring the ways in which debt management confers obligations and responsibilities, as well as complex and contradictory forms of agency, helps to reveal forms of potential for a feminist emancipatory politics. Echoing pleas for a human and solidarity-based economy (Laville and Cattani 2006; Hart, Laville, and Cattani 2010; Servet 2012), women's debt circuits hint at the potential for human debts in service of a human economy. These would be sources of solidarity, equality, and recognition, rather than hierarchy, exploitation, and humiliation. For human debts to enable the emergence of a future in their own right, it not necessary for debt to disappear, it need only escape the grip of patriarchy and private capital.

The Coming Chapters

Our research has been long and painstaking, and it has ultimately pulled us in completely unexpected directions. Chapter 1 discusses the gradual construction of our collaborative research. How did the question of women's bodies, which we had completely ignored at the outset, gradually and belatedly become a central issue? It all emerged from some of the women's spontaneous personal disclosures, as they not only wanted to talk about debt but their bodies, their sexuality, and their emotions. We ultimately combined several data collection methods, which brought both advantages and challenges. While ethnography remained our primary approach, multiple questionnaire surveys were key to capturing the materiality of debt, its evolution over time, and its deep gender asymmetries. Financial diaries, as a specific form of quantification, were instrumental in capturing the extent to which debt management constitutes real work. As it is rather unusual to combine collective ethnography and numbers, we dedicate a full chapter to the process. However, a reader eager to get to the findings can easily skip it and go directly to the next chapter.

Each subsequent chapter homes in on a key facet of this constant intermingling of debt, kinship, sexuality, and capitalism. Chapter 2 traces the gradual transformation of kinship and matrimonial payment systems over the past fifty years, their growth under the neoliberal and ultranationalist policies of the past decade, and the attendant transformation of Dalit women into housewives. These changes have been both a reflection of and a catalyst for the devaluation of women and the prohibition of so-called deviant sexuality.

Chapter 3 traces back the construction of dedicated credit markets for women and the sexual division of debt. This stemmed from a blend of deep precarity, aspiration, and the desire for prosperity and independence. Having emerged at the turn of the century, credit markets have become a pervasive reality in village spaces today. Credit providers became so successful because there was such strong demand, not only to help make ends meet and compensate for a lack of social protection but also to improve children's chances in life, and to break away from, or at least weaken, historical dependencies on high castes. For women, it is also a matter of regaining economic worth, as they are increasingly unable to find paid employment.

The subsequent chapters discuss the intimacy and everyday experience of debt. Chapter 4 examines the daily management of debt within family units and the emergence of debt work as a new form of invisible, unpaid, but highly productive work. Chapter 5 considers the multiple ways in which women collateralize their bodies to establish and maintain their creditworthiness and how, over time, they have increasingly feminized their bodies to better persuade or seduce potential lenders. Chapter 6 focuses on the indebted woman in love. It discusses how, over time, certain privileged lenders become lovers, providing a source of credit, love, care, and sexual pleasure. In the collateralization of their bodies, transgressive sexuality is experienced as immoral and therefore a source of guilt. But with lender-lovers, it is sexual pleasure that is a source of guilt. Chapter 7 focuses on debts that women take on with other women, where the circulation of money intertwines with friendship and care. Here again, we witness an intermingling of financial debt and affects.

Finally, Chapter 8 puts South Arcot in greater context, with lessons for a theory of the gender of debt. Taking a detour across time and space, we revisit the multiple ways in which ideas and norms about happy and desirable marriages, and respectable sexuality, are both shaped by and constitutive of debt and credit markets. We also consider how this intermingling produces a specifically female demand for credit, female form of creditworthiness, and female repayment ethic. We equally consider the future of debt. Since the 2008 global financial crisis, many feminist antidebt struggles have been playing out in various parts of the world. This needs to be coupled with measures and policies to break the rules of kinship and sexuality, to pull the indebted woman out of her ontological status as debtor and guilty party.

1

Intimacies and Measurement

IN 2011, OUR TEAM had already been studying the effects of credit policies on rural Dalit Tamil women for several years. One day, a non-Dalit woman named Raika called Santosh. She disclosed that she had grown close to a man who helped her a lot with her business. He loaned her money, which she was paying back, but she felt he expected a further form of compensation: sex. She didn't want to betray her family values, but she cared about her business. She was therefore very hesitant and in need of advice. Over several months, she called Santosh very regularly. She was agitated, both torn and upset, by what she was about to do. Santosh felt unable to offer her any advice but listened patiently. More than a year later, Raika decided to go ahead and start a sexual relationship with her lender, calling Santosh regularly to share her ethical dilemmas. Sometime later, a Dalit woman called Pushpurani also shared the same ethical conflict, first with Santosh, then with Isabelle. Confiding this to us was a sign of deep trust, given that women's bodies are constantly scrutinized and controlled. Gradually, other women opened up about their personal lives, doubts, fears, and sometimes joys.

To understand the indebted woman as a figure, we must dive into various forms of intimacy: those concerning sex, debt, and household finance. As Zelizer wrote in the early 1990s, family financial affairs are an "uncharted territory" (1994, 43), less well known than domestic violence or marital sex. Three decades later, we know a little more about household finance and women's debt but still very little about its enmeshment with sex. And we know little about any of these in the context of India.

Raika's disclosure was certainly the starting point for this book since it inflected our research in a truly unforeseen direction. As a result of Raika's and many others' confidences, which emerged after we had spent eight years in the field, our initial project on the effects of microcredit policies gradually turned into an exploration of the mutually constitutive relationships between financial capitalism, sexuality, and kinship. Ethnographic methodology guided our approach, "with its focus on the ethnographer's surprises rather than on a pre-formulated research plan" (Tsing 2011, x). We also made use of several tools to measure women's debt, as this is a blind spot in debt statistics, in India and beyond. We used questionnaire surveys and developed inventories such as financial diaries. As we will see, measurement and counting can also lead to surprises, provided that the categories and units of analysis used fit ground realities, as ethno-accounting encourages (Cottereau and Marzok 2012). It sheds light on unexpected female productivity and women's decisive economic contribution.

Debt is not a purely economic object involving cold calculation but a reality that is both multifaceted and very intimate. Like sex, debt is imbued with feelings and emotions, some of which are unspoken, with mysteries and secrets, both private and public. Many debts are hidden within the family space. Deep trust is required, even in a questionnaire survey or a financial diary, to successfully capture and quantify, however approximately, such a confidential reality. As we will see later, female debt is a pervasive reality, a pillar of social reproduction, and a public secret.

Accessing the intimacies of sexuality and debt, and measuring debt and its evolution over time, is the outcome of almost two decades of collaboration and relationships built up with the women and men we seek to represent in this book. Over the years, these men and women have shared a part of their daily lives with us, including their aspirations, dilemmas, and questions. We—Santosh and Venkata in particular—have become "bound by bonds of reciprocity"(Narayan 1993, 672), asking questions, listening, and responding to their own questions and doubts, sometimes getting involved by sharing information, helping people with their paperwork, or fundraising. We used an improvised "patchwork" (Tsing 2011, xi) of methods over time as new issues emerged. Before setting out why, we will explain who we are and why and how we embarked on this research, which gradually became a collective venture.

A Collective Venture

Isabelle was the starting point for this long-term collaboration. Women's debt has long been one of her obsessions. Starting out with her doctoral fieldwork between France and Senegal in the late 1990s, she observed women's crucial role in household debt management among working classes. In her subsequent fieldwork in locations ranging from Morocco to the Dominican Republic to Mexico and Brazil, the figure of the indebted woman constantly returned, taking on multiple forms. With a background in economics, she quickly acknowledged ethnography as an essential instrument for grasping the noneconomic side of debt. She started her first fieldwork in Tamil Nadu in 2003, to study the impact of emerging women's credit policies at the time. She sought assistance from Venkata and Santosh, who were both trained in sociology and were highly experienced research assistants who had collaborated with various French researchers.

Very soon both Venkata and Santosh went beyond their research assistant status to become researchers in their own right. Isabelle's research then became a collective venture, driven by diverse but converging interests. For Isabelle, a middle-class French woman, understanding what is both universal and particular about female debt is a constant concern. With his high-caste landowner family background and middle-class status, Venkata is fascinated by the transformation of his own society and the role that Dalit women play in that transformation. His ongoing questioning lies in what constitutes real change and what makes for continuity. Santosh, who comes from a middle-class and middle-caste urban family, started out as an activist in a nongovernmental organization (NGO) health and AIDS community. He grew frustrated with the NGO's lack of knowledge of the ground realities and the entrenched pitfall of portraying women either as victims or heroines. His constant concern is to better understand the complexity of gender relations.

This collective venture has enabled us to take advantage of our complementary skills and sensibilities and our diverse—and sometimes shifting—personal positions in terms of our gender and cultural and social backgrounds. Such divergent positioning has allowed us to penetrate different yet enmeshed social and intimate worlds, to access different voices and narratives, and to reduce the risks of what Pierre Bourdieu calls "biographical illusion" (1986). When people tell their stories, they sometimes highlight one or another aspect of their lives, depending on the circumstances of the discussion and the person they are talking to. Collective ethnography helps us to compare and contrast different interpretations of the same observed reality.[1]

Over time, each of us took the place that the women and men accorded us. Santosh had previous research experience in the field of AIDS and sexuality, with anthropologist Frédéric Bourdier. Santosh is a part-time researcher, and his main activity is running a dance school and fitness coaching business. This probably reflects and reinforces his sensitivity to emotional and bodily issues, which are his major contribution to the book. He gradually became the confidant of several women, and a few men, gaining access to their sexual and emotional privacy. Yet this is not what he was initially looking for. It shows that in certain circumstances, some men can just as easily access and facilitate the voicing of women's confidences. Researchers, like their respondents, are subject to multiple identities, subjectivities, and sensitivities. The identification of gender, class, color, or caste certainly facilitates confidences, lending legitimacy to the researcher's voice and who he or she represents. But the ability to instill trust and create reciprocal relationships over time are also key, as we will see (Narayan 1993).

Venkata, as a full-time researcher at the IFP, had been involved in multiple research projects in the region. His wide-ranging research focuses have included employment, agrarian change, urban–rural interactions, water management, and religious rituals. He is very sensitive to questions of power, which is probably linked to the responsibilities he holds in various collectives, ranging from unionism to Sanskrit and village deity temples. He supports his own family farm in a village near the study area, which gives him thorough knowledge of local markets and prices. He is a Brahmin and always dresses in formal pants and shirt, which makes it much easier for him to gain access to government administrations and people in power. At the same time, he breaks all the rules of impurity still very much in force in Tamil villages. He drinks the water that the Dalits offer him (the three of us refuse offered food so as not to put a strain on people's budgets) and enters people's homes and sits on the floor. Throughout the research, he was instrumental in capturing both the materiality and the political economy of debt—that is, how debt is both shaped by and constitutive of power relations.

Meanwhile, Isabelle's broken Tamil left her dependent on her two field colleagues. But she was able to adopt the role of the naïve foreigner who is able to ask "silly" questions that sometimes reveal unexpected or unseen facets of field realities. She was able to share her own experiences, from France and

elsewhere, and the Tamil villagers were often curious and interested in learning about other cultures. Comparing and contrasting was often a good way
to start discussions and debates. Over time, she became the "foreigner who
is always there." Her distanced perspective allowed her to articulate obvious
realities of the local culture that her two colleagues were not always aware
of. But Santosh's two-year stay in France and Venkata's field visits to France,
Mexico, and Brazil certainly sharpened similar analytical skills.

Isabelle lived in India for two years, in 2003 and 2004, and then returned
to France to follow her partner. She returned to India two or three times a year
while her partner took care of their two children after they were born. Isabelle
is part of a generation of French middle-class women for whom independence
is supposedly a given, but that did not prevent her from feeling guilty and constantly torn between her love of her family and her professional commitment.
Her own dilemma may explain why she is so sensitive to the anguish that the
indebted woman persistently faces.

At first, Isabelle worked separately with Santosh and Venkata, before suggesting that they combine both pieces of research as the two projects capture
a facet of the complex reality of debt. The collaboration was not always easy
since their views and interpretations sometimes conflicted. The fieldwork was
rarely collective since each researcher had his or her own field techniques.
But trust was created over time, and the collective work turned into endless
conversations. The diversity of languages used—literary Tamil, spoken Tamil,
slang Tamil, French, and English—proved a constant challenge. It forced us
to debate at length the precise meaning of terms and concepts. In the field together, our respective sensitivities and positions sometimes caused us to hear
and understand different things. Ultimately, our collective work took the form
of a long "conversation" (Gudeman and Rivera 2007) punctuated by doubts,
debates, and dissensions. Nevertheless, we reached reasonable common
interpretations.

None of us lived in a village in the study area, which consists of about fifteen villages further divided into *ceri*, the Dalit settlement, and *ur*, the main
non-Dalit village. As a result, we did not become part of the continuous flows
of exchange and debt, as some ethnographers can.[2] But staying outside local
micropolitics certainly opened the door to disclosures and secrets. Our ongoing regular visits over almost twenty years have made us familiar figures
to most of the villagers, with their web of relations and exchanges with the
outside world. As with all ethnographic experiences, we developed privileged

relationships over time with "allies" and "mediators" (Selim 2021, 154, 158)—namely, people who were always willing to talk and exchange views. Some exercise roles of authority in their community, others do not. Conversely, we became confidants on sensitive, invisible issues such as sexuality and shameful debts, as well as mediators within local communities to support their access to the world beyond the village boundaries. This included sharing information about welfare programs and job opportunities, assisting with paperwork, facilitating access to hospitals or sometimes the judicial system, or more generally to any form of organization where an intermediary is commonly needed, especially for Dalits. This included buying pregnancy tests for unmarried girls, giving tips to find a marriage partner, offering advice on school quality, helping young people find employment, and also recruiting some of them ourselves to implement our questionnaire surveys, including young women. As much as possible, we avoided lending or giving cash. But we regularly raised funds for educational support or to tackle cases of hardship, be it individual (a widow losing her house, a mother seeking to educate her handicapped daughter, a family facing a run of adverse events and sinking into destitution) or collective hardship (food distribution support during the pandemic).

The Surprises of Ethnography

Let's return to Raika's disclosure. Unbeknownst to us at the time, these disclosures would transform our research questions. Our questions had hitherto been shaped by a careful analysis of the political and moral economies of debt—that is, how debt is both shaped by and constitutive of broader power structures—while also being imbued with subjectivities and obligations. But we had completely missed the issues of sexuality. We had a feeling that sex-for-cash transactions existed, but we did not suspect to what extent, or how ambivalent they were. The use of female bodies in exchange for credit or debt repayment remains underexplored, which is precisely the motivation for this book. But feminist anthropology has long shown that women deprived of material resources often only have sex left as a resource (G. Rubin 1975; Tabet 2012).

The fact that it took us so long to understand the intertwining of debt and sexuality probably indicates two things. First, very little is known about the sexuality of Tamil women, including Dalit women. We were not immune from stereotypes, at least initially, that depicted women as either hypersexual or as simply victims of forced sex (Bourdier 2001). But as time went by, we discovered a rich sexuality. It was largely coercive but did not exclude pleasure, at least for some women, imbued with a frequent feeling of guilt due to the increasingly prevailing norms of chastity. Throughout this research, we struggled to account for these tensions.

Secrecy is the second factor. Extramarital sex is only imaginable if it is kept secret. To preserve their own reputation, as well as that of their husband and kin, and to maintain their microfreedom, women spend considerable energy concealing their extramarital sexuality, be it voluntary or forced—the boundary between the two of course being very blurred. Often, the secrecy is partial: complicity between close friends is necessary. Most extramarital sex takes place outside the village. The conspiracy entails confirming the excuses the women give for being away. The most frequent and plausible excuses given are NGO meetings; transactions at the bank or the pawnbroker; visits to doctor, hospital, prefecture, or any other government office; shopping; or visiting their mother's place. It also entails listening for rumors and challenging them. Neighbors, husbands, and in-laws are hardly fooled, but what matters is that the information does not become public, or at least does not leave the neighborhood.

After Raika, some other women—all Dalits apart from Raika, about ten in total—shared their confidences. It was unthinkable to ask direct questions or force any disclosures. But a handful of women from several villages also told us about their close circle. These women took us carefully through the workings of sexual bargaining with lenders. In return, discussions with lenders and observations of transactions between lenders and their female clients confirmed the prevalence of sex in daily debt arrangements. While we cannot give figures, it is clear that sex-for-debt exchanges are not a marginal phenomenon.[3] Just because it was mainly Dalit women who told us about it does not make this reality unique to Dalits. It reflects the fact that we were much more in touch with Dalit women, and that they had greater freedom of speech.[4] The women also shared their moral dilemmas, the tensions and contradictions they have to contend with, the suffering this causes, and the meanings they attribute to their practices and transactions. Some still regularly call Santosh to ask for advice. Far beyond their repayment difficulties, they want to express their moral anxiety over value conflicts: fulfilling their obligations as mothers and wives, forcing some of them into sex-for-debt exchanges, while pretending to uphold the norms of chastity, passive sexuality, and marital fidelity. This moral anxiety is an ongoing, pervasive concern.

Ultimately, the intertwining of debt and sexuality in the life of the indebted woman has been one of the surprises of our ethnography. Although it was by no means part of our research agenda, it gradually became clear that the indebted woman constantly juggles debts and her body, that she is fighting against the world but also against herself. This is what she wanted to talk about with outsiders like us.

Of the three of us, Santosh is the one who draws out confidences, albeit never on a premeditated basis. He has often been asked, especially by anthropologists familiar with India and aware of the sensitivity of the subject: "What tricks do you use to make women talk?" Indeed, how did this male become privy to intimate details that many ethnographers, including female ones, never could? Certainly, women confided in him because they wanted to share their own ethical concerns and were seeking a listening ear to help them accept their own dilemmas. The way they justified and framed their behavior clearly helped them cope with their predicament and certainly explained their need to confide. Yet by doing so, the women were revealing themselves, exposing their lives, and taking considerable risks by discussing acts of social transgression considered highly reprehensible, both morally and physically.

For all three of us, this question also became a methodological discussion point without a clear answer. The reason some people confide in one person over another is a complex issue. Santosh took the question back to his confidants: "Why do you disclose your intimate life to me?" They all answered: "You don't judge us." His previous experience as a research assistant on AIDS and prostitution certainly helped him become comfortable talking about sex, putting his interlocutors at ease. Although indebted Dalit women mostly confided in Santosh, Isabelle's intermittent presence probably helped build trust. It was a matter of our long-term presence, our strong personal commitment, and also our atypical sexual status—namely, a European woman traveling without her partner and a married Indian man who agreed to accompany her everywhere. We never lived in their villages, which distanced us from local gossip, and that probably also helped. Discussions took place over telephone, initially at the instigation of the women themselves. Sometimes some of them visited Santosh in his own home to be able to talk more freely. The social promiscuity of the villages prevented any confidences being made in the open.

Initially, Santosh simply listened. The women regularly raised their doubts and questions about what is wrong or good, what is acceptable or not. He gradually dared to ask questions, about both their own situations and those of the women in their orbit, treading very carefully, given the topic's taboo. In time, Santosh felt more comfortable and did not just listen. He shared his own premarital love misadventures. He also disclosed that he was sensitive to the charm of some women other than his wife but that it is not a sin. As a fitness coach for urban middle- and upper-class women and men, he receives many confidences about the emotional and sometimes sexual lives of his clients. Without revealing anything personal, he shared some anecdotes about them and reassured his confidants that their situations were not unusual. Sharing his personal experiences certainly helped. Finally, his stature—he is a former bodybuilding champion and has maintained a very muscular build—surely helped to put them at ease. In the villages, no man has ever dared to challenge him. Of course, we were careful to respect the secrets that the women and men entrusted to us. Beyond anonymity, we have altered many of the disclosures and intimate details of people's lives to preserve their privacy and dignity.

Why Measure Debt?

This surprise twist of our ethnography did not bring us to drop our initial, more classical research aimed at quantifying and contextualizing debt in the local political economies in which Venkata is an expert. No statistics existed on female debt, and we believed such quantification was indispensable to grasping the materiality, magnitude, evolution, and cost of that debt. We considered that debt's multiple realities and meanings form a social whole, which eventually becomes intelligible thanks to methodological diversity.

Quantitatively speaking, it is remarkable how little we still know about women's debt, including far beyond India. This also explains why it is not considered a problem. In a world dominated by numbers, what is not counted does not count (Waring 1999). There are three major explanations for the lack of, or biases about, quantification of female debt.

The persistence of the statistical unit of the household is the first explanation, along with the assumption that debts are managed by the household as an undifferentiated whole. According to the definition of economists and statisticians, the term "household" refers to the residential unit, to people who live under the same roof and share meals. We also use it in this sense, interchangeably with "family," reserving the term "kinship" for broader family relationships when opening the black box of intrahousehold financial responsibilities. As we discussed in the introduction, it is well known that contemporary capitalism is both shaped by and constitutive of household debt. It is also widely known that a growing proportion of household debt is not about investing for the future but rather making ends meet and compensating for insufficient income and absent or inadequate social protection. This has been well documented and widely quantified. But curiously, the gender of household debt has been virtually ignored and has defied quantification. The only exceptions are for student debt and single women's debt (Reboul, Guérin, and Nordman 2021; Reboul 2021).

Specific approaches to debt and credit are a second factor. As Scott has argued, statistics are "neither totally neutral collections of fact nor simply ideological impositions. Rather they are ways of establishing the authority of certain visions of social order, of organizing perceptions of 'experience'" (1988, 115). For many policy makers, experts, and researchers, the problem is not debt but financial exclusion. This refers to the inability of people, and women in particular, to access formal financial tools—that is, tools offered by entities regulated by law. In the Global South, a large proportion of financial practices eludes regulation, India being no exception. Much effort has as such been devoted to improving financial inclusion.[5] As a consequence, most available surveys of women's financial lives have focused on the degree of their financial exclusion (or, conversely, financial inclusion), and rarely on the amount of debt.

This is the case of the World Bank's Findex survey, the first international survey to gather gender-disaggregated financial data. The survey has been conducted every three years since 2011 across 140 countries and with around 150,000 adult participants. It has provided very detailed data on sources of borrowing, saving, transfers, and insurance. The survey shows that while financial inclusion is growing, including among women, the gender gap persists.[6] India is among the top performers: financial inclusion has more than doubled between 2011 and 2017, from 35 to 80 percent (as opposed to 69 percent worldwide), and for Indian women it has almost tripled, from 26 to 75 percent (as opposed to 62 percent worldwide) (Demirgüç-Kunt et al. 2018).[7] Like all statistics, indicators of financial exclusion are not value-free but create particular norms around desirable financial behavior. These indicators somehow create a void to be filled, a market to be created in order to wipe out an exclusion deemed undesirable. Some people may already be heavily indebted and need to get out of debt or limit it as a priority, but this is not on the agenda. The Findex survey can tell us how many women are in debt and from what sources, but we have no idea how much debt they have.

The third issue with debt measurement is data unreliability. Take the case of the All India Debt and Investment Survey (AIDIS), conducted in 1951–52 by the Reserve Bank of India and repeated six times since then. Time tracking is a great opportunity to capture the transformation of debt over time, at least at the household level (as elsewhere, the data are not disaggregated by gender). Unfortunately, the debt amounts seem quite unrealistic. The most recent AIDIS survey conducted in rural Tamil Nadu in 2012 revealed that 30 percent of households were indebted, with an average outstanding debt of around INR 32,000 (USD 500)[8] (NSSO 2014). In our own three surveys from 2010 to 2020, the share of indebted households was 99 or 100 percent, and in 2010, the closest date to the AIDIS survey, the average outstanding debt per household was around INR 90,000 (USD 1,400). Our survey focuses on a small region of Tamil Nadu, but there is no reason for debt to be higher there than elsewhere in the state. The gap is such as to make one wonder what the AIDIS data means. This problem is by no means specific to India. In contexts ranging from the United States to South Africa, people are estimated to underreport their debt by half on average (Karlan and Zinman 2008; Zinman 2009).

Debt is a sensitive, intimate, and unstable reality, making its measurement a challenge. Whatever the context, people don't necessarily want to tell strangers about their personal financial lives. Moreover, what we, as researchers, consider as debt—a sum of money to be repaid—is not necessarily qualified as such by our interlocutors. The disparity stems from what statisticians know well as social desirability bias. Respondents are likely to respond based on what is socially desirable and acceptable, and what they want the interviewer to see. The disparity is also down to a very wide range of transactions and underlying relationships. In his groundbreaking ethnography of village indebtedness in Chhattisgarh (central India), anthropologist Chris Gregory argues that the figure of the moneylender was a colonial imaginary, while the local financial reality showed a diversity of profiles and practices (1997, chap. 6). We observe a similar diversity here. Most indebted women juggle two, three, four, five, fifteen, or even more debts at once, most often from highly diversified sources, which are not necessarily termed or experienced as debt. The money will have to be paid back one day, but women (like men) do not necessarily use the term "debt."

The word *kadan*, like the English term "being in debt," refers to both financial debt and moral obligation. When people talk about their personal situation and a particular financial transaction, *kadan* may signify a feeling of pressure, stress, and possibly shame. "Exchange of money" and "help" are used more often in the first instance and convey the idea of interpersonal relations, trust, and negotiability, although this does not preclude interest rates and possible strong sanctions for nonrepayment. The terms used refer as much to what the debtors expect as to what the relationship actually is. Their expectations are not at all unrealistic: for better or for worse, negotiability is the rule in informal, unregulated debt. To describe the debt as "help" is to hope that the lender will agree to postpone the due dates and reduce the cost. Lenders are not referred as lenders but as *terinjavangal*, which is best translated as "known person," and which also refers to the idea of mutual acquaintanceship, trust, and potential negotiability. Conversely, a pejorative term, used mainly to criticize prices and sanctions deemed abusive, is *kandhu vatti*, which literally means "meter interest" or "running interest."

The English terms "loan" and "finance" are now part of the common Tamil language. "Loan" refers specifically to bank loans. Both in popular opinion and in practice, loans are reserved for the richest individuals, mostly men, and repayment is rarely considered an obligation, due to regular debt write-offs offered at the whim of political agendas.[9] "Finance" refers to the financial companies that have emerged over the last twenty years and provide micro-loans, for the most part to women. In general discussions, these transactions are qualified as debt (*kadan*) together with an adjective to specify what distinguishes these transactions from usual ones. These unusual features include, for example, the targeting of women (*magalir kadan* or *pombalaingal kadan*, which literally means "female indebtedness"), the principle of group guarantee (*kuhzu kadan* or *kuttu kadan*, which means "group loans"), and regular monthly repayment amounts (*masa masam kattara kadan*, or the English acronym EMI, for equated monthly installment). Conversely, when people talk about their own situations, they sometimes reject the term *kadan* to convey that repayment will not be a problem.

Other very common debts are determined by the lender's profile. Door-to-door informal lenders are called *thandals*, best translated as "instant," in reference to the speed and simplicity of disbursement. *Settu* historically referred to a pawnbroking subcaste. By extension, it has been taken up for all forms of pawnbroking, even though pawnbrokers are now very diverse in caste. Small reciprocal debts circulating between friends and close relatives are not qualified as debt but as *kai mathu*, which literally means "changing hands." But the obligation to repay is scarcely open to negotiation and is implicitly set at a very short deadline of a few days or a few weeks or, at the latest, when the lender himself or herself needs the liquidity. Note that not all people use these local terminologies. Many women and men refer to their lender by name (including for microcredit loan officers), by day (for door-to-door moneylenders), or by caste.

Not only is debt a multifaceted reality, but Tamil villagers have a peculiar sense of number and quantity. As anthropologist Arun Appadurai (1989) has argued, in many non-Western contexts, and rural India is a good example, it is not appropriate to reason in terms of an ordinal, continuous variable. A raw quantity often has little meaning, and so it is often expressed approximately, contextually, qualitatively, and comparatively. For example, to the question "How much money did you take from a given lender?" respondents frequently answer "far too much" or alternatively "he gave me little." To the question "How much rice did you harvest this year?" people may answer "less than I expected," "more than last year," or "less than the neighboring village." In regard to a saree or a piece of jewelry, what counts more than price is the place of purchase, which is more or less prestigious in terms of the talent of the weavers or jewelers. Value is estimated along these lines, as well as in terms of the type of event the item was purchased for, such as for a son's first birthday or a daughter's wedding.

For all these reasons, measuring debt is a serious challenge. The statistician's struggle is evocative of the experience of economist Phyllis Deane when she was developing the National Account System in Africa in the 1950s. Because of the discrepancy between her worldview and that of the local population, she had the feeling that she was faced with "a few large shapes in a thick fog" (Morgan 2011, 310).

One could simply wonder whether it makes sense to measure debt. Very clearly, what is obvious to the statistician—adding up supposedly comparable amounts of debt—is not obvious to many Tamil villagers, and the indebted woman is no exception. Many of them do not really know what their total debt is, simply because the debts are not comparable and are therefore incommensurable.

"Why do you measure and add up debts if it doesn't make sense to local people?" a fellow anthropologist repeatedly asked Isabelle. The ongoing challenge of measurement is precisely about accepting the need to evaluate and measure different objects with a common metric. We persisted with the process of measuring because the sum of the debts does represent a part of reality: it is the amount that people owe, irrespective of the moral and social meaning of each debt. Even if the debtor considers them incommensurable, these debts will still have to be repaid at some point, if only temporarily, or the nonrepayment will have serious consequences. Repaying these debts comes at a cost, which as a source of value extraction also needs to be measured. The total amount doesn't necessarily tell us anything about the lived experience of debt, as a small debt can be experienced as far more degrading than a large one. But the total amount can tell us a lot about the person's financial and material situation, and the degree of financial exploitation he or she may face. The lived experience of debt does not offer any better insight than debt as aggregation by commensuration, or vice versa. Each method reflects a facet of the reality of debt. The methodological purpose of combining quantification with lived experience is to reconstruct the diverse facets of this reality and the way they intermingle, cumulate, or oppose each other.

Measurement as a Conversation

Encouraging people to talk about their debts first requires awareness of the variety of options and vocabularies, being aware of pejorative terms and using them with care. Asking people if they have received financial help for repayment later is more probing than asking them if they are in debt. Listing all the local options also gets people talking. Other techniques include triangulation, which is asking the same question differently, in this case by asking not only how much money people owe to which type of lender but also how they have financed a particular type of expense. It is also useful to pay attention to what statisticians refer to as the "interviewer effect" since some interviewers may be able to obtain certain responses more easily than others. This was not the case here, but it could have happened.

In collaboration with two economist colleagues, first Marc Roesch and then Christophe Jalil Nordman, our team conducted three questionnaire surveys in 2010, 2016–17, and 2020–21 (between the two pandemic-related lockdowns) among about 500 households and 1,600 individuals. Part of the questions, especially those on debt, were asked individually and separately.[10]

In July 2021, Shanmugam, a small farmer from our fieldwork area, telephoned Venkata. He had been interviewed the previous week by our team for a questionnaire survey, and he had forgotten to mention a loan. He asked Venkata to include it because, he said, it gave a completely different picture of his financial situation. Venkata, as the data collection supervisor and sometimes enumerator, received many such calls during the three surveys. The interviewees would ask the team to add some loans, sources of income or assets, which they had omitted or did not want to talk about at the time of the survey. This included land sold to pay off a debt, a loan contracted from a Dalit by a non-Dalit, or a debt incurred by a man without his wife's knowledge, or vice versa.

This reveals a key facet of the method we used for our questionnaire surveys: they were conducted in the manner of conversations. Most user manuals for questionnaire surveys advocate for the neutrality of the interviewer. The interviewer is not supposed to deviate from preestablished questions and answers or volunteer an opinion or explain the meaning of the questions but let respondents interpret these for themselves. The neutrality rule is supposed to ensure comparability of responses, without interfering with the survey's administration. The neutrality rule is certainly feasible in certain contexts, and necessary when comparability is an objective. This was not applicable in our case, for both ethical and pragmatic reasons. Neutrality is a source of symbolic violence, in the sense that the rules of the game—questions, pre-answers, objectives, and uses of the data—are imposed without the respondent being able to negotiate them or sometimes to understand them (Bourdieu 2013). This is incompatible with establishing bonds of trust and reciprocity, which we consistently sought to accomplish with the men and women we represent here. Neutrality may also undermine the collection of quality data. Weary of the interviewer's insensitivity and wary of the strangeness of certain questions, respondents may answer haphazardly, deliberately give false answers to show their irritation, or demand that the interview stop. In our case, the conversational mode was the only way to obtain reasonable quality numerical data. It involved carefully explaining the meaning of confusing wording, listening to people even when they didn't answer our questions, taking the time to answer their own inquiries, and then gradually encouraging them back to the topic.

Complex family financial arrangements were another challenge to measuring debt. As previously discussed, the household is problematic as a unit since most debts are incurred on an individual basis. Yet it would also be misleading only to consider the individual as a unit since family members are often jointly responsible for debts, be it legally or informally (most often a husband for his wife, or vice versa, sometimes a son for his mother). In such

cases, lenders can turn to coborrowers in the event of a default. Coresponsibil-
ity also means other family members are likely to contribute to the repayment,
although this varies greatly in practice. It depends as much on the ability as
on the willingness of the coborrower. An effective overview of indebtedness
requires several combined indicators and units of analysis. Consideration of
the amount of household outstanding debt—what household members owe
at any given time—and the various associated ratios (debt-to-income ratio,
debt-to-asset ratio, and so forth) makes sense because some of the debt and
resources are pooled. The debt-to-income ratio, for example, pertains to the
theoretical possibility of repayment at the household level. Quantifying wom-
en's income-to-debt ratio also makes sense since women can never be sure
that other family members will help them with repayments.

A further complication is the fluidity of financial obligation boundaries.
The number of people living in a residential unit—the definition of household
we use here—is pretty much fixed.[11] It could be a couple and their children,
the so-called nuclear family. These made up 60 percent of households in our
field area. Or it could be an extended family (the remaining 40 percent). These
can include grandparents or married children, most often on the husband's
or son's side since virilocality—married couples settling in husbands' native
place—is common. Men (husbands, sometimes their fathers and sons) rou-
tinely commute to the city or to work in agribusiness but return home regularly. But the residential unit's relative stability does not preclude ongoing
negotiations over the boundaries of the financial unit, together with multiple financial circuits involving members' extended kinships, and sometimes
lovers and friends. Even within the kinship group, most of these circuits have
little or no transparency as each member seeks to honor his or her obligations
while preserving microspaces of financial freedom. Maternal uncles, for example, have heavy obligations to their sisters and nieces. Owing to the decline
in marriages within close kinship groups, as we will see in the next chapter, it
is likely that such obligations have considerably weakened. But they have not
disappeared. The circulation of money within kinship groups is ubiquitous,
through gifts or loans, and regularly conflicts with obligations to the residential unit.

Beyond this, the very idea of women having money of their own to use as
they please is inconceivable. Money is always a male or family attribute: it is
unthinkable for a woman to have her own money.[12] An important part of the
indebted woman's work is therefore to preserve her own circuits. This entails

having various forms of savings: savings at home, hidden in a box, at the back of a cupboard, buried in the garden, entrusted to a friend or relative—but above all savings in the form of loans to her inner circle, which she can recover if necessary, and gifts at the time of ceremonies, which she will recover at the time of her own ceremony. Lying about her own income when she has one, the price of groceries, or the amount of loans and repayments are also frequent tactics employed in order to force husbands (sometimes sons, in-laws, or parents) to be more generous or to work more. Men are held much less accountable for transparency over their income and expenses. Lying is therefore less of an obligation for men, but hiding part of what they earn and redistributing it to their own kin is very common. For women and men, nontransparency is a rule of management, and our survey did not intend to disrupt this. As much as possible, men and women were interviewed separately to ensure a certain freedom of speech.

Needless to say, despite these precautions, the data remain approximate, providing a quantitative order of magnitude of the realities observed. Above all, comparison over time is instructive, highlighting key changes. These measures indeed convinced us that the indebted woman was a figure to explore. In the early days of our research, we felt that debt was a growing burden for both men and women but especially women. But did our observations reveal an objective increase, or did they reflect the fact that debt had become a more visible, spoken-about reality? Undertaking a systematic analysis and delving into the financial life of each family was the only way to clear up this doubt, as the following data illustrate.

The comparison over time is indeed telling. Consider the debt service indicator that economists frequently use, which represents the amount to be repaid compared to income. In 2010, on average, households devoted 44 percent of their income to debt repayment. This rose to 48 percent in 2016–17 and 68 percent in 2020–21, after the first COVID-19 pandemic lockdown. Comparison is equally instructive since debts have grown much faster than assets, and this is especially true for Dalits and the poorest.[13]

The majority of these debts go toward social reproduction—namely, daily expenses, healthcare, education, old debt repayment, housing, ceremonies, and marriages. Social reproduction made up around two-thirds of debt purpose in 2010. In 2016 and 2020, it accounted for almost three-quarters (84 percent for Dalits and 87 percent for the poorest). In 2020–21, with the pandemic, the breakdown of social reproduction expenditures changed: the weight of marriages, which had sharply increased between 2010 and 2016, gave way to debt repayment.

As far as female debt is concerned, women bore a disproportionate debt burden relative to their incomes. In 2016, women's income made up 22 percent of household income on average, while their debt made up 37 percent of household debt. Indebted women in paid employment had nine times more outstanding debt than annual income on average, as opposed to three times higher for males. The discrepancy was greater among Dalits and the poorest households, in terms of both the proportion of female borrowers and debt volume.[14] With the pandemic, the burden of female debt has increased further. In 2020–21, it was more than half (52 percent), while the weight of their income had barely increased (24 percent).

Women also tend to use debt differently. Overall, and as we will see in chapter 3, debt for investment purposes remains limited but is much more widely practiced by men. Most importantly, as the financial diaries reveal and as we will see in chapter 4, repayments are overwhelmingly women's responsibility.

Another key indicator is the cost of debt, which can be estimated by comparing the interest paid to income, what economists call "interest servicing charge." It is a challenge to estimate the cost of debt given the negotiability of many loan transactions. As noted earlier, interest rates are not fixed, repayments are irregular, and borrowers do not always know whether they are paying off the principal or the interest. We made a rough estimate for 2016–17, with 2020–21 being an exceptional year owing to the COVID-19 pandemic. For debtors who did not know how much they paid, we applied the average cost of loans, distinguishing between each type of lender given the diversity of practices and costs. We found an average rate of about 30 percent. This means that out of every 100 rupees earned, about 30 rupees go toward paying off the interest. The financial diaries method, which we discuss in the next section, is much more accurate and yields similar results. Note here that the most appropriate unit of analysis is the household since male income can be used to pay off female debts (although this is far from being the rule, as we will see in a later chapter), and vice versa.

After each round of our survey, we shared some of the results of our questionnaire survey with the villagers. In 2017, Venkata decided to focus on the burden of female debt. Usually, villagers actively debate each result, some commenting, others disagreeing or questioning the meaning of the variables or the measurement methods. Here, suddenly, no one spoke. Venkata started again, speaking directly to some of the women he knows well. They lowered their heads and looked away. Suddenly, Venkata felt bad as he understood his mistake: talking publicly about the burden of women's debts is not welcome. While women's debt exists everywhere, it is a public secret. To openly acknowledge the importance of women's debt means acknowledging their economic contribution, their associations with male lenders outside the family, and the inability of husbands to fulfill their breadwinning role. This is all in complete contradiction with local norms of masculinity and femininity.

The questionnaire survey confirmed our observations about rising debt and the disproportionate burden on women. Long-term ethnography has revealed unexpected facets of women's debt, particularly its interrelationship with bodies and sexuality, which proves an important aspect of women's creditworthiness. In 2018, even after fifteen years of investigation, we remained intrigued by the complexity of family financial circuits, with the feeling of not having fully understood how women manage to repay these disproportionate debts in relation to their incomes, with little help from their husbands or other family members. This led us to develop the financial diaries method.

The Surprises of Quantification

Financial diaries are a counting method. The objective is to carry out a systematic inventory of all, or at least most, of the financial flows within a residential unit over a given period of time. Initiated in the nineteenth century to understand the budgets of the working classes (Le Play 1855), the method has recently been redesigned by a group of economists and implemented in various parts of the world (Collins et al. 2009; Morduch and Schneider 2017). The results have been fascinating, highlighting the complexity of the financial portfolios of the poor, who are constantly borrowing, saving, repaying, giving, receiving, and juggling a wide variety of financial instruments, even in a country like the United States (Morduch and Schneider 2017). The method has been replicated across many countries. With few exceptions, however, none of these initiatives has disaggregated financial flows by gender.

We experimented with the method, unsure of what else it might teach us. It proved extremely useful, making us aware of the broad reach of women's repayment responsibilities: women repay about 80 percent of all family debt. We had missed this in the questionnaire survey, naïvely thinking that the person to take out the loan would be the main one to make repayments. This was a big mistake, as it turns out that women largely pay back not only their own loans but those of other family members. It is unlikely, however, that a questionnaire could measure this, as men would certainly have a hard time admitting they do not pay their debts. Ultimately, the financial diaries method allowed us to understand that debt management is both real work and a central contribution to the production of economic value within the household. Echoing the ethno-accounting approach developed by sociologists Alain Cottereau and Mokhtar Mohatar Marzok (2012), the productivity of the various household members emerges in a new light. With debt flows often as great as or even greater than income, and women the primary managers of these flows, their contribution to household wealth and productivity becomes a central one. Quantification and efforts to systematize can also bring out surprises.

Though the term "diary" conveys the idea of "tracking intimate details of financial management over time" (Collins et al. 2009, 188), an interviewer comes to collect the data, visiting the household on a regular basis (e.g., twice a month over one year, in Collins et al. [2009]). If people are not used to keeping accounts, asking them to keep a diary makes little sense. While most financial diary surveys use large samples (several hundred respondents), we opted for the ethnographic method since our goal was to capture who does what at each stage of the debt, and to situate these day-to-day transactions within family members' broader sets of obligations. After several attempts, ten families were selected, including four in the study area. They agreed to collaborate, and the fact that they had known us for several years certainly helped. This sample was not intended to be representative but rather to illustrate different cases (Burawoy 1998). The ten families are typical as regards their caste, occupation, and kinship patterns and marriages. Their details are given in the following chapters.

For nine months, Antony Raj, a research assistant trained in ethnography, spent half his time with four families in our field area, chosen from the same village to avoid too much travel. He established close relations with all the family members, spending entire days in their homes, observing the transactions in progress and asking for details of transactions on the days when he was not there, sometimes spending long hours waiting for a suitable moment. As discussed earlier, some expenses and debts were common, others were not, so he had to talk to each person individually.

As in double-entry business accounting methods, the basic principle of financial diaries is to balance incoming and outgoing flows. In our case, this rule was difficult to apply, and we quickly abandoned it, as we felt it was both unrealistic and ethically questionable. Given the opacity of financial management described earlier, claiming completeness would have meant forcing people to reveal things they didn't want to talk about.

On a number of occasions, Antony felt that some of the women were involved in sex-for-debt exchange, but he could not be certain. It is unthinkable to ask, and no woman (or man) disclosed anything to him. His almost constant presence in the village certainly did not help. The sexual disclosures received by Santosh and Isabelle, let's remember, systematically took place outside the villages. For his part, Santosh developed the financial diaries method with a few women he knew well. But except for one case, which remained very incomplete, the results were inconclusive. It required a continuous presence that he could not afford but also a tenacity and obstinacy that he did not have the patience for. In other words, capturing the financial and sexual intimacy of women in debt does not require the same field conditions or the same skills and sensitivities. We had to deal with this disparate and messy method, and these different forms of learning experience (Tsing 2011, xi).

Lastly, we obviously missed many things. Our lengthy fieldwork allowed us to see, observe, and sometimes quantify things invisible to others, but there is also much we did not see or hear. Probably the most shameful, violent, and exploitative forms of sexual relations remained hidden from view, even for the most dedicated of ethnographers. These dilemmas are resolved in ways that people do not talk about such as escape, suicide, or murder. This goes without saying for the affected people, especially, of course, if they have disappeared, but it is just as obvious to their loved ones, who also seek to preserve the honor of their close circle, and their own honor by extension as they are part of that family and kinship group. Tragic cases do exist, and the media regularly report on them.[15] Our analysis focuses on more ordinary, less dramatic, but much more commonplace situations.

2

Kinship Debt

WHO ARE YOU GOING to marry your daughter to? How much will you give? Where are you going to get the money?" These are the incessant questions asked by Tamil mothers, concerned about their daughters' marriages, including among the Dalits. Concern for girls' future marriages starts at a very young age due to the increasing cost of the dowry over time. And for those trying to break the cycle of exchanges, debt takes on another form. "What rights do you have when you came empty-handed?" Pushpurani faced this recurring question from her in-laws, referring to her love marriage and the dowry she didn't bring. "His penis is locked in her vagina," her in-laws also regularly said about their own son, whom they accused of being controlled by his wife since he settled in his wife's village, in opposition to the norms of virilocality. They have never accepted their son's choice, his separation from the parental home, and Pushpurani's relative freedom of movement. Her in-laws constantly criticize her, but sometimes she anticipates their requests to show that she is not useless or unproductive. After thirty years of marriage, she continues to pay what appears to be a combination of moral and financial debt that takes the form of constant rebuke and humiliation. She also takes on multiple financial obligations for her husband's kin who live nearby. As for many other women, Pushpurani's debt is above all relentless, which our long-term ethnography has brought to light.

Through the case of Pushpurani and a few other characters, this chapter traces the radical transformation of kinship and wedding payments over the past fifty years in the South Arcot region. These transformations must be situated within the wider transformation of sexual political economies which denotes the idea of a mutual co-constitution of kinship, sexuality, wealth accumulation, and power (see the introduction). In South Arcot, this has entailed a sharp transition from bride price to dowry practices, the constant rise of dowry payments, the concomitant transformation of Dalit women into "housewives" (Mies 1998, 100–110) (or supposed housewives), and the prohibition of "deviant sexuality" (Mitra 2020, 2). In their own communities, whereas Dalit women were once valued primarily for their economic productivity and were reputedly sexually freer, it is now their purity and chastity that are increasingly valued and sought after. And it is now girls' parents who have to pay to have them married, not the other way around. This makes them permanent debtors.

As we will see, Dalit women's shift from asset to liability in South Arcot reflects men's increasing control over the economy, which itself is linked to the failure of the agrarian transition and an unstable and volatile economic environment. The shift is also a result of state policies. Not only do Indian social policies fuel aspirations for modernity without providing a safety net, but they also construct women as fragile and dependent entities in need of protection and rescue from rampant insecurity.

As is often the case, women and men inhabit, enact, and perform patriarchal norms in various ways, as we will discuss. Kinship debt is also shaped by, and constitutive of, class and caste inequalities that weigh heavily on men's shoulders. Paying the dowry involves a steep debt for many, as observed in other parts of India (Marius 2016, 60–61; Parvez 2020).[1] Although fathers, maternal uncles, and older brothers are supposed to shoulder marriage costs and debts for their female kin, women are also responsible for a large portion. Furthermore, an ontological condition of indebtedness emerges out of Dalit women's narratives, stemming from their status as women and devalued subjects. Feelings of debt and obligation, entitlement, and guilt come up again and again in testimonies and permeate financial behaviors and conducts. Female debt clearly materializes as a power relationship shaped by patriarchy, kinship, and sexuality.

The Indebted Woman in South Arcot

Since the late 1980s, India has recorded one of the strongest economic growth rates in the world.[2] This has been accompanied by a sharp decline in income poverty, which then increased again with the COVID-19 pandemic.[3] Economic growth has also been accompanied by a persistence of caste discriminations (A. Shah et al. 2018; Jodhka and Manor 2017), the rise of the Hindutva ideology (Jaffrelot 2021),[4] and a firm rise of income inequality (Chancel and Piketty 2019).[5] Over the same period, the child sex ratio has steadily declined to the detriment of girls.[6]

Tamil Nadu has long stood out from the rest of the country due to its higher economic growth, active social policies, anti-Brahmin social movements, low Hindutva presence, and less severe patriarchy. One particular notion of justice dates back to the Madras presidency under the colonial empire and the so-called Dravidian mobilizations.[7] These were rooted in Brahminic critique and considered the abolition of caste hierarchies as essential to establishing an egalitarian socioeconomic system (Kalaiyarasan and Vijayabaskar 2021, 27). While the Dravidians did not eliminate those caste hierarchies, they are the reason behind historic resistance to Hindutva and the initiation of welfare regimes (Kalaiyarasan and Vijayabaskar 2021). The less severe degree of patriarchy in the region stems from the fact that many of its diverse kinship systems all practice isogamous marriage, which is more favorable to women. This is the practice of marrying within one's close kinship circle, choosing by priority a groom from the bride's mother's side, allowing the bride to maintain strong links with her own kin (Agarwal 1994; Uberoi 1993). Although anti-Hindu social movements and less severe patriarchy still linger, they are losing ground in the region.

The same is true of South Arcot, albeit with several unique attributes. South Arcot used to be a district in the Madras presidency of British India. It no longer has an administrative existence,[8] but it still has regional significance, and the term continues to be used. Situated in the east-central part of the state, South Arcot benefits from diversified but declining agriculture, a port, a regional market, and an industrial cluster. Economic growth has been palpable there, albeit to a very unequal extent. The mix of fertile plains and semiarid areas has historically been a source of inequality within and between villages. The historic overlap between caste and class, while evolving, still exists there. Data gathered on education, income, and wealth levels in 2010, 2016–17, and 2020–21 make this clear. Education and income gaps are decreasing, while wealth gaps remain significantly high. In 2020–21, Dalits on average owned half as much as non-Dalits.[9] Dalits are no longer forced to limit themselves to farm work. Nor are they compelled to do carcass and waste work, or when they do so, it is in exchange for monetary remuneration. Intergenerational bonds of dependencies between Dalit bonded laborers and non-Dalit landowners are a thing of the past.[10] Common explanations for this are urban male migration, mostly to nearby or big cities, along with social policies and Dalit political movements.[11] These are undoubtedly valid, but this book's main argument is that women's debt is a further crucial explanatory factor.

A few Dalits have managed to climb the social ladder. Most operate as labor intermediaries, some as traders, or exceptionally as government employees. But employers and large lenders are still predominantly non-Dalit. Working for or borrowing from "lower than oneself" remains stigmatizing to non-Dalits. New forms of servitude have emerged, based on the explosion of household debt. Spatial segregation also continues, with the main village (*ur*) reserved for non-Dalits and a separate hamlet—the *ceri*—for Dalits, including better-off ones.[12] Whatever their caste, people tend to think of themselves in caste terms; their identity is heavily bound up in their caste. Both Dalits and non-Dalits have a strong sense of "them" and "us" (Dalits and caste Hindus).

As discrimination and inequality persist, Dalits advocate for their social and political standing on a daily basis. They are widely supported by local political movements, the most active being the Viduthalai Chiruthaigal Katchi (Liberation Panthers Party). Conflict recurs between Dalits and Vanniyars, a farming caste whose ritual rank is low, although far superior to Dalits, but who now control a large share of local land and businesses.[13] Open conflicts relate to the use of common land, temple management, religious ritual organization, local politics, access to government programs, and intercaste marriages and sexual affairs. At the same time, Hindu ideology is spreading, including among Dalits, from the expansion of Hindu festivals to the construction of temples. Upper castes—Mudaliyars, Naidus, Reddiyars, and Chettiyars[14]—have mostly moved away from the villages in recent decades to nearby towns, adopting urban jobs and lifestyles. Their dominance has greatly declined but is by no means a thing of the past. They maintain local control through politics and lending. Muslims and Christians are minorities in the area, although Christian-faith NGOs are present.

A quick look at everyday village life can give vivid insight into these processes. The signs of economic growth and the wish for prosperity are easy to see with improved road infrastructure and the construction of private educational institutions, wedding halls, and temples, including in the hamlets restricted to the Dalits. Housing, too, has been improved, albeit patchily.

Thatched huts stand alongside colonnaded and two-story houses, including in the Dalit hamlet. Many houses have satellite dishes installed. Some still have outdoor wood-burning ovens, while others have gas stoves. Shelters that once provided shade for livestock are increasingly being used to park motorcycles and sometimes cars. Most adults and young people, men and women alike, now have a cell phone and sometimes a smartphone. Consumer society is gaining ground, even in the most remote areas.

The villages are being emptied of some of their men, most of whom now work elsewhere. Many go to nearby cities, others leave for other Indian states, or, in some rare cases, they go abroad. Some work as security guards, restaurant staff and cleaners, in shops or private homes, or as loaders and unloaders at markets or on trucks. Some work as masons, carriers, stone breakers, or brick molders on construction sites. Others work as sugarcane cutters or coconut pickers in agroindustry, and so on. One of the backbones of India's economic growth has been its cheap, vulnerable, and circulating labor force, which moves back and forth as private capital needs it (Breman 2007; A. Shah et al. 2018; Picherit 2018). According to various estimates, informal employment—that is, unregulated and unprotected employment—accounts for 80 to 90 percent of the Indian labor force (Harriss-White 2020). Increasingly, highly educated young men struggle to find jobs, hanging out and passing the time as best they can.[15]

Over recent decades, Tamil villages have largely become villages of women and young people. We can see women working in the fields, but they are mainly Dalit, as female employment is considered degrading and a marker of subalternity. Since the Green Revolution of the 1960–80s, working women have gradually replaced men in agriculture, their lower wages somewhat compensating for Indian agriculture's low profitability. Today, however, agricultural fields are increasingly deserted or mechanized.[16] Women's official labor force participation rate, including among Dalit women, poor families, and in rural areas, has been steadily declining over recent decades. This makes India an exception among emerging countries.[17] According to our surveys, Dalit women's paid employment rate dropped between 2010 and 2016–17 from 75 to 55 percent, reaching a rate similar to that of non-Dalit women (which remains stable).[18]

Dalit women's paid work is declining, but they remain very active and much of their activity remains invisible. There is less fetching of water and wood, and the most fortunate women even have dishwashers. The manual tasks of the past have been replaced by a multitude of new tasks. With the spread of Hindu religious festivals, prayer and rituals have intensified, and women carry out the bulk of daily religious obligations, including the cost. Women must also learn to consume, and their gradual integration into consumer society calls for new skills and brings new pressures. Which type of quality or brand do you choose, where do you go to get good prices, and above all, how do you take on debt? The way in which they handle their monetary debt is the core of this book.

At this point, let's consider the transformation of their childcare roles and its implication for kinship debt. With education now a priority, they have to ensure children do their homework. This is true for both boys and girls, but the goals are different: the hope is for boys to find skilled jobs, while girls' education is mainly intended to get them a good marriage. The virginity of girls is now a major element of their credibility in the marriage market and has to be carefully monitored. Financing weddings involves anticipation and planning, such as setting gold aside and contributing to the costs of others' ceremonies, knowing others will reciprocate when it is their child's turn to marry.

Shifting Marriage Patterns

"Boy's side gives a lot of torture," we often heard. Danam's neighbor listed all the things her son-in-law's family was demanding for her daughter's upcoming wedding: "They even ask for specific brands. The only thing they haven't asked [for]," she says wryly, "is electricity. . . . They don't even know how to ride a motorcycle, [but] they're asking for one."

Indian feminist movements have long condemned dowry practices for being a central pillar of patriarchy, and rightly so. But as feminist researchers have argued, it is also necessary to consider their political and sexual economies and what they reveal and express about local patriarchal structures, to better understand their meanings and implications.[19]

During colonial times, the first compulsory dowries responded to the need to protect high-caste and upper-class women, owing to their exclusion from the property laws the colonial power set up (Oldenburg 2002; Agarwal 1994, 480–83). In a context where females are deprived of inheritances, which is still widely the case in Tamil Nadu despite an equality law, the dowry is upheld as a premortem form of inheritance.[20] This, however, assumes that the goods and cash transmitted through the dowry will actually be owned by women, which is only true in some communities (Agarwal 1994, 135–37). That is not the case here; most brides have no rights to their own dowry, which is considered the property of their in-laws. The quest for upward mobility and for stable, well-paying jobs might also contribute. Here, too, the colonial period seems to have been a turning point, when sought-after professions emerged.[21] Today, highly qualified professions such as medical specialists and IT engineers attract astronomical dowries.[22] In much of rural southern India, the postindependence dowry responded to the modernization of agriculture and to women's relegation to subsistence farming.[23] The general decline of farming and the rise of nonfarming men's income have been subsequent aggravating factors, as clearly holds true in South Arcot. Last but not least, marriage payments may also offer compensation for economic instability and volatility, as Karin Kapadia (1996) had already shown in a neighboring region. This, too, is clearly the case here, with a highly precarious labor market encountering risky and expensive investments in education (for boys) and housing.

Pushpurani, in her own words, describes with great lucidity the radical changes of the past five decades in her village, alongside the transformation of kinship rules, women's worth, income sources, and consumption needs. Her mother married her maternal cousin in the 1970s. The wedding took place at home, with a few guests; the expenses were shared between the two families, and the groom's family paid the bride price, a few thousand rupees, which was then the rule. As agricultural labor was a largely female and livelihood requisite, Dalit women were valued not only as mothers but also as productive labor, making them people of value. The son-in-law's parents were willing to pay in recognition of this value and compensate the loss to the daughter-in-law's family. Pushpurani's mother went back and forth between her natal and marital homes, both to work for her natal family and to seek help. Pushpurani does not romanticize this close mother–daughter bond or family solidarity: her mother spent her time in the fields working hard and often went to bed hungry.

Then practices and needs changed. Now, she explains, "we need more items, more money, more time." Pushpurani was born at home, whereas her own children were born in the government hospital, and her first grandson in a private clinic. Far beyond healthcare, other expenses have also exploded, including food due to the near disappearance of production for self-consumption, education, housing, and electricity. More and more money is needed, said Pushpurani, not only to survive but also to "make progress" and have a "new life" (*pudu vazhukai*). In her mother's time, Dalits were content to bow their heads—a reference to submission to the upper castes—and put food on the table. Today, they want to do what others do, and part of this integration process involves participation in consumer society.

At the same time, as previously discussed, agriculture has declined along with women's worth. Beyond agricultural decline, the drop in women's employment has reflected the rise of education, which is rather good news. But it also reflects the rise of patriarchal norms that place a high value on the housewife (Heyer 2015; Still 2015; Rao 2012). We will return to this point later, but for now we will set out the implications of the loss of women's worth in South Arcot.

The first hope for social mobility lies in nonfarming jobs, preferably skilled ones. These are mostly the preserve of men since they require mobility women are excluded from. Women's migration for work, for example in brick molding, is a last resort only for the poorest people. Yet the nonfarm economy is unable to provide jobs to most rural workers. What political economists call the "agrarian transition"—the shift from an agricultural to an industrial and service economy—has failed (Vijayabaskar 2017; Lerche 2021). Marriage has thus become a significant coping strategy in the quest for mobility. In other words, the failure of the agrarian transition at least partly explains the radical transformation of marriage rules within Dalit groups. Isogamy and bride price, which was the rule until the 1970s, has gradually given way to attempts at hypergamy—marrying into a richer family—and the normalization of a practice akin to dowry. Tamil villagers speak of "ritual expenses," or very simply, "what she brought." Wedding payments are predicated on real long-term calculations. They are specific forms of wealth circulation, which must be understood as particular responses to constantly changing economic and political contexts.

In our case, wedding payments are both shaped by and constitutive of a volatile economy that is increasingly dominated by men. Such volatility generates instability, competition, and aspirations for social mobility. For the upper classes, marriages and marriage payments mainly serve as accumulation strategies, whether to transmit or conserve capital, boost one's reputation through ostentation, or show off one's wealth and reputation.[24] For the lower classes (and castes), as is the case here, marriages and marriage payments mainly seek to mitigate risks and compensate for the increasing costs of social reproduction and the inadequacies and contradictions of social policies.

Subsidizing Males' Education and Housing

Danam illustrates another facet of the indebted woman's situation. Her case reflects the old system, the time when Dalit women were valued for their work. Married in the late 1990s, she often mentions the event with pride. Her father-in-law had hesitated over another potential bride, who had jewelry and crockery, while Danam had "nothing to bring." He chose her on the grounds that "jewelry only comes once," while Danam brought skills that her father-in-law needed, as a farm worker but more importantly as a recruiter and farm labor manager, expertise sought out by a wealthy landowner he was working for at the time. Her father-in-law was one of the last bonded laborers in their village, assigned for life to his high-caste owner along with his wife and children. As for many bonded laborers, one of his key tasks was to find and manage labor efficiently. Danam's mother, also a bonded laborer, both charismatic and authoritative, had earned a solid reputation as a labor broker and subsequently trained her daughter.

Today, bonded labor has almost completely disappeared from South Arcot, and Danam and her husband, Pushparaj, have escaped it. They even have a small piece of land that Pushparaj's father received from his landlord. Danam is in charge of cultivating the land, while Pushparaj trades in jute bags in the nearby towns. For a decade, as her father-in-law had hoped, she managed farm labor for various local landlords. With the decline of agriculture and the rise of microcredit groups, she converted her expertise from labor brokerage into managing microcredit groups.

Venkata has known Danam and Pushparaj since at least 2010, when our first questionnaire surveys were conducted. She was part of our financial diary sample, and since then Venkata has met with Danam frequently. On several occasions, she clearly explained her sense of her own situation, that of the village and the region, and prospects for the future. Women are worthless, men "only value them when they are dead"—that is, once they are no longer a burden—she said sarcastically. Danam gets by "not too badly," not only because she has three sons and therefore the prospect of as many dowries, but also because Pushparaj has no nieces and thus escapes maternal uncle duty.

Compared to their parents' situation, they had already come a long way. But Danam wanted a different future for her sons (and for herself since her sons would be her main support in her old age). She educated her sons to marry "outside" the family, considered too poor, in order to "progress." Marriages outside the family allow one to ask for more dowry. She spent 5 lakhs (USD 8,000)[25]—the equivalent of more than six years of their annual income—and went heavily into debt for her son to get a business school degree. As of April 2018 (end date of the financial diaries), Danam and her husband held three times their annual income in outstanding debt, and, on an average, over the financial diary period (July 2017–April 2018), they spent almost half (45 percent) of their monthly income on repaying their debt and around one-sixth on interest (16.4 percent). But "that's nothing," she said, since with her son's degree, she could claim "thirty gold sovereigns" from a bride's family. In 2018, thirty gold sovereigns—around 240 grams[26]—cost about 6.3 lakhs (USD 9,800). Danam's expectations are excessive, and she is likely to get only two-thirds or half at best. If her son expresses a preference for a certain young woman, she may agree to lower her ambitions. In order to reconcile young people's desires for love while keeping face, parents commonly accept compromises. What is clear, however, is that like many others, Danam invested in her son's education by roughly calculating what she would be able to demand of his future bride. The calculations included both the compensation for educational expenses and the risk involved since many young graduates cannot find jobs. At the time, her son was working as a loan officer for a financial company, but the salary and working conditions were not up to his expectations. Danam's calculations also included what she would spend on the wedding: around 3 or 4 lakhs.

In a time of very high economic volatility, children, both girls and boys, are like real commodities giving rise to sophisticated calculations on the part of parents. But as economic sociology has long shown, such calculations are not at all incompatible with the affection and love that parents have for their children (Zelizer 2005). It is very much in the name of her love for her son that Danam wants the best for him.

Today, for weddings in the villages of South Arcot, most families—Dalits and non-Dalits alike—rent a hall, invite several hundred guests, hire a photographer or even a videographer, and so forth. Other expenses include the commitment ceremony and gifts handed out to close relatives and friends. The estimates of Danam are average. According to our surveys, the average total cost of a wedding between 2017 and 2020 was about four years of the parents' annual income. These costs are most often shared between the groom and bride's families. This ratio is roughly the same regardless of caste, meaning that Dalits are no more "ostentatious" than others, contrary to local gossip. As for the dowry, borne solely by the women's side, it represents on average more than twice the parents' annual income (2.3). Part of the wedding costs are paid indirectly through guest donations (from relatives but also, and increasingly, from friends and various acquaintances). A cold accounting analysis of what is spent and received shows that, on average, the groom's side may expect a net surplus of about two years of annual family income, and it is the opposite for the bride's side.

Yoganathan, whom we also followed with a financial diary, comes from a poor non-Dalit family. His is a typical case of a man whose farm is on the decline and who failed to invest in nonfarming activities such as transport and trade, now struggling to maintain his position. He lives with his two wives, Devaki and Rani, who are sisters; their three sons; and the wife and daughter of the eldest son. Note that polygamy, though unusual, is accepted. They are of the Vanniyar caste, ranked just above Dalits in the local village hierarchy. By the time we met them in 2018, Yoganathan, Devaki, and Rani were severely indebted. Each month on average, they repaid nearly twice (1.8) their income, which in turn forced them to constantly incur more debt. Their debt had grown over the years to pay for the education of the two older sons, the hospitalization of the younger one, and various attempts at overseas employment for the eldest one. On top of this came Yoganathan's obligations as a maternal uncle, and, most recently, the renovation of their house. A few years earlier, while they were already heavily in debt for education and healthcare costs, they sold a piece of their land to pay off some of their debt, regain the trust of lenders, borrow again, and renovate their house.

We have to "keep up face," Yoganathan often said, and it's true that most neighboring houses had significantly improved over the previous decade. Thanks to debt and land sales, they now had a house with an outdoor veranda and colonnades, three rooms, and a separate toilet in the backyard. Renovating a house is a calculation about the future: a good house boosts reputation and creditworthiness, and the two are closely interconnected. "Financers don't care, they just see the house and lend blindly," Yoganathan's daughter-in-law once mentioned to us.

A good house may also attract a well-endowed bride. This is also what Danam was planning. Her house is made of clay and is thatched, but she intended to modernize it before marrying off her eldest son. Investment in housing, a heavy source of debt, also enters into dowry calculations. For example, a man seeking marriage who has a house built out of concrete and with a private toilet can ask for more dowry.

The key but ambiguous role of the state in housing policies is also worth noting. These policies emerged at the turn of the 2000s at the federal level and were reinforced by Tamil Nadu's very active state housing policy. In 2015, the BJP government announced a "housing for all" project that the State of Tamil Nadu supplements. The program provides grants to convert clay and thatched houses into permanent houses, or to extend existing permanent houses. The amounts are not negligible. After deducting bribes and various hidden costs, the grant accounts for over three years of family income.[27] According to our survey, around a third of Dalit families have benefited.[28] But the amounts are largely insufficient to cover the real costs. These subsidies therefore mainly serve as an incentive to take on debt, while most villagers have no access to any housing credit policy. By 2020, no one had access to a home loan (including non-Dalits), but about a third of them had gone into debt to renovate their homes (30 percent in 2010, 40 percent in 2020). The only options are informal or microcredit short-term loans. For many, having an attractive home therefore means juggling short-term loans repaid through other loans. This ultimately means an exorbitant cost of debt. Over the nine-month financial diary period, Yoganathan's interest payments made up 38 percent of his family's income.[29] In fact, and far beyond Yoganathan's case, it is common for construction work to pause along the way, even for several years, while the family recovers its financial health.

But if sons refuse arranged marriages, housing and education expenses will turn out to have been risky investments. "Our eldest son made a big mistake," Devaki—Yoganathan's wife—told us. Their son Kumaresan had made a love marriage with a Vanniyar girl from a neighboring village who was still in high school and a minor at the time, the legal age for marriage being eighteen. The affair caused a scandal involving the police and local caste leaders. Both families finally came to an agreement, and the bride went to live with her in-laws (and since then has had a child). She "did not bring anything" (no dowry), but her parents promised "something." It's been eight years, Devaki told us in 2018, and they hadn't even seen "5 grams of black gram,"[30] in other words, nothing.

Moreover, like many young rural graduates in the labor market (Jeffrey 2010; Vijayabaskar 2015), both sons were struggling to find stable, well-paying jobs. The parents spent about 5 lakhs (USD 7,800) on education fees (nearly two-and-a-half years of their annual income). A few years prior, the eldest son, Kumaresan, with a degree in mechanical engineering, migrated to Dubai. Once there, his salary turned out to be half of what was promised and did not include accommodation. He quickly returned, having spent more than he earned. He then planned to leave again, this time for Canada, and applied to three employment agencies. Two of them, one in Mumbai and the other in Delhi, turned out to be fake, and he lost the substantial fee he had advanced, several tens of thousands of rupees. The third employment agency, in Puducherry, was a genuine company, but after he paid the visa and airfare fees, it went bankrupt. He lost 45,000 rupees (USD 700), nearly three months of the family's entire income.

Kumaresan's setbacks are just one example of how education can prove a risky venture. According to the latest census data, 29 percent of young male graduates (bachelor's degree or higher) in rural Tamil Nadu reported not being in employment, education, or training (Vijayabaskar 2017, 70). Young people are not equally prepared for this highly competitive market and not all diplomas are equal. How to choose a "good school" is a question that villagers repeatedly ask Venkata and Santosh. In the field of engineering, for example, there is now a plethora of private schools, many of which have very poor-quality teaching and no value on the job market. English language ability is often a requirement that only expensive urban schools can provide. Interpersonal skills and contacts are often another prerequisite, which Dalits and the poor lack (Hilger and Nordman 2020). There is no level playing field.

In light of these circumstances, it is easier to understand the matrimonial tactics. In the event that they fail to ensure a decent job for their son, parents can at least try to recoup their investment by demanding compensation from the bride's parents. The dowry as such proves instrumental in creating a qualified workforce in the context of an extremely volatile and insecure labor market. Ultimately, the dowry subsidizes an unstable job market and expensive housing.

Value and Chastity

"If you come with a crown, you are like a queen." "It's like a label, you live with it." We would often hear these two sentiments. It is true that the amount of the dowry partly shapes and ranks the value and respect accorded to daughters-in-law. But another crucial aspect of women's worth is chastity. Pushpurani is regularly scolded by her in-laws for her mobility (*ooru ooru meyaraval*—literally, a goat that keeps moving from village to village to graze). This is a classic, harsh criticism, an explicit allusion to the perception that she moves around for no good reason and lacks control. When the tone rises, Pushpurani gets called a whore (*thevidiya*), including by her own mother and brothers. Although daily discussions in Dalit settlements are full of sexual and often crude metaphors, Pushpurani finds this very hard.

Historian Durba Mitra (2020) has shown how ideas of deviant female sexuality have shaped modern social thought in India while being used to describe, justify, and enforce social hierarchy between castes, classes, and religions. Precolonial times saw a large range of marriage alliances such as matrilineality (a system of filiation in which each person is related to her mother's lineage), polygyny (a man married to several women), and theogamy (marriage with a god). With only a few exceptions, all of these have gradually died out. Since the colonial period, the only legal marriage has been monogamous and patrilineal (Basu and Ramberg 2015; John and Nair 2000). In postcolonial India, under the influence of Westernization and Sanskritization (i.e., the adoption of upper castes' cultural norms), the rules of monogamy and bridal virginity, the chastity of wives, and the continence of widows became hegemonic.

In rural South Arcot, the control exerted over Dalit women's bodies by their immediate circles is relatively new. Still today, Dalit women are usually much freer in their movements than non-Dalits are. Many still work, although this trend is falling, as we have seen. The women are often allowed to come and go from their home street without anyone's permission, although their perimeter of mobility remains limited and rarely exceeds a few kilometers (though there are exceptions like Pushpurani). They spend a lot of time sitting out in their streets or at their doorsteps, chatting in between domestic tasks. Non-Dalit streets, by contrast, are usually deserted with almost no women to be seen.

Historically, Dalit inferiority was related precisely to allegedly deviant and uncontrolled Dalit female sexuality. Even today, Dalit men are often mocked by non-Dalit men for their supposed inability to control their wives, and Dalit women are often taunted by non-Dalit women for supposedly being "loose." Behind these biases lies a historical and material reality, be this the appropriation of Dalit women's bodies by higher castes or the fact that Dalit women work. Non-Dalit men's refusal to drink Dalit water did not prevent them from having sexual rights over Dalit women. In the face of non-Dalit women's mockery and insults, Dalit women often sarcastically retort that non-Dalit women are only "puppets" or "donkeys" controlled by their husbands, unable to do anything on their own and doomed to begging if their husbands disappear.

While Dalit women have always had freedom (at a heavy price in terms of physical labor, poverty, sexual abuse from non-Dalits, and all kinds of deprivations), there has also been pushback against this relative freedom. In South Arcot, control over Dalit women's bodies and sexuality has been on the rise for the last four decades (Anandhi, Jeyaranjan, and Krishnan 2002; Still 2015; Gorringe 2017). Within Dalit political movements, long known for their progressive thinking on gender, female chastity, modesty, and discretion are now presented as a symbol of Dalit male honor. Rising patriarchal conservatism is now pervasive in everyday village realities. It reflects Dalit men's desire to reclaim or assert their own masculinity, something of which they have long been deprived, and their aspiration to upward mobility (Parry 2014). Having a woman at home is a sign of respectability, both for husbands and wives. Some wives do appreciate this when it saves them from hard farmwork (Heyer 2015).

The rising patriarchy is not just expressive of the quest of historically emasculated Dalit men. With the growing influence of the Hindutva ideology, which is at once nationalist, racist, and highly patriarchal, rising patriarchy is a wider reality in India. And with the coming to power of the BJP in 2014 and again in 2019, Hindutva has become an official national doctrine, largely in effect in the second decade of our fieldwork. In Tamil Nadu, long-standing anti-Brahmin movements have long kept down the influence of the BJP and Hindutva. But today their presence is palpable. They are spreading through the growing importance of Hindu religious festivals, as previously discussed, and federal social policies. With the exception of the National Rural Employment Guarantee Act (NREGA), a massive labor program targeting mostly women, federal social policies consider women not as workers but primarily as mothers, sisters, and young girls who must be protected.[31]

Sociologist Navtej Purewal (2018) has observed that women's protection and safety is a recurring slogan of the BJP government's leading social programs, from sanitation and anti sex-selective abortion to financial inclusion. In official statements and awareness campaigns, the eradication of open defecation aims at "protecting" young girls from the risk of sexual abuse in the fields. The prevention of sex-selective abortion aims to "save" daughters. In financial inclusion campaigns, brothers are encouraged to open savings accounts for their sisters. Women are seen as helpless and dependent, while men are considered as inherently violent or protective. This is coupled with the strategic use of women's insecurity and violence through scaremongering rhetoric about rape and "love jihad." This myth has been propagated by Hindu extremists accusing Muslims (or Dalits) of seducing young Hindu women in order to convert them, buttressing the ideal of female respectability and of women being confined to the tight boundaries of family and caste.

Security-related rhetoric has translated into constant suspicion of women's morality in Dalit settlements in South Arcot, as though they were the primary culprits for this insecurity. Women's movements, gestures, words, and looks, are constantly observed, scrutinized, and judged. The "paranoid distrust" discussed by anthropologists S. Anandhi and Karin Kapadia is an everyday reality (2017, 12). Permanent houses are built with the motive of protecting young girls from the risk of assault. Everyday conversations are full of gossip and suspicion about women's "morals." "Easy," "unruly" women are heavily criticized and insulted. The English term "item" is frequently used, or the expression "hot hand" (soodu kai). Divorce, which was once relatively common among Dalits, has become rare. Young girls now all go to school, often by bus, which naturally makes their mothers proud but also anxious. "If they [men] could tie us up, they would," says Praba, a neighbor of Pushpurani's, while keeping a close eye on her own daughter. For young girls, any rumor about premarital sex could harm their future prospects, and a child born out of wedlock puts the whole family to shame. We encountered several cases of suicide and of running away. Conversely, men are regularly taunted if their wives or daughters have reputations for promiscuity. Pushpurani told us that she probably never got so angry with her mother as when she called Pushpurani's husband a pottai. Pottai literally means "female" and by extension refers to men who are weak, incapable, and impotent, both sexually and materially.

As we will see throughout this book, sexual morals do not stop female extramarital sex from happening, more often out of necessity than choice. Extramarital sex is sometimes the only way to make ends meet for the family, given the shortcomings of husbands and the erosion of kinship solidarity.

The Diversity of Kinship Debts in South Arcot

As we have seen, the sexual political economies have radically transformed over the past fifty years in South Arcot. Dalit women are now in permanent debt to their kin, removed from production, reduced to a status of "dependent," to a reproductive role, and to a liability weighing heavily on the finances of their parents, brothers, and uncles. "Just born, and she already has the entire world on her shoulders," as we were once told about a newborn girl.

Although kinship debt is omnipresent, rampant, and permeates women's subjectivities and behaviors, including financial behaviors, it takes on multiple forms, including for men. Kinship debt expresses gender differentiations but also caste and class differentiations. We will illustrate such diversity in terms of the cases of various individuals. We have already met some of them—Danam, Pushuprani, and Yoganathan—others are new, and we will come back to them throughout the book.

Danam proudly recalled that for her marriage, her in-laws did not ask for anything because they were banking on her economic value. But her case is an exception and reflects a bygone era: a dowry is now obligatory. The dowry that brides bring on their wedding day dictates their future financial obligations.

Some arrive "empty-handed" as a result of a "love marriage" contracted outside the rules of kinship. Love marriages are in fact increasingly common—Kumaresan's case is by no means an exception. In our 2020–21 survey, 117 marriages had been held over the previous three years, and 85 percent were described as "arranged." This, however, included love marriages that parents later agreed to in order to maintain the family honor and in hopes of recovering a dowry. Kumaresan's parents have received nothing so far. Meanwhile, their daughter-in-law is regularly asked to borrow money from her own parents to pay off part of her in-laws' debts. "She has no choice," Kumaresan swiftly said, "since she hasn't brought anything."

Pushpurani also had a love marriage. This was about thirty years ago, in the early 1990s. At the time, the event had caused a scandal, so there was no way the families could reach an agreement and no dowry was paid. Since then, Pushpurani has had to pay her debt in another way. When we met her in 2004, she quickly spoke of the burden of her in-laws. She would regularly reminisce about the drama of the wedding. "They see me as nothing, their son's life is ruined. The mother-in-law was asking me, 'Are you going to play [referring to the fact that she was very young]? What is the use of this marriage?'" She kept telling us that despite her lack of education—she could not read or write—she wanted to show she could be an "asset" (*sothu*). As we will see throughout this book, Pushpurani took on the financial obligations of many lineage events to compensate for what she failed to bring on her wedding day. Her desire for social mobility seems to be driven by the constant humiliation inflicted by her in-laws. Her lender-lover was instrumental in her financial juggling, lending her cheap money and being flexible on the terms. But this deviant sexuality was also a source of guilt that locked her into an unpayable debt (see chapter 6).

Conversely, contributing substantial wealth is no guarantee, as its control and use frequently remain the preserve of husbands and in-laws. The case of Raika, from the Vanniyar caste, illustrates this well. She married one of her cousins in the mid-1990s. Her parents had given twenty sovereigns of gold, then about two years of family income, which was relatively high in her community at the time. Raika saw her marriage as a "constant nightmare." She called her husband lazy and was subjected to his obsessional jealousy. Like many young girls, she had expected romance and love from marriage, but she quickly turned into "a police officer to make him work." Everything had to be constantly negotiated. If she needed clothes for the children, he would buy the cheapest possible; she wanted her son to go to engineering school, he wanted him to have bare-bones training; she wanted *dosais* (pancakes stuffed with vegetables or meat) for breakfast, he would just buy *idlis* (rice cakes). Initial help from her brothers steadily dried up as they got married and had their own obligations. And Raika did not want to fall apart in front of her sisters-in-law. She had no control over the jewels she brought to the wedding—"If I were a beggar, do you think they would have given you all that gold," her husband regularly asked. Above all, in view of her own parents' efforts to marry her off properly, she felt obligated to respect family values. She constantly thought about divorce but couldn't bring herself to go through with it. She would feel guilty about ruining the family reputation. Prompted by an NGO, then with the crucial help of her lover, she developed a small computer services business in a nearby town. This became a space of microfreedom, an opportunity to escape marital and family control, including sexual control, and a source of financial autonomy. As with Pushpurani, her deviant sexuality also trapped her in a sense of unpayable debt. In her own words, she aspires to be a "pure mother," but she constantly wonders if she is not a whore instead. As will be seen later, both her moral breakdown and her husband's hold on her also reflect the increasingly difficult quest for respectability of a declining social group. Raika is married to a handweaver, a profession that has long been highly respected among the Vanniyars but which is now under attack from industrial (and Chinese) competition.

Sexual political economies are not only intertwined with patriarchy. They reflect and reinforce class inequalities of which men are also victims. A man who has sisters will find it more difficult to marry since sisters are seen as a burden to be married off and supported throughout their lives. Maternal uncles are also supposed to take care of the marriage of their nieces. And throughout

life, the simple fact of having sisters or nieces translates into specific obligations. However, some men delegate at least some of these to their wives. Yoganathan's first wife, Rani, would complain: "I've spent all my life giving gifts
to these four sisters, and each sister has daughters," referring to her husband's
obligations as an elder brother and maternal uncle. Beyond the risky investment of raising sons discussed earlier, Yoganathan bore heavy obligations as a
maternal uncle. During one of Isabelle's visits in 2019, Yoganathan was visited
by one of his sisters, who asked for help with her newborn granddaughter.
Yoganathan retorted that his duty ended with his nieces. But she insisted, and
two days later he finally gave her 2,000 rupees. This is not even "accumulated
capital," Yoganathan's wife lamented, as there would be no "return." By this
she meant there would be no reciprocal giving, as is normally the case for
maternal uncle obligations. Far beyond Yoganathan's case, and as we will see
in chapter 3, women incur just as much debt as men do for ceremonies, and
they do so as mothers, grandmothers, sisters, and sometimes sisters-in-law (as
the case with Yoganathan's wife). In a nearby region, a joint study with Isabelle
Agier and Ariane Szafarz concludes that the primary factor in women's indebtedness, "all other things being equal," is the number of daughters (Agier,
Guérin, and Szafarz 2012, 364). If, adopting an econometric analysis, we take
women with identical wealth levels, occupations, and education, the number
of daughters they have is the greatest factor for them getting into debt.

Chandran, a Dalit man, is a further example. His own debt, he said, was
having three sisters in his care. We met him in 2005 when he was a social
worker for a rural development NGO (which would later turn into a microcredit organization). He opted for a love marriage that almost cost him his
job. The NGO blamed him for setting a bad example for women and instill-
ing "modern" and "unrespectable" ideas. To compensate for his love marriage
and the lack of a dowry that could have helped finance his sisters' marriages,
he promised his parents that he would take care of them himself. Ten years
later, he continued to struggle with the debts contracted to secure his sisters'
marriages. His salary was low and irregular, depending on the NGO's projects and the funding it could obtain. Over his many discussions with Santosh,
he mentioned two extramarital affairs with well-off women who had helped
him access cheap funding. His wife was aware of the affairs, but when she
complained, Chandran would retort: "You brought nothing [to our marriage],
what the hell have you brought to me?" He made it clear to Santosh that he had
no choice and needed mistresses to solve his financial problems. At no time

did he evoke any feelings of guilt. Unlike the indebted woman, the indebted man enjoys sexual freedom.

Womanhood as Debt

From Pushpurani, Raika, Chandran, and Yoganathan, we can see there is no one outcome or destiny. Women and men both regularly seek to break free from patriarchal norms, paying a high price in the process. Wedding alliances and payments take many forms and cannot be understood in isolation from the set of rights and obligations that bind members of the kinship group and extended sociality (Carsten 2000; Narotzky 1995). What is striking, however, is that in each scenario, women felt indebted, liable, and guilty. Feelings of blame and guilt were often explicitly voiced. The women used the terms "debt" (*kadan*, which refers to both moral and financial debt), "gratitude" (expressed as an obligation of thanks [*nandri*]), or "guilt" (*vetkam*). Well beyond verbal expressions, however, feelings of debt and guilt permeated women's daily routines, driven by an obsession with fulfilling their obligations and unfailingly meeting their duties.

Pushpurani, who got married with no dowry, seems to have contracted an infinite moral debt to her in-laws. Raika, as someone very well endowed, feels morally indebted to her own parents. Her dowry is actually a burden that stops her from walking away from her cross-cousin marriage. Chandran, as a brother, had the duty to marry off his sisters properly. His love marriage prevented him from recovering a dowry that could have been used to marry off his sisters, but he managed to discharge his moral debt thanks to his wealthier mistresses. He did this openly, and his own wife was not allowed to complain since she came without a dowry. Yoganathan, as a brother, was also morally indebted to his sisters, but he deferred much of his financial debt to his two wives. As will be seen later, they bear the bulk of the obligations.

Danam's marriage respected old kinship norms when Dalit women were still considered active economic contributors. She now complies with new norms and will benefit greatly since she has three sons. A few years ago she was still expecting one of her sons to pursue land cultivation, and she would have looked for a bride who could assist him (while still demanding a dowry, which has become a rule regardless of the bride's productive status). Now, she has come to terms with the fact that farming is out of fashion. In a few years' time, she said with regret, Dalit women would be like Reddiyar women (the highest caste in the village), locked up at home, just opening and closing the front door to visitors. This exaggerates the inactivity of upper-caste women, which includes multiple pursuits and responsibilities—social and religious rituals, invitations, and social relations, sometimes also lending—most of which are invisible to outside observers. But Danam is right about the unenviable productive inactivity of high-caste women, which seems to shrink the horizon for Dalit women in an economy increasingly monopolized by men.

We should also keep in mind the weight of religious debt. As mentioned earlier, prayer and rituals are becoming evermore prevalent among Dalits, and the responsibility for this is placed on women's shoulders, especially for daily piety. This means prayer and respect for priests' prayer instructions; on auspicious days, drawing *kolams* [ephemeral decorative drawings made with powder] in front of the house to attract the good eye and chase away the evil eye; cooking, fasting, and following specific hygiene rules in accordance with religious prohibitions, astrological requirements, and the lunar calendar; following specific dress codes when visiting the temple; and placing offerings both in the family's place of prayer at home and in temples.[32] Echoing an ancient belief dear to Hindu theology about the "auspicious" woman (Fuller 2004, 23), women describe this as an additional family obligation, supposedly to ward off bad luck, ensuring the husband's well-being and good fortune, successful education and marriages for the children, pregnancy for the young brides, and so forth. As Pushpurani pointed out in a very pragmatic way, it is as if their devotion had to compensate for their supposed lack of economic contribution.

We will have opportunities to discuss the intertwining of women's moral obligations and financial debt throughout this book. For now, what lessons can we draw from this incursion into the rules of kinship and sexual political economies? Putting kinship back at the heart of the economy, as in the anthropological tradition, casts a different light on debt as a power relationship.[33]

Far beyond anthropological and crucial philosophical approaches based in questions of class, caste, or, in other contexts, race (see the introduction), womanhood reveals itself as an ontological condition of moral indebtedness. The devaluation of Dalit women, and their sense of devotion and self-sacrifice, are of course nothing new. But their economic devaluation and the repression of their bodies reinforce and entrench this sense of indebtedness within their selves and their flesh. Debt first and foremost reveals itself as a power relation shaped by patriarchy. Financialized capitalism feeds on this patriarchal debt and in turn strengthens it. As we will see in the following chapters, women's economic devaluation and the repression of their sexuality are the foundation to understanding their demand for market credit, how they boost their creditworthiness, and how they experience indebtedness and the ethics of repayment.

3

The Sexual Division of Debt

IN OCTOBER 2004, MISS Mary was working as a pastor and as the head of a small rural development NGO for rural Dalit women's empowerment. She would try to explain to the Dalit women she encountered that microcredit was a "poison" that would never solve their problems. The Dalit women would strongly disagree, claiming that she could never understand because she was not married. The women would say: "Our husbands keep asking us what we have brought back from home." This refers to the ongoing support that wives' families are supposed to offer in compensation for their lack of inheritance and low economic value. "Microcredit will mean we have something!" Miss Mary eventually gave in and ran government microcredit programs for almost a decade before they were replaced by a range of private financial companies.

By June 2017, Pushpurani had access to market credit, as did many women in her neighborhood. Learning of this sort of credit gave her the confidence to borrow from various informal sources elsewhere, including an upper-caste man in a neighboring village. She hand-delivered an invitation for her son's wedding, hoping to foster good relations with this lender. She described the following scene to us: As she stood at his front door, invitation in hand, he ironically exclaimed, before even greeting her: "In the time of your mother and grandmother, women like you would come in through the back door." Pushpurani understood this allusion to the time when Dalit women worked for the upper castes and were asked to carry out all kinds of domestic services for their masters, including sexual ones. Since that episode, she continued to borrow money from this man but categorically refused to go to his house. She does not think he would assault her, as it could create a high-profile scandal that the Dalit political parties would condemn. But the mere fact that he looked at her with sexual desire felt unbearable. She would often repeat: "We need money, but we also need dignity."

The indebted woman is a product of the capitalist credit market. But the rules of kinship and caste interdependencies closely shape female credit markets. The emergence of microcredit was a turning point in the feminization of debt in South Arcot. Microcredit was launched by NGOs at the turn of the twenty-first century and went on to receive public policy support. It was initially designed to help fight poverty and emancipate women and subsequently transformed into a commercial product (Nair 2005, 2012). In numerical terms, the microcredit market has been successful. About half of the families have access to one or often more sources of microcredit in South Arcot today. Ninety percent of clients are women. In India as a whole, women make up 98 percent of microcredit clients, as opposed to 80 percent worldwide.[1] Microcredit advocates had long thought that the purpose of setting up or strengthening small businesses is to drive women's demand for credit. But they now acknowledge that microcredit is frequently used to smooth consumption, allowing women to better manage their budgets and be empowered within their households.[2] Microcredit's critics argue that microcredit is mostly an expensive debt that simply helps poor women to make ends meet. It includes and entraps them within the exploitative global financial market.[3]

We concur more with the critical analysis overall, but greater complexity is required. As discussed in the previous chapter, shifting kinship norms, along with changes in livelihood patterns, seek to make housewives out of Dalit women. Far from microcredit advocates' entrepreneurial ideals, here microcredit just fuels this "housewifization" (Mies 1998, 100–110) since most of the credits are put toward social reproduction needs. Beyond that, women use credit access to assert their authority as good budget managers and stay-at-home mothers, thus regaining worth in the eyes of their families and kinship groups. This is what was being requested of Miss Mary. Microcredit allows women to partially fulfill their family obligations, or their kinship debt, as discussed in the previous chapter.

Interestingly, however, the indebted woman does not limit herself to a narrowly defined housewife label. Over time, she gained access to larger amounts as the microcredit market expanded. Thanks to her microcredit experience, she gains creditworthiness with other lenders. She uses the debt money not for economic investment but for social investment, aiming, with varying success, to improve her children's chances in life. She redefines the status of housewife in her own way and uses debt not only for survival purposes but as "potentiality," to use anthropologist Julie Chu's term (2010, 5). And the indebted woman is not content to use income from her husband. She tries, again with varying success, to have him work to pay off their debts.

Microcredit's success has thus gone hand in hand with the transformation of kinship rules discussed in the previous chapter. Microcredit's success has also hinged on the caste system, as Pushpurani's experience suggests. It has a further potentiality: to stop endless caste debt. Caste debt used to lead to financial dependency and disposable bodies of either sex, including sexually in the case of women. Microcredit advocates are not entirely wrong to praise the emancipatory virtues of microcredit, albeit with one strong caveat: a potentiality may or may not materialize. Neither sexual dominance nor dependency on high castes has ended, as the following chapters will show, but both have shifted and reconfigured. As we will also see, under no circumstances do market credits substitute for other forms of debt. On the contrary, the indebted woman desperately needs to borrow from family, neighbors, informal private lenders, patrons, and lovers to repay her microloans, and vice versa. As is often the case, the market does not eliminate but displaces domination and creates new forms of classification and hierarchies (Fourcade and Healy 2013). The reconfiguration of caste debt above all results in the feminization of debt.

More fundamentally, market credit radically restructures the financial landscape. Out of choice or constraint, not all Dalit women use microcredit, but most are now highly indebted and are able to attract lenders. Microcredit's greatest success has been to prove the creditworthiness and discipline of women, who are now the target market for many lenders. Women's debts, however, are specific. They are both expensive and degrading, and they require seamless repayment. The reconfiguration of financial markets has made for a sexual division of debt, confining women to debts that men do not want. Here we can see a constant trait of capitalism, based not only on the sexual division of labor but the sexual division of debt. As we will see at the end of the chapter, history can be instructive here. It shows that the sexual division of debt runs alongside capitalism and the male breadwinner model.

The Rise of the Indebted Woman

"We shouldn't have to continue to depend on one single person. Before, if we didn't go to the *ur* [the non-Dalit neighborhood], there'd be no food. We depended on them for everything," Danam reflects on her childhood as the daughter of a laborer attached to a high-caste landlord (*padiyal*). To this, a neighbor listening in on the conversation from a distance retorts that slavery (*adimai*, "to be at someone's feet") is no longer being under one person but under multiple people at once. Danam and her neighbors, who are watching the conversation, laugh and acknowledge that the man is right, but one thing has changed: the money is flowing. You have to pay it back, but getting it is now very easy. "In the past, you had to beg for cash, but today the money comes ringing at your door," we were often told. Just a few hours in a village are enough to observe the almost frenziedly industrious, mainly male credit agents in action. They now go door to door to their mainly female clients. Danam told us that her mother had barely been able to borrow ten rupees. Nowadays, Danam regularly accrues three or four microloans and about ten additional informal debts. Her rather cooperative husband works hard to help her pay off her debts, but it is not enough, and she constantly has to go back into debt to pay off the regular installments on her microloans.

The expansion of debt opportunities in South Arcot has been surprisingly rapid, mushrooming in a twenty-year period. It is equally the outcome of a long process involving Indian rural colonial-era public policies, current so-called financial inclusion policies, and new private actors, from lending castes to contemporary global capital finance companies (some but not all still owned by the lending castes) (Kar 2018; Radhakrishnan 2022). During the colonial period, British officials and Christian missionaries were already condemning the working poor's "congenital" and "extravagant" debt (Pouchepadass 1980, 167; Hardiman 2000; Cederlöf 1997). Programs began emerging to regulate or standardize the poor's finances, whether to tackle the scourge of usury, curb overindebtedness, or encourage monetary saving in the name of thrifty household management. After independence in 1947, various measures upheld the British legacy via credit unions and later by subsidized credit policies (Gregory 1997, chap. 6). With the (relative) liberalization of India's banking and financial system in the 1990s, public policy shifted toward incentives for the financial inclusion of so-called excluded populations.[4] Whereas women

were often left out of previous programs (Dreze 1990; Harriss-White and Colatei 2004), since the early 2000s they have become the main target.

Financial inclusion policies first took the form of self-help groups (SHGs).
These consisted of ten to twenty members, most often women, and aimed to
educate their members on how to manage their savings, circulating those savings among themselves, first as internal credit, and then as access to a cheap
bank loan. In the absence of physical collateral, the social pressure of the
group and solidarity between members served as collateral. The SHG concept
emerged in the late 1990s from within NGOs involved in rural development
and social rights. It was then championed by male and female social workers,
often with training in public education and lengthy experience as volunteers
and activists. Some NGOs strongly criticized the very idea of microcredit as
running against a more radical transformation of gender inequalities, and as
incompatible with the unity necessary for a broader struggle. This was the
"poison" that Miss Mary was referring to in our opening vignette. Some of
these NGOs ended up converting to microcredit under the pressure of their
donors, who saw microcredit as an opportunity to make concrete, visible impacts. Others changed their minds under pressure from rural women who
strongly demanded microcredit. This was the case with Miss Mary, who re-
luctantly gave in to keep the trust of the Dalit women she had been trying to
help for about a decade.

In contrast to the official rhetoric, women do not want to start businesses
using microcredit. They wish to assume the status of housewife and smooth
over household expenses, in new supposed self-sufficiency. When asked to
compare their situation with their mother's, a similar scenario often emerges:
a maternal uncle had been responsible for protecting his nieces, and after marriage, these women could regularly seek help from their parents or even go
back to their parents' home in the event of conflict or financial stress. Today,
says Pushpurani, "When a girl gets married and comes to a family, the family
sends her there and thinks she will be happy; when it goes wrong, the wife does
not want to show this to outsiders, she does not want to damage the status of
the family . . . this would be degrading to the entire family; and it leads her
to manage on her own." Pushpurani is probably romanticizing the generosity
of the maternal uncle here. It is certainly true, however, that support from a
woman's birth family is no longer a given. With the transformation of kinship rules and the emergence of the dowry, the kinship support that Dalit
women historically enjoyed after marriage is subject to ongoing controversy

and conflict. Many Dalit women must now manage on their own, and it is credit access that allows them to compensate for the decline in family support.

In the early 2000s, the SHG model was replicated on a large scale with the help of international funding and the federal and Tamil government in India. A key step was the inclusion of SHGs as a priority sector in banking regulation. Even though the banking industry has been greatly liberalized, banks are still required to allocate part of their portfolio to priority sectors. This legislation is a powerful incentive for banks that have very little experience with women clients, let alone rural or Dalit ones. Partnerships with NGOs avoid direct contact. By assigning SHGs as a priority sector, banking regulators have probably played a key role in boosting rural women's creditworthiness, particularly for Dalit women.

This all allowed the indebted woman to take her first steps, not without difficulties. Of course, Dalit women have probably always been indebted, including monetarily speaking.[5] What changed is that female debt became legitimate among a range of actors including NGOs, public administrations, and banks. But other actors needed to be convinced: husbands and local leaders, who were often lenders themselves. In 2003, when we started out with our fieldwork, the first SHGs were just emerging, and the process was often painstaking. For husbands, this new cash opportunity raised interest but also suspicion. The procedures were time-consuming and impinged on women's already busy schedules. Men also had a very negative view of the group as a potential generator of rumors, talking points, and challenges. Social workers above all had to persuade husbands that the time involved would benefit the entire family. Chandran, a social worker who created and participated in hundreds of SHGs, was known for his ability to bring women together but also to convince men of the SHG's legitimacy. In the early years, he considered this the most difficult part of his work. Over time, SHGs became transmission belts for various public programs that were aimed solely or primarily at women. These included subsidies for housing, livestock, and daughters' weddings. The SHG movement also involved various awareness and training sessions such as entrepreneurship, leadership, empowerment, or financial literacy. The broadening of the SHGs' mission allowed them to gain legitimacy, especially with men, while raising new points about the potential emancipation of women.

Village men held contrasting positions. Some sneered, scoffed, and did not see SHGs as a threat to male power. This attitude was most common among Dalit men, who generally had less control over their wives. SHGs would be nothing more than "big shit," "smoke and mirrors," "a one-man show and the next day there's nothing left." Other men, however, were adamant that their wives should not be "brainwashed." "The goat may graze, but it must not leave the field." In other words, SHGs should not go beyond the limits imposed by men on their wives. Many women were never part of SHGs. Some were considered unreliable at repayment and thus excluded by NGOs, while others were forbidden to participate by their husband or in-laws. In extended families, it was common for daughters- or sisters-in-law to participate on paper but only as mere nominees. This was the case of Jothi, the daughter-in-law of Devaki and Yoganathan. It was also the case with Pushpurani's sister-in-law. Although she did not share the same home, she lived in the adjacent house and left the management of much of her own financial affairs to Pushpurani.

Social workers also strained to convince various dominant local groups. We discuss this in depth elsewhere (Guérin and Kumar 2017a), but here we will set out the key points. Each village is its own local political arena with its own economic—controlling labor and debtors—and political issues. These include controlling voters for political parties, congregants for churches, and the "beneficiaries" for competing NGOs. Each NGO therefore has to skillfully build its legitimacy and persuade people that these new forms of credit do not threaten the existing order. Over time, two trade-offs emerged: existing lenders realized that women were a new niche for their own markets, and power networks (political parties, often in association with powerful businessmen; some churches) built alliances with NGOs. They offered support, and sometimes resources, via privileged access to public programs. In exchange, NGOs committed to sending women to mass events run by political parties, businessmen, and churches. The women were thus required to participate in political rallies, and their willingness to do so partly determined their eligibility for microcredit. Being freer and less demanding than non-Dalit women, Dalit women were given priority.

After a chaotic and often conflicting legitimization and coalition process, the indebted woman became an accepted figure. In the early years, the debt amounts were limited. SHG internal loans were initially a few hundred rupees, then a few thousand. SHG bank loans rarely exceeded 20,000 rupees (USD 300). The sum remained limited as it was split among ten to twenty women, unless the women took turns signing for it. The debt money was mostly put toward small daily expenses. Over time, the women learned the financial jargon. They learned to compare costs (at a price of 1 to 2 percent per month, SHG loans have an attractive cost). Most importantly, they learned to pay back in fixed installments since this is the basic rule of microcredit and radically distinguishes it from all other sources. Restating the rhetoric of microcredit advocates, microcredit officers justify female targeting by the female repayment ethic. "Women always pay better," they say repeatedly. This learning process came to transform the financial landscape and a real sexual division of debt then emerged.

Male Debts, Female Debts

Until microcredit started, Dalit women had to rely on local sources of credit, whether from their landlords, neighbors, or relatives. The only outside sources were door-to-door lenders, known as *thandal* ("instant"), who came to the home to lend and collect and very often specialized in women, who were seen as "sober and compliant" (Harriss-White and Colatei 2004, 259). Some Dalit women also borrowed from high-caste women by pawning their brassware, or gold for those who had any. As the SHGs developed, so did door-to-door lending and pawnbroking.[6] Door-to-door lenders, who offer small amounts of unsecured money that can be repaid weekly, are very useful for repaying microcredit installments, which usually require payments biweekly or monthly. For pawnbroking, the principal is repaid in one lump sum over time up to one year, giving borrowers some breathing room. Microloans are frequently used to recover pledged assets, and vice versa. Microcredit is also used to purchase small amounts of gold for pledging at a later date. In the early 2000s, each village would have one door-to-door lender or, in rare cases, two. Twenty years later, at least one door-to-door lender comes per day, and they are referred to by the day they come on. Sometimes even more turn up.

The pawnbroking market has equally exploded. It was historically the preserve of non-Dalits and was used to finance farming, but it has now been opened up to Dalits. Dalit women no longer pledge their goods to non-Dalit women but to specialized stores in nearby towns. In Panruti, the nearest town where Danam and Devaki go, there used to be a dozen pawnshops in the early 2000s, and they were all reserved for non-Dalits. Now, twenty years later, there are about eighty pawnshops, and many target women, including Dalit women. Given the ongoing context of scarcity and the constant mismatch between incomes and expenditure, budget management is a constant race against time. As these three debt sources work over different time frames, they are far more complementary than competitive. The more SHG loans increase (in 2020, the average amount per SHG was around 200,000 rupees [USD 3,100], more than double one year of household income), the more the other sources are needed. Women also borrow from relatives, neighbors, grocery shops, their landlords, and local elites. But the particularity of door-to-door lenders, pawnbrokers, and SHGs is that they almost exclusively specialize in female loans. Dalit men have also expanded their options, however: most now work outside the village, which widens their social networks and boosts their opportunities for borrowing.

After the indebted woman learned the business of lending through SHG loans, she gained access to global financial capital. In the mid-2010s, the SHG movement fizzled out. Financing was drying up and international funders were turning their attention to poorer regions of India. Indian government funding was also getting scarcer, and NGOs found it increasingly difficult to obtain a license for international funding. At both federal and state levels, the Indian government sought to regain control over development activities and civil society (Picherit 2015; Kumar 2019). This control was already prevalent with the Indian National Congress (INC) around the 2010s but was severely reinforced when the BJP came to power in 2014. Many NGOs disappeared altogether. Others tried to convert into profit-making financial companies. We were regularly asked to take shares. By 2020, the supply of microcredit mainly came from commercial entities.[7] In local terminology, "finance"—the local term for microcredit companies—has replaced *kuzhu loans* (group loans).

Many microcredit organizations are now listed on the stock exchange and are financed on the global financial capital market. As also observed in the neighboring state of Karnataka, loan officers have a radically different profile and mission compared to the SHG movement's social workers (Kamath and Joseph 2023). They have degrees in finance or marketing and the objective is clear: "We have to catch the market," to quote them. In most cases, the group guarantee is still required since it is the only collateral women have. Unlike SHGs, however, getting approval for finance does not require prior savings or attending any group meetings. For Dalit women, who lack both money and time, these new rules are very welcome. The costs are higher (officially around 2 percent monthly, often more due to multiple additional fees), but the amounts are much more attractive. SHGs are now considered "pocket money," we often hear. And without the support of NGOs, Dalit women have a hard time collecting savings. Microcredit providers readily offer individual loans of

50,000 60,000, or 70,000 rupees (from USD 800 to USD 1,100), the equivalent to 60 to 90 percent of a Dalit household's average annual income. Some SHGs have persisted, especially among non-Dalits, who find it easier to collect regular savings. Most Dalits' SHGs are disappearing. But the key function of the former SHGs should be noted. Both Danam and Pushpurani used the trusted women of these old SHGs to create the joint-liability groups needed to qualify for "finance." The loan officers have also grasped the value of assistance from former SHG leaders and often turn to them first when opening a new market in a village.

In March 2020, outstanding credit was valued at around USD 30 billion, three times as much as ten years earlier (Sa-Dhan 2020; 2010). Of course, compared to the size of the Indian financial market, these amounts are trivial. But compared to the amount of money in circulation in Dalit neighborhoods, the amounts are far from negligible. They are also quite high in relation to Dalits' incomes, especially Dalit women's incomes, as we have seen in chapter 2. The indebted woman has turned into an active player in global financial capital while also actively contributing to the local credit market. Table 3.1 reflects the sexual division of debt sources. Women clearly specialize in microcredit, and even more so in pawnbroking, while men borrow far more often from banks (with banks remaining marginal), from "well-known people" (local elites who lend out their surpluses), from labor recruiters and employers, or from their friends, neighbors, and family. Regarding moneylenders, our quantitative data do not indicate a difference, but women specialize in door-to-door lenders, while men deal with lenders in their workplace. The survey do not include debts under 500 rupees and thus considerably underestimates the myriad of small debts that tie neighborhood women to one other. Interestingly, however, men are much more dependent on their kin for debt. This seems to confirm the chapter's opening vignette, in that women have demand for microcredit and make use of it (like other sources of borrowing) to compensate for dwindling support from their own families.

If we look at the share of debt sources not as a percentage of users but as a volume of debt, the trends are similar. If we distinguish by caste, non-Dalit women are more dependent on pawnshops and SHGs, while Dalit women are more dependent on finance and local elites.

Survival debts, meant to help with day-to-day expenses, are of course the indebted woman's lot. Purely economic investment debt remains a male privilege, or at least mainly available to non-Dalit women, as Table 3.2 shows. But

Source of loan	Male (% indebted to)	Female (% indebted to)
Well-known person (local elite)	57.1	18.7
Relative	34.2	12.9
Friend and neighbor	14.8	4.0
Labor recruiter, employer	19.2	2.5
Pawnbroker	3.7	75.3
Moneylender	14	11.8
Microcredit (SHG or finance)	3.3	29.6
Bank	12.3	4.8

Findings show 57.1 percent of men are indebted to "well-known people."
Source: Authors (NEEMSIS-1 survey, 2016–17, Observatory of Rural Dynamics
and Social Inequalities in Rural India).

Table 3.1. The sexual division of debt by loan source.

Loan used for	Male (%)	Female (all) (%)	Non-Dalit female (%)	Dalit female (%)
Production				
Farming	17.3	11.8	18.3	5.45
Nonfarm business	11.7	6.0	7.0	5.0
Social reproduction—daily survival				
Daily expenses	44.0	56.6	53.1	60.0
Debt repayment	9.2	22.2	20.7	23.6
Health	19.4	17.8	15.5	20.0
Social reproduction—long term				
Housing	21.2	24.5	23.0	25.9
Education	18.5	19.6	18.3	20.9
Ceremonies	47.2	33.5	31.9	35

On their outstanding debt at the time of the survey, 17.3 percent of men have incurred at least
one debt for farming. Source: Authors (NEEMSIS-1 survey 2016–17, Observatory of Rural
Dynamics and Social Inequalities in Rural India).

Table 3.2. The sexual division of debt by loan use.

Dalit women borrow important amounts of money to renovate their homes, educate their children, and marry them off, whether paying the dowry for daughters or the ceremony for sons. Men look on their wives' "small" debts with disdain, suggesting that they only serve to improve daily life. The women themselves remain discreet, probably to preserve male honor. This is where counting and questionnaire surveys are so useful. Our quantitative surveys show that debt put toward long-term social reproduction—housing, education, and ceremonies—is taken out almost equally by men and women. Debt emerges as a true potentiality, which the indebted woman seizes to move forward and improve her children's future.

This was the case of Pushpurani, who kept investing in housing, education, and ceremonies to compensate for the absence of her own dowry. In many others' cases, too, Dalit women not only balance their budgets but seek to improve their children's life chances. Economists term this "opportunity debt." But these are risky investments, and it seems more apt to use the terms of certain anthropologists: to speak of "potentiality" (Chu 2010, 5), or even "social speculation" (Zaloom 2019, 26). Recall, too, the case of Danam, who wanted to provide her sons a good education in return for obtaining a good dowry for them later (see chapter 2). The sought-after potentiality was "progress," starting with an exit from caste dependency. Beyond kinship debt, caste debt also motivates attitudes toward debt and credit.

Breaking Caste Debt

Pushpurani's opening vignette depicts the remnants of a caste dependency that was long conceived of as an endless debt. Caste oppression remains vivid in memories and bodies, and permeates the attitude of Dalits, women and men, toward debt and credit. In Brahmanism, the mere fact of being born creates an original, congenital debt (Kāne 2012, 416; Malamoud 1980, 50; Graeber 2011, 57). One's birth entails a debt to the future, which can never be repaid in full but must be repaid in part. Besides sacrifices, prayers, and veneration to gods and elders, which are open to all, the repayment methods depend on gender and caste: transmission of religious knowledge (only for Brahmins), funeral rites (only for men), begetting boys (for women). While neglected in Indology research, the burden of debt seems to be most severe on women and non-Brahmins.

The theology of debt has historically found its direct expression in finance (Malamoud 1988; Kāne 2012). In medieval India, civil law precisely set out how debt transactions should obey the caste hierarchy: the lower the caste of the debtor, the higher the cost of the debt. A creditor must "take two, three, four and five per cent interest per month, not more, according to the order of the *varna* [caste group]," the Laws of Manu read, considered one of the most authoritative books of the Hindu code (Kāne 2012, 421; Malamoud 1988, 191; Chatterjee 1971, 26–28). A creditor is forbidden to use force if his debtor is of higher status (Malamoud 1988, 194n).

Well beyond cost, debt acts as a social marker. Rules of commensality, purity, and marriage are often considered the main caste boundaries and caste hierarchy markers. Anthropologist Jean-Claude Galey (1980), drawing on the ethnography of a village in the Indian Himalayas, argues that debt generates relations and distinctions between debtors (most often lower caste or non-caste) and creditors (higher caste) similar to those of commensality and intermarriage. There is a circulation of debts, as there is a circulation of women and food. In Galey's view, an inferior status as debtor is a defining feature of lower castes (1980, 137).

In contemporary South Arcot, though steeped in a long-standing anti-Brahmin ideology, debt also acts as a profound hierarchical marker. Local agrarian systems were historically predicated on the one-sided dependency of agricultural workers, who were often Dalits, on their masters (Cederlöf 1997). This is now in the past, but some traces remain. Danam's father and father-in-law were both *paddial*—that is, attached to their landlord. "We never saw cash in those days," Danam recalled from her childhood. They received three servings of *ragi* (finger millet) a day, and rice only on festival days at harvest time, and very occasionally cash.

Balakrishnan, a Reddiyar from a nearby village, employed many *paddial* until about twenty years ago. He explained to us that his job was to oversee the work done but also superintend consumption and social and religious rituals. "If [they] ask for more money, it means that I have to increase wage, so it is necessary to control their consumption; now it's over [the *padiyal* system has ended], they can buy whatever they want." Life-cycle events, however, most often involved a debt that was never repaid but which maintained the dependence and made any form of exit impossible. This unpayable debt was often transmitted down the generations and served the clear political and material objectives of reproducing a precapitalist accumulation mode, and the symbolic domination of ruling castes. Debt repayment was primarily supplied by Dalit bodies, through the labor of men, their wives, and their children. This included agricultural work, with manual irrigation a major component; maintaining livestock, plantations, and housing; and cleaning fields and yards (the interior of houses being carefully proscribed due to untouchability norms).

The appropriation of Dalit women's sexuality was another component of caste debt. As in other parts of India, control over Dalit women's sexuality was long part of a range of domination techniques. It was a source of both sexual play and pleasure that non-Dalit men forbade themselves from having with their own wives. It was equally brandished as an ideological tool asserting the inferiority of Dalits, as the supposed sexual deviancy and sexual availability of Dalit women was flagged as a symptom of their moral depravity (Mitra 2020).[8] This has far from completely disappeared, although men and women Dalits now seek out sexual probity, precisely in a bid for respectability (see chapter 2).

This past history was what Pushpurani brought up in this chapter's opening vignette. Adhering to capitalist credit markets is imbued with the memory of caste dependency in terms of access to credit, freedom of consumption, and control over women's bodies. The past two decade's deep shifts in the financial landscape are expressive of a constant desire to break away from a caste debt long considered as endless.

A similar observation holds concerning the sexual exploitation of Dalit women, which is sometimes denied and sometimes exaggerated in discussions with the villagers, whatever their caste or gender. In local beliefs and imagination, a Dalit woman who is able to borrow money must have slept with her lender, even for a few rupees. "What other guarantee would she have to offer?" we were repeatedly told. It took us a few years to understand that for Dalit women, preserving their reputation was one of the biggest advantages of market credit. It was more difficult to accuse them of sleeping with a loan officer, formally dressed and accountable to his organization. Well beyond the case of Pushpurani, Dalit women keep repeating that they need money but also "dignity."

In other terms, both Dalit men and women experience the expansion of their creditworthiness as a form of emancipation in itself, given a past where creditworthiness meant pledging their bodies, as workers or as sexual objects, and the use of any kind of loan was tightly controlled. The hoped-for emancipation remains tentative, and Dalit women are paying a high price for it. The mitigation of caste debt is mostly reflected in a feminization of debt, and the collateralization of their bodies now takes multiple forms, as we will see in chapter 5.

"Now We Are Trustworthy"

Microcredit has supplemented rather than replaced this preexisting myriad of informal debts. The Brahmanical theology of debt remains alive within these informal debts. "You don't borrow from anyone lower than you," the villagers often say. Even today, it is highly unusual for an upper-caste person to borrow from a lower-caste person, let alone a Dalit.[9] To ask an upper-caste person whether he or she is indebted to a Dalit can be considered as an insult. "They won't take water from us, do you think they would take money?" the Dalits often say. Pushpurani, who borrows a lot but also lends actively, is never approached by non-Dalit women. "They have never asked me for a single rupee," she says.

According to our survey data, while it is still very rare for non-Dalits to borrow from Dalits, it does occur and is worth noting. The transactions are done discreetly to avoid social stigma. This is what Devaki does thanks to her grocery store, which brings her into regular contact with Dalit female customers. Yet Yoganathan, her husband, regularly states that borrowing from Dalits would be the height of degradation. Getting into debt with Dalits to host a prestigious wedding, for example, where lenders are often publicly thanked at the time of the ceremony, remains unthinkable. "I would rather not marry my daughter than borrow from them [Dalits]," says Anja Pulli, who is a daily agricultural laborer from the Vanniyar caste. "Getting money from outside your caste degrades yourself, your own family but also your own caste," he explains.

While the caste-based debt hierarchy persists, one notable transformation is that Dalits now borrow a significant portion of their debt from other Dalits. This certainly represents a break from the late-twentieth-century rural Tamil financial landscape.[10] In 2010, among loans for which the caste of the lender is known (as in most informal loans), 54 percent of the loans borrowed by Dalits came from Dalits (and the rest from non-Dalits). In 2016–17, this share rose to 70 percent.[11]

The mitigation of caste debt has stemmed from multiple factors. In the villages, some Dalits have experienced social mobility, often working as labor recruiters, sometimes as traders, and exceptionally as permanent employees.

This has enabled a surplus for investment into lending. Such mitigation clearly reflects increasing internal differentiation among Dalits. Male migration allows men to expand their networks and their borrowing options among their peers. Microcredit also contributes since women often use their micro-loans to lend to their peers.

It is worth noting that, given the continued expansion of the amount of debt, non-Dalit lending to Dalits continues to flourish, although its share is decreasing. This certainly explains why the growing importance of these financial organizations has not met with strong resistance from local leaders. The decline in non-Dalit lending is relative, yet far from negligible as it expands the range of choices. As we have seen in the opening vignette, Pushpurani could not stand being subject to the disdain and humiliation of a high-caste lender, who seemed to enjoy pointing out her origins as a materially and sexually dominated Dalit woman. She avoids going to his house to avoid derogatory remarks, knowing that as a Dalit and allegedly "impure" person, she has to wait at the doorstep. The other high-caste men she borrows from (Naidus or Mudaliars) follow the same norm.[12] She rejects this humiliation ("They don't want me in their house, they won't get my money.") and asks to meet them in a public place, often the office of a small, informal financial company, which is more neutral and where caste status is less apparent.

Being eligible for loans that do not require the collateralization of their bodies is of itself a source of recognition and dignity for Dalit men and women. "Money is pouring in," Dalit men and women are often heard to say, or "I can borrow from anywhere," highlighting the contrast to their former situations of unilateral dependency. "Now we are trustworthy," the women say about the influx of credit they can now access, with their newfound recognition as creditworthy individuals.

In contexts of strong oppression, such recognition deserves acknowledgment of its true value. The memory of the endless debt on bodies is erased, translating into unprecedented self-confidence and hope for the future. In postapartheid South Africa, James (2015) has shown how Black communities' high propensities to borrow stemmed from their aspiration for democratic equality, for integration into consumer society and social mobility, and their optimism and faith in the future. Assessing the degree of optimism among individuals or social groups is of course difficult, but we have noticed a major shift in the villages we have visited over the past two decades. Debt is clearly part of this story. Quite often, debtors, whether men or women, rarely experience or consider high levels of debt as a sign of shortsightedness or wastefulness but as symbols of boldness and courage. But the burden of debt weighs differently on men and women. The sexual division of debt generates its own hierarchies.

Capitalism and the Social Hierarchy of Debt

Dalit women are on average far more indebted than men in relation to their income, as has been repeatedly pointed out.[13] Their newfound creditworthiness is a source of pride but also a heavy burden of responsibility. This responsibility is all the more onerous since women often repay their husbands' debts, as we will see in the next chapter.

Dalit women, as we have seen, partly specialize in small survival debts, intended to put food on the table, buy soap and detergent, clothe children, pay bus fares and doctor's bills, put oil in the motorcycle, repay old debts, and so forth. Given that the breadwinner model continues to emerge among Dalits (see chapter 2), this kind of debt is deeply emasculating. Added to this is the public dimension of women's debt. This is typically the case with door-to-door lending and microcredit. It also partly applies to pawnbroking, as women can rarely go alone to visit pawnshops in neighboring towns. Creditworthiness is valued, but going into public debt just to make ends meet is degrading, especially as the slightest repayment problem also becomes a public matter. In the new emerging sexual division of labor in South Arcot, survival debts are made a housewife's responsibility and a woman's task. Although considered female debts, survival debts are sometimes used for substantial investments such as housing, education, or ceremonies. As is often the case, gender categories reflect both the realities and the norms of inferiority that society seeks to assign to women.

"We are shameless" (*Vetkamey illai*) is how Dalit women often justify their status as indebted women. "We can ask, the men cannot." This point came up again and again in discussions about the sexual division of debt. "We are safeguarding men," Pushpurani told us when first asked. She explained that as men are constantly moving around, they would be widely insulted and lose their reputation if they defaulted on their debts. If the debt burden is on women's shoulders, the loss of reputation is limited to the neighborhood as women largely stay in one place. Her husband, Kandan, made it clear that he refuses to borrow from his neighbors because of the risk of losing his reputation if something went wrong.

Parvati, also a Dalit, explained how borrowing small amounts would be degrading for her husband: "Men don't want to be bothered with small expenses. He has a good position, he can't beg like that. People would say, 'What kind of income does he have?' 'What kind of man is he?'" Parvati compared debt to serving food. It is hard to think of a man not being served, and she did not want her husband going around asking for money; she would feel bad.

The women are also all too aware, when it comes to microcredit, that men would never agree to the many conditions that lenders lay down. "Men can't stoop to that," says Pushpurani. She lists all the difficult constraints involved, which we also regularly witnessed. These include attending meetings to set up the microcredit groups; meetings to pay back the money; visiting and negotiating with those who don't pay; seeking compromises, finding money; going to the agency to pick up the money and waiting in line at the counter, sometimes for hours, without food or drink. Pushpurani calls this work "social help" (*samuga uthavi*).[14] "It is a sacrifice," she says, "and it is not for men." Over time, the loan conditions have become much more flexible. The SHG operation was extremely time-consuming, which probably led to its demise. While its empowerment goals were certainly commendable, the endless meetings, the frequently unnecessary training sessions, and the NGO's various expectations exasperated the women. These meetings and trainings are no longer mandatory with the market providers and only timely repayment matters. Nevertheless, the women must still form groups, regulation of which includes chasing after bad payers when there is no other choice and putting up with harsh words and insults when payments are late. "Even in the event of death, cover up the bodies and then pay," was something we often heard from loan officers. Maintaining creditworthiness, as we will see in the following chapters, requires constant, time-consuming relationship building.

To obtain cash, women continue to line up at the microcredit branch. They are often forced to wait outside, sometimes for several hours, publicly exposing their need for liquidity. The commercialization of microcredit has also resulted in zero tolerance for bad payers. Because of the lack of physical collateral, microcredit providers have two enforcement tools: social pressure and the promise of a new loan. The women are so desperate for cash that they try to maintain their good-paying status at all costs. But late payments are common. Beyond social pressure and peer conflicts and tensions, they have to put up with intimidation and persuasion techniques from loan officers, who themselves are subject to strict profitability targets. "I lost my youth," said Ravi, who had been working as a loan officer for a few months when Santosh first met him. He was considering quitting, sickened by the daily harassment he was forced to deploy to compel women to pay back their loans. In West Bengal, anthropologist Sohini Kar has discussed in depth the crucial and uncomfortable role of loan officers. She describes them as "proxy creditors" since they do not own the capital but are responsible for repayments (2018, 86). Some lenders use harsh words or threats, while others forge strong emotional bonds that personalize the debt relationship and act as a powerful repayment incentive (2018, 97).[15]

Zero tolerance in terms of default culminated at the time of the COVID-19 pandemic. While bank clients, mainly rich and non-Dalit men, were granted first a moratorium and then debt cancellations, microcredit clients, mainly women, had to fight to have the moratorium respected and were not granted any debt cancellations, despite repeated requests.[16]

The transformation of the uses and meanings of pawnbroking is also in-structive. Pawnbroking was the historical preserve of the upper castes and classes, of those owning assets, mainly gold, that could be pawned to invest in agriculture. The poorest people and the Dalits, owning almost no gold, would pawn their brassware to local landlords who would exploit them by charging ridiculously high rates. When local economies started to become monetized, even the poorest families began to buy gold—as ceremonial wedding pres-ents, as emergency savings, and as an investment in the future, notably for the weddings of future generations. Over time, gold ownership and pawnbroking became more democratic and extended to Dalits, while becoming specifically female, as pledging gold for social reproduction rather than production pur-poses was seen as disreputable.[17] On the eve of microcredit repayments, at the start of the school year, or during religious festivals such as Deepavali and Pongal, pawnshops overflow and long lines are common. Mostly Dalit or poor women are seen there. It is not that non-Dalit and less poor women do not need cash, but they try as much as possible to avoid public exposure by bor-rowing more discreetly.

The Tamil case in some ways echoes transformations in the morality of debt during the emergence of industrial Europe (Roberts and Zulfiqar 2019). The history of European industrialization shows how survival debt, intended to make ends meet, was gradually erected as a marker of class and gender but over a very long time. Preindustrial Europe was a credit society. Not only were many transactions done on credit, but credit was a true "cultural currency," in the words of historian Craig Muldrew (2001, 83). Over time, and under the influence of a bourgeois morality of responsibility and foresight, debt became a reflection of the incapacity and improvidence of the working classes. With the rise of the male breadwinner model, debt also become a female matter, both "women's work" (Lemire 2011, 14) and "a damning sexual stereotype" (Tebbutt 1983, 36). In the first half of the nineteenth century, when industrial pauperization was taking its toll, pawnbroking exploded. Microcredit did not exist, which is obviously a central difference, but pawnbroking became an almost exclusively female market. Borrowing and repaying occupied a large part of the time and energy of working-class women, who went back and forth between their homes and the pawnshop, sometimes several times a day. Like gold today in South Arcot, jewelry, watches, clothes, linen, blankets, dishes, irons, and candlesticks were in constant circulation. They were appraised not only for their intrinsic value but also for their value on the credit market.

As in the Tamil countryside, certain periods—weekends, eves of holidays, strikes—saw an influx of requests. As discussed by feminist historians, working-class women crowded the sidewalk waiting for their turn (Lemire 2011; Tebbutt 1983). The richer ones looked at them with disdain. The public display of their need for cash carried the taint of disorder, and the lines described by historians in front of the London pawnshops are eerily reminiscent of what we see in Tamil country. The poorest people are not troubled, but those who want to maintain their dignity bow their heads, ashamed of publicly exposing the inability of the men in the family to earn enough and their own inability to manage the family's finances properly.

Contemporary Tamil villages are not Victorian England. It is, however, striking to note a similarity of processes in the emergence of capitalism: in both cases, the proletarianization of the workforce involves survival debt that is largely female and inevitable to compensate for the insufficiency of wages, the absence of protection, and the incapacity of spouses. This survival debt is both degrading and emasculating because it expressly symbolizes that lack of self-sufficiency. Microcredit, initially conceived as a tool for the emancipation of women, is primarily contributing to their "housewifization" (Mies 1998, 100–110). Its primary impact is to have feminized the local credit market, with providers now convinced of women's creditworthiness and their impeccable repayment ethics.

To widen the focus to other contemporary societies, the female face of survival debt seems to be a constant in capitalist societies. Whether it is the "full-time micro-management of every dollar and debt" (Thorne 2010, 185), painful trade-offs between arrears and mounting bills, negotiations with aggressive or humiliating bailiffs or collection agencies, demanding rescheduling, seeking debt advice, or filing for personal bankruptcy, women are very often on the front line. In the United Kingdom, working-class men who live alone find it very difficult to manage their debts and seek advice, out of "male pride" (Goode 2012, 333). In the United States, men refuse these financial tasks, deeming them "upsetting or bothersome" (Thorne 2010, 185). In France, bailiffs turn primarily to women to collect rent arrears (François 2018, 48), and women are overrepresented in the management of personal bankruptcy proceedings (Perrin-Heredia 2018, 202n19). In the United Kingdom, overindebted women motivate each other through virtual support groups for "no spending days" and regain their status as good savers and managers and therefore as good mothers (Montgomerie and Tepe-Belfrage 2017, 662). In Argentina, Brazil, Chile, and Paraguay, women are the linchpins of daily debts that keep family finances afloat (Schijman 2019; Narring 2022a; Han 2012; Schuster 2015). Borrowing to manage scarcity and facing the humiliation of creditors is deeply emasculating. Then as now, for decision makers and employers as well as husbands, women's indebtedness emerges as a comfortable solution. It not only precludes questioning the inability of men to earn a decent wage, but it also avoids challenging the inadequacy of wages paid by employers and the inadequacy or absence of social protection. It is also worth noting that in the subprime loans that led to the global financial crisis of 2008, women—primarily women of color—were overrepresented, either as clients, as in the United States, or as management over delinquencies and evictions, as in Spain.[18]

In capitalist societies, there seems to be a certain universality to the specialization of poor women in humiliating and degrading debts, even if the debts take on different forms depending on the context and the period of history. The sexual division of debt acts both as a marker and a revealer of gender hierarchies. The sexual division of debt is particularly conspicuous in South Arcot, whether in terms of the debt-to-income ratio, the sources of debt, or its uses. The sexual division of debt is as much the doing of lenders, who see women as a captive and docile clientele. The men have left these degrading and now emasculating debts to the women, and the women themselves have embraced it, seeking to regain value through debt. Beyond the liquidity needs that result from a volatile and unequal job market, there is a kinship debt and a caste debt to contend with. Women try to pay off kinship debt by getting into more and more new debt. They try to extricate themselves from the caste debt by submitting to the rules and constraints of market credit. All this is akin to real work, as we will see in the next chapter.

4

Debt Work

"**I SPEND ALL MY** time managing and adjusting debt," said Pushpurani, "so how do you want me to work?"[1] When we first met her in 2004, she was juggling various sources of income. She traded sarees that she purchased in Chennai and resold locally; she had also been taken on as an agricultural worker. She equally traded subsidized food products sourced from state-owned shops. Her suppliers were mostly high-caste women who were eligible for these food-stuffs but did not want them due to their poor quality, so she resold them in her neighborhood. She gradually ceased all these small trading businesses to focus on household finance.

The indebted woman works hard at debt management. It emerges as a specific form of unpaid and invisible work that is, however, crucial to the social reproduction of households and society and capitalism as a whole. Feminist studies have sought to uncover the multiple forms of women's invisible work and have gone a long way to foreground what feminist Silvia Federici calls the "secrets" of capitalism (2009, i). Female debt work is one of capitalism's secrets that is just beginning to be revealed.

As societies monetarized and families increasingly came to depend on cash and the market for social reproduction, new kinds of domestic work emerged. These have included managing family budgets through wives' "financial wisdom," as discussed in depth by Zelizer on the early twentieth century in the United States (1994, 41). Managing budgets to the penny, shopping for the lowest prices, and finding the best deals were then decisive skills for a good mother and spouse. In fully monetarized societies, "moneywork" is more relevant than ever and remains a female prerogative (Perrin-Heredia 2018, 202). As societies financialize and debt becomes the condition of "having" and "the only way to live well" (Schuster 2015, 106; Wilkis 2017, 35), the home becomes a place of complex financial practices and calculations. This in turn requires specific domestic work.

This argument is not entirely new. Allon's (2014) analysis of the transformations of capitalism explores successive forms of unpaid and devalued female labor, arguing that new forms of domestic work have emerged under financialization. In Paraguay and Honduras, detailed ethnographies explore the considerable time and energy that women spend managing, calculating, anticipating, seeking help with repayments, and devising reborrowing techniques (Schuster 2015; Hayes 2017). Extending far beyond so-called natural domestic skills, this requires real innovation, diversification, and persuasion. Closer to home, in West Bengal, Kar defines "credit work" as "every set of practices that women engage in to access, maintain and repay loans" (2018, 123). Here, too, she discusses in depth the multiple skills and time such practices require.

The "counting" financial diary method enables us to better examine the content of debt work and quantify its productivity. Feminists have long been fighting for the value of domestic work to be counted, and for work to be counted differently, in order to better measure women's economic contribution to capitalism. In financialized economies entrenched within the sexual division of debt, counting debt and the work of debt is an extension of this struggle. As we will see, debt management in South Arcot has become a real, invisible, devalued yet highly productive form of work. The high volume of transactions, the time invested, the routine and repetition, and the required skills all amount to a true form of unpaid, invisible labor. Indebted women, who are often illiterate although less so than before, will juggle five, ten, fifteen, or even more loans at a time, with different durations and costs, often without a paper trail. An unavoidable skill involved in such debt work is therefore cognitive. It demands both mental arithmetic and a compelling "art of memory" (Yates 1999). Debt work also entails intense "relational work" (Zelizer 2005, 35) and relational skills, including seduction. This results in highly unequal interest debt servicing (the amount of income put toward paying interest). Some women manage to negotiate very cheap loans, while others spend a large proportion of their family income on interest payments.

The issues of relational and seductive skills will be addressed in the next chapter. We focus here on the materiality of debt work, in the sense of its contribution to the household economy. As we will see, the very idea of "housewife," which is increasingly used to describe Dalit women, is completely misleading. When debts make up a large proportion of family cash flow (half on average) and women manage a large proportion of it, especially in terms of repayments, their economic contribution to the household economy becomes critical.

Approaching debt as work and labor is not just about deepening the narrative on women's unpaid work. It equally has the potential to tell a different story about present forms of accumulation and womanhood. Debt work becomes consubstantial with contemporary financial capitalism, both generating value for the financial industry and enabling private capital to pay low labor wages. As a state of mind, which comes on top of the moral kinship debt discussed in chapter 2, it is equally inherent to Dalit women's subjectivity and sense of femininity.

Counting Women's Expenses and Debt

Venkata and Isabelle talked with Kumaresan, the twenty-year-old son of Devaki and Yoganathan, whom we met in chapter 2.[2] We asked him about the way expenses and income were managed within the household and shared between men and women. He laughed and said that his mother was not responsible for anything and that she had to ask him even if she just wanted to "buy an ice cream." In other words, according to her own son, Devaki made no economic contribution to the household economy and therefore had no decision-making power. But counting precisely who pays expenses and debts tells a completely different story.

The first thing the financial diaries revealed was the existence of relatively distinct male and female financial circuits. This showed that the idea of pooled financial flows, implicit in most statistical surveys, is an illusion. For simplicity, we grouped male flows together, separately from female flows. Most male flows were the husbands', but they could also include those of sons. Similarly, female flows could include the flows of daughters or daughters-in-law. We did not measure cash savings kept at home because it was too sensitive a subject. Each household member, including adolescents, tried to preserve a microspace of freedom by saving discreetly. But it seemed that the amounts were very limited. Both male and female villagers preferred to save in gold, or by lending to others (although the amounts were limited in relation to their indebtedness level) or sometimes using savings clubs. We will return to female lending in chapter 7, but our focus here is female debt management.

Another crucial lesson from the financial diaries has been the key role that women play in rotating family cash flows. As we saw earlier, women take on a greater share of debt in relation to their income (see chapter 2). It is all the more instructive to examine their contribution to household cash flow management given the context of high monetary velocity. Tracking nine months of all the financial flows of Devaki's household using the financial diaries, we observed that the combined income (from daily agricultural wage labor) and loans of Devaki, her cowife, and her daughter-in-law accounted for nearly 40 percent of household expenses (including repaying debts). Nearly a quarter of the expenses were paid from the grocery store, jointly run by the two wives and the daughter-in-law and where men regularly lend a hand. Men (the husband and two of the sons) covered the remaining 37 percent.

Pushpurani, who stated in this chapter's opening vignette that she had stopped working to manage her debt, probably bore over 80 percent of household expenses.[3] Danam, whom we also met in chapter 2 and who was part of our financial diary survey, had a personal income of under 10 percent of the household's income. Yet she bore the responsibility for paying 40 percent of the expenses.[4] The gap was even more striking with Parvati, in the third of our financial diary households. She came from a Dalit lower-class background, was in her thirties, and her husband would regularly migrate to the neighboring state of Kerala to carry out unskilled labor. She had two small children and a negligible income (0.7 percent of the household income) yet covered 57 percent of household expenses.

It is worth noting that in some cases incomes were pooled, managed, and spent jointly, especially with respect to family businesses. As we have just seen, this was the case with some of Devaki's grocery store income. It was also the case with most of our fourth financial diary household's income. Kamatchi, a non-Dalit higher-class woman according to local standards, raised dairy cows and her son sold the milk. Most of their expenses were covered by the milk sales.

Of course, men's income and reputation (mostly husbands and sometimes sons) may help boost women's creditworthiness and their capacity to pay back if the woman earns very little or no cash. Indeed, the men often pointed this out. It is only partly true, however. Most loans were clearly identified as falling to a particular family member, even though some loans may have been jointly negotiated. In our diaries, this was Danam's situation. She had taken out part of her loans in the presence of her husband. If husbands do not help repay, and the women have little or no income, they repay by taking on further debt. They use the term "rotation" for this ongoing juggling process. Danam's income made up less than 10 percent of the household income, but she could count on her husband, who turned out to be very cooperative and provided much of the cash she needed for repayment (73.3 percent). She could also somewhat rely on her kin, and her brothers and father contributed 5.2 percent. She managed the remainder (20.5 percent) on her own, which meant borrowing from elsewhere. By consistently doing so, Danam was managing to pay back almost half (47.5 percent) of her loans (the rest came from her husband) despite having almost no income. In Devaki's household, women made 60 percent of their own loan repayments. The two cowives provided most of it, and the daughter-in-law contributed a minimal amount. Devaki and her cowife had sources of income, but their debt was such that they, too, spent their time taking on new debts to pay off old ones. Kamatchi, meanwhile, managed her repayments with the money she jointly earned with her son from the milk business.

Men also borrow to pay off past debts but less frequently. In our NEEMSIS-1 data (2016–17), 9 percent of male loans were paid off by new debt, as opposed to 22 percent of female loans. This constant rotation left women enmeshed in multiple, complex debt circuits. Figure 4.1 illustrates the rotation process for the loan E, borrowed by Devaki from a local moneylender. She repaid loan E using nineteen new debts (D, T, P, AB, and so forth), some of which were also used to repay various other debts (AJ was partly used to repay Z, which in turn was used to repay L, and so forth). Loan E was connected to twenty-six other debts.[5] Juggling has two critical implications: complex management, as women manage many loans at once, and the accumulation of costs.[6]

This constant juggling may come in striking contrast to Western middle-class monobanking practices. Note, however, that there is nothing exceptional about South Arcot. Debt juggling seems to be a constant reality among the working classes, and it seems it is most often, though not always, borne by women. In Paraguay, women say they "bicycle" (Schuster 2015, 7) or "recycle" loans (Hayes 2017, 28). In Brazil, they "cover a saint and uncover another," or solve one problem by creating another (Badue and Ribeiro 2018, 268). In Senegal they "bury a hyena, dig up a hyena," or "open and close drawers"

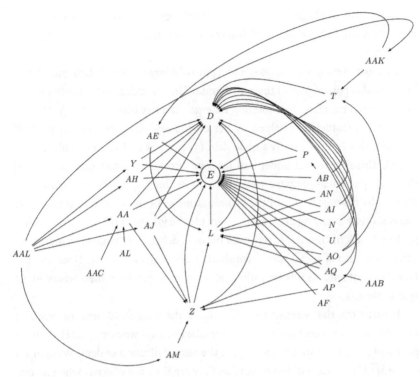

Figure 4.1. Juggling debt.
Source: Elena Reboul (Financial Diaries Data, 2018, Observatory of Rural Dynamics
and Inequalities in South India).

(Guérin 2006, 555). In Argentina, they "undress a dead person to dress another one" (Schijman 2019, 76). In Vietnam, they are "taking from here to pay
there" (Lainez 2019, 819). In Chile, much of the juggling involves department
store credit cards, which circulate extensively among family and friends (Ossandón 2017). In the United States, women are also in charge of managing
working-class budgets, which consists mainly of knowing which bills to pay
first, which to postpone, and "assessing the best strategy for juggling the creditors" (L. Rubin 1976, 108–9). In Mexico and Cambodia, female debt juggling
also brings in male migration, which is regularly resorted to in order to "clear"
debts (Morvant-Roux 2013, 184; Bylander 2014). This is also the case in South
Arcot, as we will see later in the chapter. Such juggling can entail financial
vulnerability, as well as "processes of creative adaptation to constraints on
the local financial market," as noted by economist Emmanuelle Bouquet and

colleagues on Madagascar (2013, 211). These components of juggling—male migration (mainly nearby and internal), vulnerability, and creativity—are found here.

In South Arcot, women do not just pay off a large share of their own debts, but they also pay off part of their husbands'. This includes women with little or even no income. Here, too, rotation emerges as a key coping strategy. Danam and Devaki (sometimes helped by her cowife and daughter-in-law) paid off almost a third of the family's male debt (31 percent and 32.7 percent, respectively). This rose to just under half (45.6 percent) for Parvati. Only Kamatchi does not pay back—or pays very little—male debts, probably for reasons of status. She belongs to one of the richest families in the village, and while her son is secretly accruing debt, mainly outside the village, it is scarcely an option for him to ask his mother to pay back his own debts. Repayment is a marker of gender but also of social status, combining here class and caste. Note that the reverse is not true, as it is very unusual for men to pay back their wives' loans (see Table 4.1).

It turns out that women pay off most of the household debt, between 50 percent and 90 percent according to the diaries. That women specialize in repayment is another striking feature of the sexual division of debt. Women act as kinds of "providers of last resort," as they are the ones who pay when no one else is willing or able to do so (Allon 2014, 16). When it comes to borrowing, women specialize in predatory and degrading forms. When it comes to repayment, all debts merge and repayment turns out to be a female prerogative.

If we look not at the volume but at the frequency of loans, women's share rises further since on average their loans are half the size. Figure 4.2 shows the

	% of male loans settled by women	% of female loans settled by men
Kamatchi's household	3.2	7.3
Devaki's household	32.7	0.0
Parvati's household	45.6	0.2
Danam's household	31	1

In Kamatchi's household, 3.2% of male loans are settled by women. Source: Authors (Financial Diaries Data, 2018, Observatory of Rural Dynamics and Inequalities in South India).

Table 4.1. Who repays the debt? The sexual division of debt repayment.

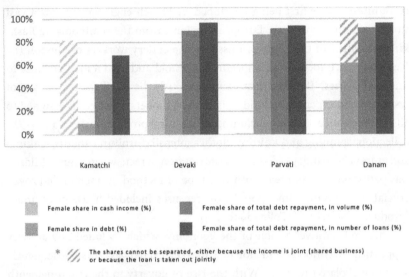

Figure 4.2. Female specialization in debt repayment.
Source: Authors (Financial Diaries Data, 2018, Observatory of Rural Dynamics and Inequalities in South India).

discrepancy between women's share of income, indebtedness, and repayment. The majority of loans, both in number and in volume, are on women's shoulders. This is all the more the case at the repayment stage. As previously discussed, economists and development experts have typically focused on how women's credit is rationed (see chapter 1). But it is also crucial to question the disproportionate representation of women in matters of debt repayment.

Bias in Accounting

Kumaresan used to mock his mother for having to beg for money to cover every little expense. He was apparently unaware of his mother's (and her co-wife's) crucial contribution to the household finances. Over the financial diary period, the household's debt was three times its income. The two women took on more than 40 percent of this debt, repaid nearly 90 percent in volume, and 96.6 percent in number of loans. But Kumaresan was no more blind to women's economic role than social scientists and poverty experts have been. The standard statistics have ignored any economic contribution to the household other than monetary labor. However, this was not always the case. In nineteenth-century Europe, statistical surveys of household income and consumption were first being developed. A French engineer oversaw a vast survey spanning thirty-six European regions, from the seminomadic Bashkir pastoralists of the Urals in Russia to the cutlery workers of London (Le Play 1855). Each focused on a specific household and used a method close to financial diaries. The investigators meticulously dissected their wide sets of resources and expenses, in kind or in cash. A monetary price was assigned to all of the resources in kind, including agricultural production; food and wood collection; spinning and knitting clothes; utensil, furniture, and toymaking; and animal husbandry fodder. The contribution of men, women, and children was painstakingly counted. With this type of method, women's role proved crucial. At the same time, population censuses included housewives under "productive activities" (Folbre 1991, 464).

This "substantive" vision of the economy, which included any activity supporting livelihoods and not just market exchanges, was subsequently forgotten (Polanyi 1977, 19). With the rise of poverty in the late nineteenth century, budget surveys of poor households proliferated, both in Europe and in the United States. Women (and children) still played a crucial economic role, through nonwage income, self-consumption, and savings. But male wages gradually became the supposedly deciding factor for standard of living. Inspired by the middle classes, the normative ideal of the male breadwinner and the housewife took precedence over any scientific consideration, and women were gradually reduced to a "nurturing" role (May 1984, 363). Employment and national accounting statistics took the same path. Despite the protests of feminist groups, household productivity quickly disappeared from the imagination of statisticians. Women were labeled "unoccupied" or "dependents," then finally disappeared from national accounts systems (Folbre 1991, 464).

According to employment statistics compiled by the World Bank (2021), 22 percent of adult Indian women were employed in 2019. In our own household surveys, which replicate this statistical bias by focusing on paid work, nearly half of adult women consider themselves employed, and one could easily infer that the other half therefore are "unoccupied." But when you see the women moving about, getting up at the crack of dawn, going to bed last after making sure everyone's stomach is full, homework is done, visitors are received, and debts are paid, it's hard to consider them "not working."

Ignoring the value of unpaid labor gives a completely truncated view of wealth. If we take unpaid labor into account, the wealth of the richest countries suddenly increases by 20 to 40 percent (Benería, Berik, and Floro 2015, 207). In the same vein, reducing work to wage labor gives a completely truncated view of work. Instead of asking people whether they "work," and rather than looking at the time spent on income-generating activities, whether in cash or in kind, the importance of female labor shoots up compared to the usual labor force surveys. This is particularly true in the Global South (Benería, Berik, and Floro 2015, chap. 5), and it doubles in India (Hirway and Jose 2011, 77). One of this book's key arguments is that this effort to value women's work must also include debt, both as an economic flow and as specific work. Taking debt flows into account leads to an entirely different view of women's economic contribution to household economies.

Valuation as an economic flow can take several forms, including contribution to expenses, as we have just done, and contribution to the households' turnover. Turnover is the criterion used by Jonathan Morduch and his colleagues to account for the financial dynamism of the poor. It is the sum of all the financial flows of a household in a given period. Morduch and his colleagues call this ratio the "cash flow intensity of income" (2009, 32). They observe that for the poor, this ratio is often higher than one, and can even be as high as three for small traders. They conclude that "lower incomes require *more* rather than *less* active financial management" (2009, 33). Low and irregular income is in some way compensated for by a high velocity of money and incessant borrowing, repaying, saving, and giving.

In our case, this is even more true for women (see Table 4.2). If we only consider women's incomes, the ratio easily reaches extremes since women's income is often low. It ranges from four for Devaki and her cowife, who manage multiple debts but also earn income from the family grocery store, to nearly four hundred for Parvati, who has almost no income. If we consider as women's income the share of male income that men concede to their spouses (which is rarely a given as we will see in the next chapter, and for which women very often have to negotiate and beg), the ratio is of course lower: it ranges from three to four (2.9 for Danam, 3 for Parvati, and 3.7 for Devaki). In Devaki's household, where both men and women are heavily indebted for multiple reasons (housing, health, sons' education, husband's obligations as maternal uncle), the ratio for men is slightly higher than for women. As seen earlier, however, this does not prevent women from making most of the repayments. Kamatchi's ratio was not calculated since too much business turnover data were missing.

	Ratio of financial flows to own income		Ratio of financial flows to own income + intrahousehold transfers	
	Female	Male	Female	Male
Devaki's household	4	5.2	3.7	4.6
Parvati's household	398.4	0.3	3	0.3
Danam's household	23.1	0.9	2.9	0.9

Source: Authors (Financial Diaries Data, 2018, Observatory of Rural Dynamics and Inequalities in South India).

Table 4.2. The productivity of debt; female and male turnover.

The Routine Work of Debt

Measuring time allocation has been instrumental in making women's work visible (Benería, Berik, and Floro 2015, 200–205). Time use surveys have high-lighted severe inequalities in terms of "individual disposable time" (Folbre 2006, 196). They have shown that specific categories of people's time, and that of women in particular, is "infinitely elastic" (Elson 1993, 238). These surveys have also allowed the concept of "time poor" to emerge—namely, the idea that some people more than others face competing claims on their time (Vickery 1977, 37).

Well beyond the case of Pushpurani in this chapter's opening vignette, Tamil Dalit women consistently stressed how time-consuming debt work is. The amount of debt, and particularly the number of debts indebted women juggle alongside their responsibilities as "last resort" payers, makes it a real job in the sense of repetitive, routine, time-consuming tasks that require real skills.

Take the case of Devaki and her cowife, Rani. Several years ago, during the agricultural season, they used to combine two daily activities. In the morning, they carried out formal work transplanting and sowing seeds, paid at a fixed rate. In the afternoon, they did more informal work, negotiated case by case both in terms of the price and the nature of the task, which mostly consisted of cutting grass for livestock and clearing weeds. But for some years now they had only been doing the morning work. Venkata asked Devaki if this was because she was too old. No, she said, it was "to pay the finance," which meant looking for the money, negotiating, and asking other women to pay off their debts in her store. It was a full-time job on the days before the microcredit repayment deadlines. On other days, she would have been able to do the paid work, but the landowners required consistency.

Rani, one of the women in our quantitative survey, said that "negotiation is my everyday time." She did not have a paid job. Until recently she had spent her time cooking and taking care of the house. Now she was regularly juggling about twenty loans at a time. These were small amounts, but they had to be constantly negotiated. She managed the family's cash flow by juggling between pledging her jewelry for a short term, as beyond one month the price increased, between microcredit with monthly payments, and between numerous small debts contracted in her neighborhood. The duration was even shorter for the neighborhood debts. If the loan lasted less than one, two, or even three weeks, it would commonly be called a "hand-to-hand exchange" (*kai mathu*) and would be free of charge. The rotation of these myriad debts was time-consuming. She said she no longer had time to cook and had delegated this task to her two daughters. At the same time, she didn't complain; not being in the kitchen suited her perfectly.

The work of the indebted woman is a routine activity, with peaks in the days leading up to microcredit repayment dates and at times of high expenses. When Pushpurani was preparing for her son's wedding, raising the money became a full-time job in the three months before the event and then a regular repayment job for a couple of years after the event. For Danam, who managed several microcredit groups (four at the time of the survey), debt work was also almost a full-time job. The day before each repayment deadline, she would spend part of her day dashing everywhere to make sure members had their cash ready and helping them to find extra cash if needed. Part of her job was also to motivate the women to stay in the group. As we will see in chapter 7, she needed these group peers to ensure her own eligibility to microcredit.

Financial diaries partly capture the extent of this routine work by measuring the number of transactions with lenders (borrowing, repaying, lending, and collecting repayments). Women managed on average between 2.6 and 9.5 transactions per week, compared to 0.3 to 1.2 for men. Some weeks would be relaxed, as Devaki told us, while others were "hell." Devaki had as many as thirty-one transactions to make in a single week. For the other women, the busiest weeks involved around ten to twenty transactions.

But financial transactions with lenders only constitute a marginal part of debt work. We have already discussed the time spent building one's creditworthiness for microcredit (see chapter 3). Other ethnographies from various parts of the world have come to a similar conclusion.[7] Negotiation, management, and repayment are just as time-consuming for other debts. Taking on a debt first means identifying a potential lender by researching them, comparing pros and cons, and finding a guarantee if necessary. It then involves meeting with the lender, sometimes many times, and convincing him or her to give the money. Widespread mobile phone use now saves time. With long-time acquaintances and for small amounts, some dealings can be done by phone. For large sums and new lenders, however, face-to-face conversations are necessary. It is more respectful and, as Pushpurani said, easier to sense the emotional state of the lender and respond accordingly. But the borrower's time is elastic. For the lender, stalling the borrower is part of the game. It is a way of both signaling the asymmetry of power and feigning possible cash flow shortfalls, which allows the lender to be firmer on both the duration and the cost. When repayment comes around, debt work involves collecting the sum, which in turn means approaching other lenders. This, as Danam put it, means "grabbing, begging, pleading." It also entails maintaining and cultivating relationships, including by offering various small favors. As we will see in the next chapter, this involves constant relational and emotional work.

The Productivity of Female Debt

Over three months in 2008, social scientists Alain Cottereau and Mohktar Mohatar Marzok (2012) tracked all the flows in and out of a Spanish family, in cash and in kind, and the time each family member spent on each activity. The simple fact of counting differently gave an unusual picture of the household's economy and the productivity of its members. The housewife was officially unoccupied except for some undeclared childcare, yet she was in fact the most productive member thanks to shopping around for "good plans," spending a significant portion of her time on this (the equivalent of 180 hours annually). These good plans included buying directly from producers, making do with secondhand clothes, using hairdressing schools (cheaper than going to regular hair stylists), and choosing stores based on discounts and special offers, even if it meant walking long distances. Measuring the money saved (compared to the market price), the housewife "earned" 16 euros an hour, over three times as much as her husband (who ran an undeclared handicraft microbusiness, i.e., he does not pay taxes) (2012, 215). The housewife's income—in the form of money saved—made up almost a third of the household's resources.

A 1990s ethnography in Cairo also gave a rough estimate of the savings made from "efficient shopping" by housewives, who spent considerable time choosing the best prices and lining up for subsidized food, saving about 30 percent on family expenses as a result (Hoodfar 1997, 179).

We do not have time-use data to accurately compare the productivity of different family members. However, given the great disparity in credit costs and their negotiability, it is clear that a good debt manager can make significant savings for the household. Remember that the interest servicing charge absorbs almost one-third of household income. But there is variation between households, and half of them (the median value in statistical terminology) pay less than 15 percent. As such, some households are doing quite well, while others bear a very high interest burden. This disparity is also apparent in our financial diaries data, in which interest servicing charges absorbed 16 to 38 percent of income. The weight of the interest charges depended on the amount of debt, of course. Of our financial diary families, Devaki's family paid the most interest with respect to their income, and this was partly related to a considerable debt load. The weight of interest charges also depends on the material creditworthiness of a given household. Fixed income and physical collateral make it easier to access cheap credit. Pushpurani's husband, for example, was able to borrow from his company at 1 percent monthly. But that does not explain the whole story: negotiating skills are also crucial.

The main sources of debt include microcredit, pawnbroking, door-to-door lenders, employers and labor recruiters, local "well-known people," friends, and relatives. Microcredit, pawnbroking, and door-to-door lenders are almost exclusively sources of female debt, while the others are used by both men and women, with the exception of bank loans. A sizable proportion of interpersonal loans, such as those from well-known people, friends, and relatives, is free of cost. Men benefit more than women from this since they use more interpersonal loans. In our quantitative survey, one-third of male loans were declared as free compared to one-quarter of women's. Of course, the financial cost is only part of the cost, and the relational, emotional, and sexual costs can be considerable, as we will see in later chapters. However, it is useful to look at financial cost when assessing the degree of financial exploitation.

With the exception of microcredit, all other loans are negotiable, which can make a big difference in terms of price. For debts to well-known people, friends, and relatives, the negotiations are over the amount, followed by the price and the repayment terms. When a price is fixed at the outset, monthly repayments are not consistently met and skipping a deadline does not necessarily mean extra cost. Borrowers pay on the basis of their ability and the lender's need for liquidity. In the end, the cost of these interpersonal debts might turn out lower than originally set.

Pawnbrokers and mobile lenders display similar flexibility. In theory, both have fixed prices and fixed repayment terms. Pawnshops charge 2 to 3 percent per month, with interest due monthly until the borrower can repay the principal. Most door-to-door lenders charge 10 percent of the principal loaned, deducted initially from the loan amount, and the principal is repaid daily or weekly over 100 days. In practice, however, some pawnshops allow some of their clients to skip certain payments, without carrying over to the next month. Equally, some door-to-door lenders allow some of their clients to skip certain payments, again at no extra cost. Financial diaries show that for half of these loans, repayments are frequently postponed. For example, when Devaki's family's grocery store was closed and her income dried up, she managed to postpone repayment to three door-to-door lenders for three months while not yet having repaid anything. By doubling the length of these debts, she cut the cost in half.

Let there be no mistake. Our goal is not to romanticize interpersonal and informal loans. Some are very expensive and an obvious source of financial exploitation. Yet others are very flexible and quite cheap. Moreover, in all cases, negotiability usually takes place at the point of repayment. Since women make the bulk of the repayments, they are more often called on to use their negotiating skills.

With adequate data, female debt productivity could be measured in terms of savings, by calculating the capacity of indebted women to negotiate lower rates and longer terms and comparing the total cost of credit to a market price. The lack of data precludes such a calculation, however. But the productivity of female debt can also be assessed in terms of opportunity. Thanks to their negotiating capacity, some women manage to raise considerable amounts with little or no income or physical security.

Pushpurani's house renovation is a case in point. Santosh failed to trace all of her financial flows, but he was able to reconstruct the complex process of financing her home renovation. In the space of five years, she completely renovated her house and completely paid it off. Pushpurani regularly made fun of her husband for being unable to borrow anything despite earning around 30,000 rupees a month (USD 470), about three times the average male salary. She was not entirely right since he had obtained cheap loans from his company. But he did contribute very little to the household's debt. She started the home renovation in 2010. The work was completed in 2013, but it took her another two years to pay off the debts. The house cost 1.65 million rupees (USD 26,000), which at the time represented almost four years of the household's income (from Pushpurani's husband and son). The house was largely financed on credit, along with savings clubs, a grant from the state government housing program (INR 10,000 [USD 160]), the sale of jewelry (INR 15,000 [USD 235]), and the sale of two cows (INR 25,000 [USD 390]). The renovation cost about half that sum (INR 885,000 [USD 13,800]). The rest went to interest charges, with 53 percent overall credit cost. The debts rarely lasted more than two or three years (exceptionally, five years), and Pushpurani regularly had to take on new debts to pay off the old ones. She juggled a total of twenty-one loans, ranging from INR 10,000 to INR 170,000 (USD 160 to USD 2,660). Microcredit and a loan her husband contracted from his company made up a marginal share of the debt (10 percent each). The rest came from personal relations, mostly men, including her lover (more on this in chapter 6).

It is interesting to compare Pushpurani's financial package with the conditions of the banking market. In 2020 in India, housing loans cost around 9 percent annually. Credit granting rules require that monthly repayments should not exceed one-third of the borrower's income. Pushpurani's husband was, therefore, able to qualify for a loan with monthly repayments of INR 10,000 (USD 160). For a principal amount of just under INR 1 million (INR 885,000 [USD 13,800]), the repayment would be spread over ten years, with a total cost of about 40 percent. When Santosh mentioned this option, Pushpurani retorted that she was not at all interested in paying less over a longer period. "Imagine what I can do with ten thousand rupees in monthly repayments for five years," she exclaimed. Besides, three years after she finished paying for her house, she arranged her son's wedding by borrowing about INR 800,000 (USD 12,500) over two months.

Moreover, even if she were interested, her husband would not be eligible since the banks required an initial capital of at least 20 percent of the borrowed capital. Neither Pushpurani nor her husband had any liquid savings. As seen in chapter 2, jewelry and ceremonial expenses are the main form of savings. For Pushpurani, productivity is not measured in terms of savings but opportunity, in this case successfully carrying out a housing project that would be impossible under normal market conditions, even for a middle-class household.

Debt Work as Labor

If we ignore female debt work, it is difficult to understand how Tamil workers reproduce themselves, and indeed how capitalism operates, sustains itself, and thrives. As sociologist Maria Mies argues, the unpaid and devalued work of social reproduction has a "timeless material dimension as well as an historical one" (1998, 58). It emerges only in historically specific forms or regimes of accumulation and is both shaped by and constitutive of specific forms or regimes of accumulation. In economies of indebtedness, as in many contemporary societies, debt is clearly a social reproduction task, on an equal footing with cleaning, cooking, caring, and so forth. Not only is debt a specific form of work, it is also a specific form of labor, in the Marxist sense of a productive and useful activity for capital—namely, the generation of surplus.

Debt labor generates surplus value in two ways in our case, the first being through interest payments. These feed the Indian financial industry, which is partly, but increasingly, financed through global capital. Payments to local lenders are reinjected into the local economy. We have seen the high interest that households pay, and women probably play a large part, both because of their specialization in certain loans (microcredit, pawnbroking, door-to-door lending) and due to their role as lenders of last resort. Second, female debt labor generates surplus value for private capital by indirectly subsidizing male labor income. It is because wages are far below the socially necessary costs of reproduction—by this we mean the minimum amounts that a family needs to survive—that villagers, and women in particular, have to go into debt. On average, debt flows represent the same value as income flows; for one rupee earned through paid work, each family borrows at least one rupee, for which interest may have to paid. Yet the borrowed amounts constitute savings for employers, who can afford to pay wages well below subsistence levels. In other words, debt, and the labor of debt, acts as an indirect subsidy for private capital.

It is well known that Indian labor wages are among the lowest in the world (ILO 2020, 106). One of the major arguments of feminist research is that "female productivity is one of the preconditions of male productivity" (Mies

1998, 58). In South Arcot, and probably in other parts of India, female productivity in debt labor certainly explains male labor productivity.

Note, however, that male and female productivity are inseparable. As seen earlier, men's income is rarely sufficient but is nevertheless useful. An essential component of debt work is to put men to work, whether husbands or sons, and sometimes daughters before they marry. This clearly translates into the proletarianization of labor, as argued in various critical analyses of financialization (Federici 2018; Adkins and Dever 2016). In Ahmedabad, in the state of Gujarat, overindebted women juggle multiple odd jobs. The priority is to "do something," as they themselves say, regardless of the wage or type of task, in order to cope with the debt (Nair 2020). In our quantitative survey, nearly one-third of both men and women said they were working more to pay off their debts. Women, however, have fewer job opportunities and many frequently say that debt "forces husbands to work." Pushpurani has the great privilege of being able to rely on the regular salary of her husband, who has a permanent job and gives her almost all of his pay. Pushparaj, Danam's husband, is also very cooperative. He is a jute bag seller and tries to sell more when Danam runs out of cash to meet her debts. Yoganathan talks a lot but works little. His two older sons have had to take low-paying, undereducated jobs to pay off their parents' massive debts and relieve their mother's stress. Parvati's indebtedness conditions her husband's migration to the neighboring state of Kerala as a coconut cutter. He leaves as soon as the pressure to repay becomes too great. Seasonal migration and debt bondage in brick-molding plants (which mostly employ husbands, wives, and young adults) and sugarcane cutting (which mostly employ men) are forms of debt proletarianization. Workers receive a significant advance on wages (around 1 lakh in 2018–20 [USD 1,500], or one year's average family wage). In return, they must work until the debt is fully repaid, tolerating deplorable working conditions. While these forms of debt bondage have long been a response to job scarcity, they have increasingly been used to pay off other debts over the past decade.[8]

In nineteenth-century industrial Europe, economists understood the key role of women's productivity very well. They insisted on the need to give housekeeping education to women so that they could manage family budgets and maintain a warm, homey environment that would encourage men to stay at home rather than waste their pay on alcohol, tobacco, gambling, and other immoral expenditures (May 1984). This in turn allowed for competitive wages and a disciplined workforce. The debt economy is a further step in the family's role as a "social factory" that acts as the very foundation for surplus value production (Mies 1998, 31).

South Arcot seems to be a textbook case, although it is not exceptional. We have already discussed the prevalent juggling practices that other researchers have explored in other parts of India, Cambodia, Vietnam, Brazil, Chile, Mexico, Paraguay, Honduras, Senegal, and Madagascar. The extent and nature of financialization in all likelihood shapes the content, intensity, and gendering of debt and finance work. For example, in highly financialized countries such as the United States, Australia, and the United Kingdom, debt work consists of understanding and managing complex credit, savings, and insurance contracts for housing, healthcare, children's education, retirement, and utility bills. A growing number of bill payments for utilities such as water, electricity, and transportation are being securitized—that is, securities that can be sold on the financial market. The line between debt and payment is increasingly blurred, and households have to make complex calculations to choose the contract that suits them best (Bryan and Rafferty 2018, chap. 3). The poor also have to juggle these complex financial tools, so it is likely that here again women are at the forefront (A. Roberts 2015; Allon 2014). To a greater extent than men, they also have to deal with fringe banking, which operates under the radar of traditional banking rules. Loans from such businesses are easily available and unsecured but expensive (Schmitz 2014, 67–68). In places such as France, where access to credit is tightly regulated (but also limited) and social protection is state-run, debt work mainly involves managing bill and rent arrears, neighbors helping each other out, and filing for bankruptcy (Perrin-Heredia 2018; François 2018). In contexts of hyperinflation, where several currencies are usually in circulation, debt management demands other forms of complex calculations. They consist of converting, switching currencies, and constantly anticipating price changes and differentials (Neiburg 2006; Luzzi and Wilkis 2018).

Debt Work as a State of Mind

Feminist struggles to accord value to women's domestic work are not just about time accounting. Another crucial concern is to denounce the disqualification of women's work skills. Minutia, repetitiveness, care, dedication, concern for others, patience, and also charm and seduction are supposedly naturally acquired feminine traits, deployed at home for general care and domestic work.

But these types of skills are found in many women's jobs that are considered unskilled since the skills in question are considered natural.[9] The devaluation of women's work, whether paid or unpaid, is one of the most obvious characteristics of the way capital exploits women.

In South Arcot, women's specialization in debt and repayment seems to be a continuation of their natural role as mothers and wives. Many indebted women compare themselves to "ATM machines," as if all they have to do is push a button and the money comes out, without anyone questioning how the machine works. When the men are asked about the sexual division of debt, many discount the difficulty of the task. "Just ask," they often argue. "You're better at asking," they often retort if their wives complain about being tired of dealing with lenders.[10]

Development experts also have a narrow and mostly truncated view of what debt work is. Like many other indebted women, Devaki had to attend three days of training before receiving her first microcredit loan. Part of the training was dedicated to financial literacy. Like the financial literacy sessions that were developed in abundance over the past decades, one module elaborated on the concept of good credit. According to the trainer, credit is good if it improves one's financial situation and bad if it worsens it. Devaki chuckled and wondered how to apply this rule to her own case. "What calculation should I do, my financial situation is always bad," she told us. Above all, the indebted woman's calculations are much more complex than an accounting comparison between an interest rate and a return on investment for a given loan. Debt work does involve calculations. Choosing the best financial options—or the least worse—demands constant sophisticated reasoning, much closer to the image we have of an entrepreneur than of a housewife. These calculations can include the economic features of the debt such as financial price, suitability to income streams, flexibility of repayments, and the financial penalties for non-repayment. They may also take what economists call opportunity costs into account (i.e., the loss of other alternatives when one alternative is chosen) and transaction costs—namely, the total costs of a given transaction.[11]

But from a classical economic perspective, the key distinction is that the "frameworks of calculation" are broader, to use anthropologist Magdalena Villarreal's expression (2004b, 71; 2014).[12] They include not only financial considerations but social and moral ones that are situated in time, space, and also bodies, as we will see in the next chapter. To the indebted woman, the valuation of a given loan only makes sense in relation to her overall financial, social, and moral obligations. The indebted woman has two obsessive concerns that she pursues relentlessly: building and maintaining her creditworthiness and limiting the financial, social, and moral costs of the debt. Moreover, these two concerns are both short-term and long-term. "I have to think about my daughters' marriage," Praba explained when we asked her whether she had paid back the 500 rupees she owed her neighbor. By this she meant that she could not afford *not* to pay back and endanger her reputation, and by extension her creditworthiness, which would be crucial to borrowing large sums for her daughter's wedding.

Calculations about debt require what historian Frances Yates calls an "art of memory" (1999). Despite the number of loans, most indebted women keep few written records of their transactions. Ceremonial debt is an exception. Accounting for ceremonial gifts and countergifts is an ancient practice that was historically performed by assigned individuals, often from among the leading castes. These are the debts from which it is impossible to escape, except to suffer social opprobrium. Microloans are the most transparent transactions when it comes to financial debts. Each borrower receives a booklet listing the due dates and the amount of principal and interest. Door-to-door lenders also hand out a booklet stating the capital loaned, the interest initially paid, and each repayment is then noted. Some but not all pawnshops issue a receipt with the amount of principal loaned, and rarely the price. Written accounting is very rare for the myriad of interpersonal loans. Some indebted women keep a written record of an upcoming due date, such as a note on a calendar, or a chalk mark on the kitchen wall. Overall, however, very few women write down their debts and their due dates. And yet it is very rare for them to forget. Regardless of issues around illiteracy and limited reading and writing, indebted women often say that mnemonic techniques are more effective. For them, counting debts means constantly "impressing" images of people, events, and places into their memories (Yates 1999, xi). "I constantly think about how I'm going to pay it back: How could I forget it?" they told us on multiple occasions. "This topic never gets out of your mind. If I don't repay, they will come and shout anyway. It is always in your mind, you will never forget it," Danam once told us.

As we will see in chapter 7, many everyday social relationships are forged out of mutual indebtedness. Debt is embedded into these daily relationships, and every interaction or discussion involving the lender is an opportunity to reactivate the memory of the amount owed, as Pushpurani explained: "I could recall my entire credit, from whom I have taken under what condition and the interest for that, by seeing the face, it automatically reminds me of the complete aspects of my settlement." By "face," she mostly means the mood of the lender that day, generosity or firmness, understanding or glare. Sensoriality helps to fix the memory. Pushpurani started counting and memorizing as a teenager when her mother asked her to help her memorize her own debts. Today, it is her daughter Savithri who helps her.

Like many domestic tasks, it is difficult to measure the time spent on debt as it is such a mental burden. It is more of a constant concern than an occupation in the strict sense. Debt work is often a secondary activity, combined with many other tasks, including daily socialization, whether it be neighborhood interactions, shared meals, or participation in ceremonies. It is more a "state of mind" (Budig and Folbre 2004, 59) than a concrete, material activity per se. For many women, it is a permanent concern, a constant cognitive load, which runs through their heads and eats at them. The women themselves frequently used the English expression "mental tension." During the first wave of COVID-19 and the first lockdown (March–September 2020), Venkata and Santosh checked in with villagers by phone. For women, the issue of reimbursement was the primary source of stress. "How am I going to pay my finance," they kept asking. The drying up of nonagricultural income has made repayment a real challenge and a source of considerable stress. Faced with the intolerance of some lenders, some women hid, locked their doors as if they were absent, or took refuge in their native families to avoid opprobrium.

As we saw earlier, the primary form of women's debt is a moral debt of kinship. It entails the devaluation of women as women, as unproductive and therefore a liability. Beyond a permanent feeling of guilt, the moral debt of kinship very clearly translates into financial debts, which women take out both to make ends meet and to fulfill their obligations as mothers, to pay their daughters' dowries, to compensate for the absence or insufficiency of their own dowry, or to invest in boys' education. The devaluation of women also explains how they have come to specialize in survival debt, considered degrading and emasculating according to the male breadwinner ideal. Lastly, women's devaluation and permanent feeling of obligation and guilt can also help explain their specialization in repayment. When Venkata and Isabelle shared one of the salient findings of the financial diaries with Danam—namely, women's hyperspecialization in repayment—she wearily responded, "It's marked on our foreheads," as if it had become part of their condition and subjectivity as women. Being a good mother and wife meant paying off the family's debts, in a never-ending process given the discrepancy between their work incomes, needs, and aspirations. When debt implies the pledging of bodies, feelings of guilt over transgressive sexuality heap on top of kinship and financial debt, as we will see in the next chapter. The debt of the indebted woman is not only infinite, but it also becomes unpayable.

5

Bodily Collateral

"**WHEN I GO TO** see a man to ask for money, it's like walking across thistles. When a man gives [lends] me ten rupees, he looks me up and down from top to bottom. He never looks me in the eyes. He just checks my physical worth. . . . Kids are hungry, 'what is she doing?' people ask. No one will ask, 'what is he doing?' We must be accountable with money, but to whom can I account my own feelings?" Pushpurani, like many others, tells us here what is most stressful and humiliating about the act of getting into debt. On the one hand, there is the risk of sexual harassment, which is constant with some lenders. On the other hand, there is the risk of raising their community's suspicions. As Pushpurani comments, "When men only get thirty thousand rupees when they have an income, and women get ten times more, of course it raises the question." Pushpurani has features and a physique that men find attractive. Over time, she has also learned to be assertive, confident in her words, and as such to inspire trust. Like non-Dalits, she now wears lingerie and beautiful sarees. Her physical appearance, gestures, and body language are considerable assets in her negotiations with lenders. There are days, however, when her own body disgusts her, and she feels like covering her head to avoid those perverse looks. But she also wonders how she will manage when she gets older, as she knows these assets only last for a while. Other women are much less fortunate, and seduction does not suffice; the sexual act is the only way to build and maintain their creditworthiness.

We know from feminist scholarship that male appropriation of women's bodies and work is at the heart of both patriarchy and capitalism, and their intertwining. Through their work of procreation and care, women produce workers.[1] Through their emotional work, and far beyond care work, women facilitate consumer comfort in many services (Hochschild 2012). Through sex work of various kinds, women facilitate business deals and male migration (Hoang 2015). From ethnography, we also know that the agent–victim binary is "a dead end of sorts," as argued by anthropologist Nicole Constable (2009, 57). Within specific patriarchal orders, women navigate and negotiate their bodies, their emotions, and their lives as much as they can. Far from being opposites, paid sex work and married sex, coercion and freedom, are more of a continuum of fluid and interconnected positions (Tabet 2005; Constable 2009).

This chapter explores the central but underexplored role of women's sexual and emotional work in credit markets. How do they cope and try to make the most of them? While sex and often forced work as a means of repaying debt has been amply documented,[2] sex work in the ordinary fabric of creditworthiness and repayment remains unexplored. Historians of preindustrial Europe have probably paid the most attention, noting the key role of women's sexual reputation in their creditworthiness while discussing many other factors, emphasizing that sexual probity could also sustain men's creditworthiness.[3]

In South Arcot, debt work is not just about financial management and calculation. As the indebted woman lacks material resources, she frequently uses her own body as collateral, a security that the lender can use throughout the transaction. The indebted woman is also supposed to respect the moral codes of virtue and chastity. This all requires specific techniques and disciplines of body exposure, and the management of feelings and emotions. In other words, the debt is embodied and entails intense sexual and emotional work.

In India, male appropriation of women's bodies is nothing new, even more so for Dalit women. Historically, the sexual rights of upper-caste landlords over Dalit women were commonly accepted. This was both shaped by and constitutive of Dalit financial dependence and inferiority. Dalit activism has greatly reduced this, including in South Arcot. Yet sexual domination has taken on other forms. Sexual and debt dependency on higher castes have shifted toward multiple forms of debt and sex-for-debt exchanges with men of diverse castes.

The collateralization of the bodies of indebted women takes on various forms, operating both within and outside the marital space. It involves multiple sexual acts, such as smiling, charming, touching, oral sex, and penetration. It leads to a variety of compensation, and although the collateralization of female bodies primarily helps build and maintain creditworthiness, it can also be a source of comfort, recognition, and love (see chapter 6).

Using one's body to attract and seduce lenders is not a given from the outset. Over time, the indebted woman changes her appearance and becomes more feminine. New beauty norms emerge. The shifts in beauty standards result from a desire for modernity and social mobility since an alleged absence of "femininity" is precisely one of the markers of inferiority and Dalitness (Mitra 2020, 41). These shifts in beauty standards are also connected to the needs of the credit market. Microcredit organizations actively contribute to this process. While the supposed idea is to transform poor women into self-employed entrepreneurs, their actions mainly promote feminization and the dissemination of new norms of femininity. The discipline of repayment primarily translates into a discipline over women's bodies.

Emotional work is probably the most challenging skill in debt work. The indebted woman must be able to be seductive while minimizing the risks of forced sex and preserving one's reputation and self-esteem. Women negotiate these conflicting imperatives in different ways. Some have given up on their respectability, while others spend considerable energy on it. Marital status, physical appearance, learning techniques, and ethical choices help to explain these variations. Reiterating a historical constant of patriarchy, the indebted woman's body proves to be both an asset and a stigma.

Tying Up One's Husband with One's Saree

In February 2008, Santosh and Isabelle were taking part in the regular gossip of a group of Pushpurani's neighbors, sitting in front of one of the group's verandas. As usual, the latest rumors came up, with one woman criticizing a recent wedding as not up to standard, another commenting about a man who crossed the line by beating his wife too hard, another criticizing a young girl for going too far, too often, in showing off to a young man from the neighboring village. Saktipriya joined the group, sweaty and disheveled. Her saree was untidy. The others laughed, asking her what she had to negotiate with her husband—a welder on surrounding sites—to put herself in such a state.

The whole group laughed, and one of them pointed out that Saktipriya knows "how to tie up her husband in her saree."

Rajam, another of Pushpurani's neighbors, was in her late thirties at the time of the discussion and a "housewife" married to a bus driver. She explained to Santosh that she absolutely needed 24,000 rupees (USD 375) to buy three gold sovereigns for her little sister's wedding. Her parents-in-law had argued that one sovereign would be enough. When Santosh saw her again a few weeks later, he asked her if she had managed to get the money. Another neighbor, who was listening in on the conversation, commented that Rajam had probably pushed her husband into the bedroom and given him a good *puja* (prayer). Rajam laughed and said that she actually managed to persuade her husband to find the money behind the backs of her in-laws.

These two examples reflect a routine reality for Dalit women. The conjugal space is first to be used by women for sex as a currency of exchange. It is commonplace to make a contrast between prostitution, the exchange of sex for payment, and conjugal sex, supposedly only governed by affects (the romantic marriage of so-called modern societies) or by kinship rules. Going against that binary opposition, anthropologist Paula Tabet (2005, 1991) has proposed conceiving of a continuum of sex-for-money exchanges, which anthropologists today widely refer to as transactional sex.[4] Paying for a prostitute, offering a meal on a date, and falling in love with or marrying one person over another are all interactions that involve the norms of female and male sexuality, the division of labor, and unequal access to resources. Women often have limited access to material resources and monetizing their bodies is the only option if they want to obtain something. Beyond prostitution, interactions between sexuality, intimacy, and the economy are nothing exceptional and are part of the ordinary fabric of sexuality and monetary exchanges (Zelizer 2005).

We have previously discussed how women's bodies and sexuality are negotiated in matrimonial alliances in South Arcot. Marital relationships are also scattered with constant negotiations for sex, goods, services, and favors. Sex is a precious resource for the indebted woman in the constant search for liquidity. Debt work demands making skillful use of her sexual capacities.[5]

Devakumari resented her mother-in-law's omnipresent bids for control, whether over how she dressed or about when she got home too late. She regularly negotiated with her husband through "pillow magic"—in other words, sexual favors—to get him to intervene with his own mother. Saraswathi tried to do the same to convince her husband to let her daughter marry a man of her choice. The subjects of these negotiations include education and marriage expenses for daughters, using sex to convince fathers to agree or spend more, women's personal spending such as on expensive sarees, outings such as visiting birth families or going to the movies, avoiding getting (too badly) beaten for behavior that has made the husband angry such as being out too late, not preparing meals or doing so badly. The negotiations also include debt repayment. As repayment deadlines near and become more pressing, some women push their husbands to work more or waste less, while others use pillow magic to make them more understanding and generous. A key challenge is to give pleasure without being too innovative, which could be taken as a sign of extramarital relations. Refusing sex is also part of the repertoire of action, although risky since many men readily resort to marital rape.

Of course, the men are not puppets and sex remains a tactic that allows for very marginal gains. It does not always have the hoped-for effect and remains a "lottery," Kasturi told us. Saraswathi's husband had not worked for many years and was depressed and alcoholic. Saraswathi had gone into debt to maintain a certain standard of living and to educate her daughters. Santosh had known her for several years and had regular discussions with her during the first lockdown of the COVID-19 pandemic in 2020. She was fed up with being the only one responsible for a debt that was crushing her. She was urging her husband to go back to work and begging him to find the 5,000 rupees (USD 80) needed to pay back the weekly installments. He promised that he would one day. He was so kind and considerate that she wondered whether "it would start to rain in the dry season." She agreed to have sex, which they hadn't had in several months. Their relationship was so conflictual that she didn't even use sex as a bargaining chip anymore. He himself did not seek it out, and it seemed that depression was causing erectile dysfunction and low desire. The next day, he came back completely drunk, without the money. Once again, she had been fooled.

Chandran, meanwhile, understood his wife's tricks perfectly. Changing the sleeping arrangements between parents and children, such that there are no assigned beds, facilitated the tactical use of sex. Normally, Chandran's wife would sleep with the children; when she wanted something, she would put the children in another bed. "If there is only one pillow, I know she is going to ask for something." So, without telling us whether he played along, he let us know he was not fooled.

Sex and Creditworthiness

Any lender requires collateral before lending. Usually, collateral is a physical asset such as real estate, savings, or a regular salary. Sometimes it is a social asset such as a personal guarantee or a joint guarantee group, as in the case of microcredit. In practice, this "social collateral," to use anthropologist Caroline Schuster's term (2015), goes much further: far beyond mutual aid within their microcredit group, the obligation to repay permeates all of their social relationships. Friends, neighbors, and relatives are constantly solicited to help with repayment, finally absorbing part of the credit risk. We will provide examples of this in chapter 7. When women have no physical assets, and their social assets are fragile or insufficient due to the extent of their debts, their body becomes their main guarantee. It is used as a sort of collateral—namely, as an asset used as security for a loan. The lender (or a third party) can seize that collateral and sell it to recoup some or all of the losses.

Santosh was talking at a tea stall with some door-to-door lenders, the ones we often saw on motorcycles, going from door to door once a week to collect their dues. The men were exchanging information about each other's clients, who were mostly female. They identified their common clients, those who were easy to deal with and those who were more difficult. The discussion would often turn to sex: "How easy is she?" "Can I have my way with her?" After witnessing this informal discussion, Santosh would question the lenders, but few would openly admit to this being a criterion for lending. But observing daily transactions, not just with door-to-door lenders but with any type of male lender, made it clear that female clients were partly judged by their sexual appeal and their likelihood of consent. Conversely, some indebted women would sometimes offer sexual services to different types of lenders to gain access to loans, negotiate larger amounts, reschedule repayments, lower the price, or sometimes to clear the debt.

The collateralization of bodies takes many forms, from flirtation and smiling to sexual intercourse, depending on various factors. It is very difficult to obtain precise and systematic information on this type of transaction. The subject is very sensitive, even among the women themselves. The women will talk about their lovers, about the men with whom they have built up long-term relationships. We will return to this in the next chapter. But speaking about sex-for-money exchanges, considered close to sex work because it is occasional and casual, remains deeply taboo. However, by cross-referencing the testimonies of some women, their neighbors, and lenders, we were able to get a rough idea of these arrangements. The transactions varied greatly, and the key factors seemed to be the expected payoff, the woman's attractiveness, her economic creditworthiness, and the lender's profile.

Indebted women negotiate on a highly uneven playing field, starting out with their looks and bodies and the extent to which they meet local beauty standards. In dowry negotiations, women's physique is already a key criterion. According to local gossip, dark skin and a tall build drive up the price. Tall women are thought to be difficult to control. For their creditworthiness and eligibility to credit, a smart look can bring down the price. "For the same amount, one woman can get away with a smile, while her neighbor would have to perform oral sex," we were once told. The lenders themselves admit they are more or less demanding depending on a woman's "attractiveness." Such is the case with Veerappan, a Dalit man, former NGO fieldworker, and casual lender: "When I see her, I feel something in my body," he said about a woman to whom he regularly lends money on highly advantageous terms. He would never ask her for sex; a simple smile is enough. He considered that the women at a strong disadvantage were those who were dark-skinned, ill-at-ease with their bodies, and poorly dressed, with unkempt hair and a stern demeanor.

"I have flesh on my body," said Varalakshmi, in her thirties, explaining how her seductive power made it easy for her to negotiate. And she added: "Women over fifty or sixty can't get anything." She was not entirely right, however, as we met a number of older women who were perfectly able to borrow. Yet one thing is certain. The terms negotiated differed, and above a certain age, women's bodies were rarely part of the deal. "You have to do the maximum at the right time," said Pushpurani, aware that her seductive power to borrow wouldn't last forever. In one of the Dalit settlements where we spent time, it was common knowledge among the women that Shenbagam, who was sunny, graceful, and elegant, could get much better terms than her neighbors. "She is always served first," her neighbors complained, with a certain sense of irony.

Women's physical appearance aside, sex can offset poor material creditworthiness. Women from households with a poor reputation commonly encounter sexual pressure. This can occur when their husband is seen as drunk or lazy, when there is no steady source of income, and when a household is already highly indebted and reputed for its inflated aspirations. Women may have to use their bodies to convince a dubious lender. Sex can also take place when a debt is due, to clear a debt, or to postpone repayment.

Some lenders complain about women's charm tactics. As one once told us, "Women are always trying to please me. For instance, when a woman comes out of her kitchen, she'll normally straighten herself [her clothing] before talking to me. They don't do that: a technique to show they're open." By this he means that when women don't straighten themselves, that's a sign that they are open. There is no doubt, however, that many of these situations are highly oppressive. Many women do use their seductive power. But they have scarcely another choice since their body is often the only resource they have.

Single women, whether widowed or separated (which is rare but happens) are certainly more likely to engage in these kinds of transactions. Not only are they often less creditworthy since they lack male income, but there is no risk that the lenders will run into their husbands. "It's like being weighed up," Shanthi explained. Male lenders would scrutinize her "from head to toe, from front to back." For their part, women constantly size up potential lenders in terms of their risk of sexual abuse. "That one probably won't harass me," Janaki explained when talking about how she chooses lenders. She carefully assesses lenders' reputations and personalities based on word of mouth, often hesitating before approaching a new one, especially if she's unsure she can make repayments. Some women only choose female lenders, but these are not available everywhere. Female lenders might also exert other pressure such as asking for free domestic labor or publicly exposing late payments, particularly if they are non-Dalits.

Beauty and Cleanliness

The body of the indebted woman is not given, it is built, to cite the pioneering reflections of anthropologist Marcel Mauss on the "techniques of the body" (1993b, 373). Western modernity has seen the progressive emergence of beauty as a form of capital, especially but not only for women (Wacquant 1995). With the decline of arranged marriages, a physical appearance that meets beauty standards is increasingly necessary for access to a sexuality that is now elective. Physical appearance may also be used to satisfy the needs of private capital. Studies from across the world have brought to light the productivity of beauty, whether to find a salaried job or to be an efficient seller.[6] In our case, the rise of new beauty norms is partly connected to the construction of credit markets. The transformation of beauty norms is also expressive of the recon-figuration of caste relations and Dalit women's will to extricate themselves from their status of women of little virtue, which is considered a marker of their inferiority. The indebted woman must be able to use her body effectively, without being called a whore, since chastity is a prerequisite for respectability. There is a fine line and, as we will see next, being able to navigate that line is an integral part of debt work.

In twenty years, we have seen the norms of beauty transform. By beauty norms we mean ways of dressing, covering up, body and skincare, expressing oneself, and moving in space. Interestingly, microcredit NGOs have actively contributed to the construction of these beauty norms. When Dalit women are asked to compare microcredit to other sources of borrowing, some explic-itly state that microcredit gives them more "dignity." By this they mean that the language used is more respectful and that there is less risk of being called a whore if they do not repay. It can happen, however. On several occasions, we heard tired loan officers, under pressure to perform, calling their clients whores or advising them to prostitute themselves to repay their loans. But this is not the norm. More importantly, the formally dressed loan officers of microcredit organizations, representing a reputable agency, inspire the local community's trust. Microcredit is perceived as a respectable loan, whereas women usually face constant suspicion of wrongdoing with their bodies in order to obtain credit. The body remains an element of creditworthiness, but creditworthiness criteria are changing. For women, the techniques of the body are taking on other forms.

When she was younger, Danam, whom we have already encountered sev-eral times in this book, had at most two or three sarees, like most other Dalit women. She had one or two for daily life and another for ceremonies. She would wear the same saree all day long, including working in the fields. The sarees were cotton, and the women would wash them on the spot, in ponds or in a well, and dry them immediately. Cotton sarees started being replaced by higher-quality polyester ones, first in the 1990s with government policies to distribute free sarees to poor women. Then the textile industry began using street vendors to tap into this huge market of poor women in rural areas. High-quality sarees are now the norm for special occasions such as ceremo-nies or formal procedures or appointments, including loan negotiations. By local standards, "high quality" means good-quality cloth that is thick enough not to crease and well cut with well-designed patterns. A saree of this quality

costs INR 800 to INR 1,000 (USD 12 to USD 16), or five to seven days of daily
farm wages. The cosmetics market has also expanded greatly, boosted by wide-
scale contact with television and advertising and the packaging of exorbitantly
high-priced products sold by weight into small sample sizes, making them
seem more affordable. Here, too, government policy support was instrumental, with the distribution of free televisions to poor women in the mid-2000s.

Now, when the loan officer visits the microcredit groups that Danam man-
ages, she asks all the women in the group to dress appropriately, with neat
hair and some jewelry. Her son, a loan officer, explained to her that this is a
criterion frequently used by his colleagues as a sign of seriousness and creditworthiness. Some women complain that they need money to buy the proper
clothing and items to look the part, but Danam suggests that they borrow
what they need from their neighbors, which is indeed what we frequently
observed. Far beyond Danam and her group, creditworthiness now involves
having a respectable appearance.

Taking care of one's appearance is also a necessity to deal with bureaucra-
cies and to improve eligibility for social programs. During our fieldwork, we
regularly had to interrupt a discussion because a woman had to go to work,
cook, take care of her children or her elderly parents, or prepare for a visit
from a lender or an official from a public social program. Here, too, getting
ready meant washing, styling hair, and applying makeup. It also meant don-
ning a good-quality, not-too-shabby saree and putting on jewelry; those who
didn't have these would borrow from their neighbors. When we saw women
busy taking care of their clothes, this was often a sign that a moneylender or
official was expected.

Microcredit NGOs, themselves in a constant quest for credibility, have
done much to encourage women to work on their appearance and learn new
body skills. We previously discussed the rise of NGOs in the early 2000s in
chapter 3. The NGO field is highly competitive, and impact and good practices must be constantly proven, both in terms of international donors and
the Indian state, which was an active funder of microcredit in the early 2000s.
NGOs publish reports and sometimes conduct field studies for foreign donors.
With the Indian government, eligibility criteria are closely tied to religious
or political affiliations and other allegiances. Organizing field events with
donors and their target population—microcredit clients—is another key criterion for boosting credibility. At this time, microcredit was still considered an
effective tool for entrepreneurship and successful women entrepreneurs were

selected to speak at these public events. In practice, the success stories were very rare.[7] As such, the women who were called on to share their experiences were selected for their ability to look presentable, for their skill in speaking comfortably in front of a group, and for their willingness to play the game by not voicing any criticism. Women were often also asked to take part in public events such as politicians' visits, demonstrations, awareness campaigns, and fairs. On these various occasions, NGO staff would not hesitate to coach the women on their appearance.[8]

Some women played along while others refused. Raika's case is instructive on this. As we saw in chapter 2, Raika had been running a computer center business since 2004. When we first met her in 2005, she was just starting to get involved in the activities of an NGO specializing in supporting rural women's entrepreneurship. The NGO selected her to start this particular business and offered her a microloan and a cheap space in a covered market devoted to women entrepreneurs. She was able to read and write but had never used a computer. Despite its promises, the NGO offered no training or help finding contracts. Like many other rural development NGOs, it had embarked on supporting women's entrepreneurship to benefit from public subsidies or international funding, without any expertise in the area. Raika grew increasingly at odds with the NGO due to its unfulfilled promises. She was also exasperated by the way women were being instrumentalized. She was convinced that she had been chosen because she was one of the "presentable" women. "I was nicely dressed, that is why I got this loan." "Scruffy women" are never selected, she told us. Ironically, as she told Santosh and Isabelle, the only training she had received was on her appearance. "They also train the women they select in how they should dress. The NGO staff kept telling me, 'You must dress like this, you must dress like that.' We were just used as window dressing for the NGO." Since getting the loan, she must have attended a dozen public events with state officials. The conflict reached its peak when the NGO official asked her to put flowers in her hair. Her husband was extremely suspicious and took a very dim view of his wife's business since it involved so much contact with men, be they officials, suppliers, or clients. Her husband thought that women who wore flowers in their hair, other than at ceremonies, signified that they were whores. The head of the NGO did not want to listen and claimed that taking care of her appearance was a sign of "good value." "If it is to have two *thalis* [necklaces that symbolize a woman's married status], what is the use of NGOs," she told us. By this she meant that the NGO was acting like a husband

and telling her what to do. Exasperated, Raika left the NGO and decided to run her business by herself. (As we will see in the following chapter, the support of her lover would prove decisive.)

With such selection criteria, Dalit women are clearly at a huge disadvantage. Raika was a non-Dalit, as were all the women selected for the NGO's entrepreneurial program. In another NGO we observed between 2004 and 2010, the issue of the caste-based selection of women was a regular source of conflict between the non-Dalit director and his predominantly Dalit fieldworkers (three out of four men). This NGO was set up by Brahmin families in Chennai and had close relations with the local upper castes (mainly Reddiyars and Naidus) in its villages. The director came from a well-established local family. The director often rebuked Perumal, a Dalit fieldworker in charge of Dalit women, because "his" women were poorly dressed and not "presentable." In 2007, Santosh attended a staff meeting for selecting candidates for entrepreneurship loans. The director only chose non-Dalit women. When Perumal challenged this decision, the director replied: "If they [Dalit women] don't impress me, how do you think the bankers will be impressed by them? These women are simply not presentable!" Perumal tried to argue: "They all come from a colony [Dalit hamlet], so how can you expect them to be presentable?" He reminded the director that the NGO was there precisely to help them "improve their lives." Perumal did not get his way and the director remained adamant. Perumal could have argued that wealth, economic networks, and family experience in business are all factors due to which non-Dalits, on average, are more successful at entrepreneurship. But the director was not concerned with such considerations. He was convinced that "presentable" women would be far more capable of repaying their loans. "They [Dalit women] don't know how to take care of themselves and look good, so how can you expect them to manage a loan?" he said.

The NGO director's comments reflect a broader reality of discrimination toward Dalits on moral grounds. Dirtiness, impurity, and the inability to meet obligations and pay debts are seen as symptoms of a common problem: a lack of ethics. Even today, non-Dalit women often gossip about the dirtiness and impurity of Dalit women, and they sometimes use these stereotypes as an insult to Dalit women. Non-Dalit women condemn Dalit women for being dirty, for not cleaning their clothes, or for not washing clothing soiled from menstruation separately. This is taken as a Dalit-specific sign of negligence and irresponsibility and the reason for their supposedly poor repayment practices.

It follows that for many Dalit women, taking care of their appearance is not just a matter of solvency but about breaking down anti-Dalit stereotypes. When Pushpurani spoke about her multiple setbacks with lenders, she constantly referred to sexual harassment from male lenders. She also talked about the disdain and contempt of non-Dalit female lenders. In 2018, she once told us: "From day one we are Dalits, always like that, what do to?" Then she imitated non-Dalit women's typical remarks about Dalit women: "You *paraiyar* [the main Dalit group in South Arcot], you never have any regulation, restriction, regularity, you forgot who gave the money and once you need money you'll come here as a dog and stand here."

We have to understand Miss Mary's motivations in the light of this, as an NGO director trying, often clumsily, to transform the bodies of Dalit women. She constantly asked Dalit women to be "beautiful" and to dress in an elegant, colorful way, as if they were going to a festival or a wedding. She also asked them to be clean, to shower before coming, to not have sweaty underarms, and to put flowers in their hair. One day in 2008, while Santosh was attending the preparation of a public event with the district collector (the equivalent of the prefect), some of the women sneered and laughed at Miss Mary: "Who are we supposed to attract?" they asked. "Is it a beauty contest?" one of them asked. Miss Mary admitted her own contradictions, as she was also constantly critical of the fact that the women were being used as puppets or dolls. The justification she gave was that this was the only way that "work gets done" and that unfortunately women's appearance, especially for Dalit women, is the only way to show that they are "strong," "well-educated," and that they are now "knowledgeable." In the mid-2000s, when Miss Mary's NGO began managing microcredit programs in partnership with banks, several bankers complained about Dalit women visiting the bank branches: they were "too noisy" and "smelled bad," she was often told. "They sound like a herd of goats," Santosh overheard on one of his bank branch visits. When Miss Mary had to select a woman or two to meet bankers, she came to choose the most "presentable" ones, capable of "impressing" people, like Pushpurani or Shanti, who regularly refreshed their wardrobes and wore elegant makeup. Others were never invited, even though they were very active leaders in their own village. This was the case of Esther, who deliberately refused to make any effort, arguing precisely that she was not a "doll." In rationalizing her own choices, Miss Mary said of Esther: "She looks like she just woke up."

Pushpurani willingly complied with Miss Mary's recommendations. In the early years of our discussions, as she was starting to become involved in the NGO, Santosh congratulated her on her dressing. Pushpurani replied, a little embarrassed, that Miss Mary had asked her to dress up. As a result, she would attract the insistent gazes of the male staff at the NGO and had to avoid being alone with them. Santosh and Isabelle regularly discussed with Pushpurani the tactics she used to maintain her creditworthiness. As the opening vignette shows, she readily admitted that she pays attention to her body. She was very well aware that the techniques that allow her to be persuasive are not only a matter of dress code, makeup, or hairstyle but also of gesture, oral expression, and looks. This is what Bourdieu called "embodied capital," which he considered a reflection and a catalyst of social differentiation, both class and gender. Embodied capital is an "enduring way of standing, speaking, walking, and thereby feeling and thinking" (2000, 291).[9] Pushpurani, in her own words, perfectly understood the importance of embodied capital. When she spoke to lenders, she expressed herself with "firmness" and "courage," while avoiding arrogance and vulgarity. Women who can't speak, she explained, are not taken seriously. Those who are shy and ask with their heads down give the impression that they are unable to find money on their own.

When Pushpurani, born in the 1970s, reflects on the specifics of her generation compared to her mother's, born in the 1950s, she explicitly mentions the need for women to use body language (*aala kavukkarathu* [literally, "turning men inside out"]), which is crucial to convince a man to provide help or a loan. This is obviously not something completely new. As mentioned earlier, caste domination was historically based on sexual domination and the appropriation of Dalit women's bodies by the upper castes. This did not prevent Dalit women from negotiating with their bodies as best they could, including with Dalit males. Esther had the reputation of using the "old techniques": she was always disheveled, dressed in old, worn-out, cheap cotton sarees. She managed teams of Dalit agricultural workers, including men. According to local gossip, she frequently raised the flap of her saree to show her legs to encourage the men to be more efficient.

Sexual coercion by the upper castes has declined greatly. Yet with the expansion and monetization of social reproduction needs and the aspirations for modernity and social mobility, the uses of Dalit women's bodies have transformed. Today, echoing philosopher Michel Foucault's concept of discipline (2004), sexual coercion is less about the exercise of violence than the creation of norms that people, and women in particular, strive to adopt or enforce. In a nearby region of Tamil Nadu, social scientist Kalpana Karunakaran

(2017) described in detail the Foucauldian discipline of repayment that micro-credit organizations impose. Ethnographies from various parts of the world point out similar processes.[10] In South Arcot, financial discipline meets bodily discipline in a continuum of sexual acts, from charm to sexual penetration. Compared to the historic sexual oppression of Dalit women, it seems that the oppression has both lessened, as high-caste men's sexual rights over Dalit women are a thing of the past, yet also proliferated in light of the need for cash. Lenders are now multi-caste, including Dalits.

Respectability and Guilt

Collins and her colleagues used financial diaries to conclude that the poor face a "triple whammy": incomes are low but also irregular and unpredictable, and financial tools are absent or inadequate (2009, 16). The indebted woman faces a further double whammy: being forced to use her body to maintain or boost her solvency, all while maintaining her respectability. And this is a matter both of self-respect and of reputation. The indebted woman is thus forced to make constant calculations and arbitrations between what is nec-essary to build or maintain her solvency and what is morally desirable. Her dilemma is reminiscent of historian Clare Crowston's (2013) discussion of the completely different context of eighteenth-century France. While reputation and creditworthiness were one and the same, women constantly had to use emotion and seduction to enhance their reputations, without losing their virtue and sexual probity. Access to credit, in financial or social terms, was predicated on women's ability to reconcile these contradictory imperatives.

The indebted Dalit woman faces similar contradictions. She is supposed to be attractive and persuasive without showing any sign of indecency or vulgar-ity. Sexual probity and moral virtue, let us recall, are a precondition for respect-ability. To express this, Pushpurani explained to Santosh and Isabelle: "You should not run fast, you should not run slow, you should run at their pace." We also heard her regularly criticizing one of her neighbors, who "goes to a moneylender as if she goes to a marriage." In other words, she does too much.

When indebted women compare today's situation to what they experi-enced fifteen or twenty years earlier, before the financial landscape diversi-fied, they appreciate the broader market. They can more easily turn down an intrusive or aggressive lender. Public insults, which also contributed to the reputation of "easy" Dalit women, have become much rarer.

But the needs are such that the pressure comes "from another side," Push-purani told us. For her, the most complex task of juggling debt is this constant pressure on her body and her respectability. In her countless conversations with Santosh, this issue came up repeatedly. She was constantly managing five to ten loans of several tens of thousands of rupees, which she repaid regularly, leading her to "rotate" lenders. She mostly took out loans from men. The women she knew lacked capital, except an NGO manager who regularly loaned her money while asking her for multiple favors in return. With men, the sexual pressure was pervasive. She said that every time she approached them, the men tried to "push" or seduce her. Escaping this pressure and maintaining her respectability were the priority criteria in her own calculations. For example, in 2018 she owed 50,000 rupees (USD 780) to a lender who lived in the next town. From the beginning she did not like him. He stared at her insistently and spoke sarcastically as if making fun of her. A few days before the repayment date, he would call her to offer to postpone the payment, without any additional cost. "Just come and see me," he would tell her. It was clear to her that the implicit condition for the postponement was sex. A few days later, the lender saw her on the road and offered to take her on his bike, insisting heavily. She refused, explaining to Santosh that she had to, or rumors might spread among many lenders that she was an "easy borrower." She decided to pay back as quickly as possible and was determined never to borrow from this man again. In another case, the man was a long-term lender. He had never tried to seduce her, but she regularly felt his insistent looks, and he invited her into his house.[11] She got to know his wife and made sure the wife was there whenever she went in. It is even more awkward if lenders know the women's husbands. At the slightest misplaced gesture or glance, the lender can easily complain to the husband that his wife has tried to seduce him or threaten to tell the husband as much.

As far as we know, Pushpurani had only had extramarital sex with her long-time lender/lover. The next chapter discusses the ethical dilemmas that this deviant sexuality creates. With all the other lenders, it seems she had managed to play the seduction game without being forced to provide sex. But this required effort and attention at all times: smiling but not too much, answering personal questions without saying too much, agreeing to go to their homes but making sure their wives were present. As the opening vignette shows, this game disgusts her. There are days when she wishes she could disappear, become a *sadhu*—that is, an ascetic who has renounced all material life. During the COVID-19 pandemic lockdown, when most negotiations were done over the phone, she had a much harder time convincing her usual creditors. Most of them had financial troubles, of course, but it certainly seemed that the telephone was less conducive to the game of seduction.

Saraswathi's case also illustrates the constant arbitration the indebted woman faces between her financial needs and her reputation, which in turn shape her creditworthiness and her own ethical framework. Saraswathi, as we have seen, did not expect much out of her husband. She said she was disillusioned with men and did not want to owe them anything. She did not trust men at all. It seems, however, that she had a lover, but she did not want to talk about it. When Santosh discreetly asked her if she would ever offer sex to pay off her debts, she first replied that she would do so "only for 5 lakhs," a very large sum (USD 7,800, more than five years of the average annual income for a Dalit family). She was still young—around thirty-five-years old—and she regularly attracted attention. Over the course of our discussions, however, she ended up confiding to Santosh that it had happened with the supervisor of the textile unit where she had been working since her husband no longer brought any money home. She had started working there a few years before our discussions. In the first few years, she had been very cautious. She was wary of men; her daughter was young, and she didn't want to damage her reputation. Over time, she became friendly with the supervisor. He encouraged and complimented her, which she was not indifferent to, as her husband has not done so for a long time. Then the supervisor loaned her money—INR 25,000 (USD 390)—and told her to pay it back "when she could." She quickly realized that he expected something else and that he was looking at her differently. Her financial situation got worse. She felt that she would have a hard time paying off this debt but refused to think about doing so sexually. She was constantly thinking about her daughter and refused to make any mistakes. She feared that the supervisor would use her and blackmail her. She finally gave in to his advances. We don't know what kind of sex she offered him, but it obviously cleared up the debt and she managed to set down her conditions: it would be one time only. She didn't want to depend on him. Saraswathi's natural charm had already earned her a bad reputation. Her neighbor regularly warned Santosh, telling him that Saraswathi "talks like honey" and risks "bottling him" or, in other words, might seduce him.

Anthropologist Svati Shah (2014) describes sex work in the slums of Mumbai as a public secret that is both ubiquitous, on every street corner, and also constantly concealed, including by the women themselves who never use the term. Here, the moral stigma of sex outside marriage condemns the indebted woman involved in sex for debt to silence and subterfuge. As previously discussed, very few openly talk about their dealings. We gradually learned to identify the tangible signs. For example, a woman would suddenly clear or postpone a debt repayment and claim she was helped by her mother-in-law or had taken out a microloan. A close friend would cover for her by pretending to have been with her. In other cases, seeing a woman in tears after meeting a lender, her saree slightly rumpled, one could assume that a sexual act may have taken place, whether seduction or something else.

Some women do not care about their respectability for the simple fact that they have already lost it. Leila, for example, was one of the few Dalit women we met who openly acknowledged her sexual freedom. When she got married, she already had a lover, whom she continued to see, in full view of everyone. She had five children, and there was a lot of gossip about who the father of each child could be. Her lover died over ten years ago, and her husband more or less deserted the house, so making ends meet was a constant struggle. A friend of Pushpurani's son warned Santosh not to give her anything, "or she'll take your penis." Pushpurani told us that, indeed, Leila regularly offered oral sex to lenders. She had a bad reputation and was already a certain age—around fifty years old—so her bargaining power was weak. We don't have the details of the transactions, but it seems that she was offering oral sex to pay off small debts of a few thousand rupees. As a single woman whose husband had deserted her long ago and whose lover was dead, she no longer felt the need to protect her respectability.

For most of the other women, maintaining respectability was a constant preoccupation. The main challenge was to create time and space for the sexual act, running the risk of being discovered. Sex never took place at home, which would be far too unsafe given the dwelling density of Tamil villages; keeping out of sight of neighbors was a constant challenge. The most common places were surrounding woods after nightfall and at cinemas (for those women allowed to go). Women sought out cinemas that were not too crowded, where they would sit in a corner and where their relations may be limited to oral sex. Women with more freedom of movement had the option of going further afield to a cheap hotel room.

It is likely that most husbands were not fooled. In echo of the observations of anthropologist Jonathan Parry (2014) for another part of India, a husband would turn a blind eye because he knew that his wife's hard work and the pledging of her body helped balance the family budget. Sometimes husbands were even complicit, and the wives knew that they knew. Saraswathi, for example, regularly broke out in rage when her husband would ask her to go and handle the loan officers at the door, when he otherwise scrutinized and judged her every move. Her husband's hypocrisy and cowardice were only reflections of the powerlessness and emasculation of many Dalit men, themselves victims of an unstable economy. It was certainly no coincidence that Saraswathi's husband was depressed, alcoholic, and regularly suffered from erectile dysfunction. While debt embodiment principally weighs on women, it does not spare men. For women, however, debt embodiment is much heavier to deal with, both sexually and emotionally.

Feminist history has shown how beauty and sexual attractiveness are eminently diverse and shifting realities, while very frequently being both a stigma and an asset (Tseëlon 1995). Sociologist Beverley Skeggs (1997) notes that in many circumstances, femininity means being beautiful without being vulgar, crude, or exhibitionist in a way that would make the woman a seductive threat. For indebted Dalit women, who over the past fifty years have lost both their economic and sexual autonomy, managing these conflicting imperatives is a real challenge. This is a crucial component of debt as a state of mind, as discussed in the previous chapter, and we have already discussed the cognitive load of memorization and financial calculations. Added to this comes a huge mental and emotional burden. First come feelings of repugnance and suffering as a result of coercion and the sexual seduction process. Second comes a specific form of emotional work, seeking to keep up one's respectability.

For sociologist Arlie Hochschild, emotional labor consists of managing feelings "to create publicly observable facial and bodily displays" (2012, 7n). Many jobs, which are often carried out by women, involve a strong component of emotional labor, from flight attendants for the well-being of travelers to childcare workers for the children they look after. In South Arcot, the indebted woman must constantly flaunt her body to persuade her husband or lenders. But she must also constantly deal with her own emotions and ethical dilemmas. This is another crucial component of debt work. As a result of this constant emotional effort, women complain of sleep problems, anxiety, and various pains. We never encountered any suicides, although the media regularly reports cases among indebted women (and men). Mental health in Tamil Nadu remains severely overlooked, both among medical staff and local populations. Obviously, we did not pay sufficient attention to mental health, and it is certainly a topic that deserves more consideration.

Debt does not spare male bodies, of course, and it can lead to exhaustion, imprisonment, or even death. In South Arcot as elsewhere in India, various forms of bonded labor and wage advances are practiced, mostly affecting men (Breman 2007; Guérin 2013). Employers and recruiters can leverage workers' indebtedness to enforce harsh working conditions and meagre wages. As mentioned in the previous chapter, in recent years the household debt boom has fueled these labor arrangements, with the wage advance being used to pay off other debts (Guérin and Venkatasubramanian 2022). The suicides of overindebted Indian farmers in cotton areas are a documented and publicly acknowledged tragedy. As in-depth ethnographies have shown, debt becomes unbearable owing not just to its financial cost but to the combined impact of overdependency on single crops; uncontrolled techniques, farm input costs, and climate; and a sense of irreversible decline (Mohanty 2005; E. Shah 2012). The suicides of male government employees laid off in the wake of privatization are not discussed as widely but have been equally, if not more, problematic (Parry 2012).

In the United States, imprisonment for debt, though illegal, has resurfaced, with a notable increase since the 2008 financial crisis (LeBaron and Roberts 2012). More data are needed, but it can be assumed that both men and women are affected. Honor debts and financial debts, which can be astronomical, can easily lead to the murder of debtors in the male-dominated economies of crime (Feltran 2020, Narring 2022a). But given the social hold over women's bodies and their limited resources, the incorporation of women's debt vastly exceeds that of men.

As mentioned earlier (see the introduction), the collateralization of women's bodies is obviously nothing new, from ancient forms of dispossession to wide-ranging contemporary arrangements. It is worth noting, however, that women's bodies are sometimes seen as collateral and sometimes as a risk. In the United States in the 1970s, the credit market targeted white men while women, regardless of their status and income, were highly discriminated against (Hyman 2011, 195). The bodies of middle-aged women were not an asset but a risk due to childbearing, and bankers required a certificate of nonpregnancy before granting credit (Thurston 2018, 144).

Female bodily collateral moreover takes on multiple forms, which can only be understood in terms of the set of rights and obligations within which women are embedded. For contemporary neoliberal Chile, anthropologist Clara Han (2012) has discussed in depth how, in a context of strong economic precarity, state violence, and the traumatic memory of dictatorship, women's debt is embodied chiefly in anxiety, depression, mental disorders, and sometimes suicide. In the drug trafficking–plagued Brazilian *favela* of Vitória, the embodiment of debt is deeply gendered. It involves the infliction of physical violence onto male bodies, sometimes leading to death, and psychological violence onto female bodies (Narring 2022b). Mothers and grandmothers not only manage daily household debt but their sons' and grandsons' trafficking debts. These men are sometimes murdered or condemned to flee from the traffickers and moneylenders. Here, too, the stress of the debt leads to depression, addiction, and cardiovascular disease (Narring 2022a, 229). In South Arcot, men's increasing control over labor income has met with chronic economic precarity and strong aspirations for mobility and sexual respectability aimed at ending Dalit inferiority. Dalit women have found themselves caught in a vice, forced to go into debt to take on their new status as housewives and pay their kinship obligations, while engaging in deviant and transgressive sexuality to maintain or improve their solvency.

The indebted woman deals with these impossible demands as best she can and to varying degrees, using trickery, lies, and subterfuge. Sex-for-debt exchanges help to boost and maintain creditworthiness and apparently help the indebted woman to pay off some of her debt, both the financial ones and the ones owed to her kinship group. At the same time, the transgressive quality of these exchanges strengthens a moral debt through feelings of shame and guilt. Ultimately, since she is deprived of financial and sexual autonomy, the indebted woman is condemned to an unpayable debt. We turn to this in the next chapter.

6

Debt and Love

PUSHPURANI FELT CONSTANTLY GUILTY about her extramarital relationship with her lender/lover, Ramesh. She regularly justified herself, pointing out that the money went to her household and not to personal needs, which in any case were minimal. She also insisted that she had no choice, as Ramesh was lending her money her family needed, and she was paying it back. This earmarking clearly helped her feel less guilty. Yet her moments with him were precious to her. She was able to express things that she could not share at home. "He gives me what I'm missing in my life," she once told us, meaning material and emotional support. Her feelings of guilt also extended to her pleasure, including sexual pleasure, which she willingly admitted.

Raika had been in an extramarital relationship with a man for almost fifteen years. Without the loans he regularly provided, she wouldn't have been able to run her business or keep the family finances afloat, let alone pay for private school for her two children. Her husband, a weaver, had not been able to retrain after his industry folded. She spoke hesitantly about her affair to Santosh, as if expressing it out loud were unthinkable. And she was obsessed with judging her own behavior: "Am I a whore?" she would constantly wonder to Santosh.

Far beyond the cases of Pushpurani and Raika, the lenders of many indebted women gradually become their lovers. By tracing the interweaving of intimacy and economics, we could observe how feelings of love and gratitude developed over time. Feminist research has stressed the "historical meaning

132

and construction of love, its performance and authenticity" (Constable 2009, 54). These subjectivities are shaped by structural constraints, and they emerge out of changing state policies and political economies, bringing into play needs for resources, identity issues, and power relations. In South Arcot, it is certainly no coincidence that the indebted Dalit woman falls in love with Dalit men who are able to lend her money. But a relationship of monetary debt does not preclude affection, love, and care. Intimacy and economics are in no way the imagined "hostile worlds" of Western morality, as Zelizer has amply demonstrated (2005, 20).

It is also worth noting the ambiguity of these relationships. They are essential sources of comfort, care, recognition, and sometimes sexual pleasure but also sources of deep moral conflict. The indebted woman in love is constantly torn by feelings of guilt and shame that eat away at her from the inside, haunt her, obsess her. Her ethical dilemmas are simply the reflection of a colonial-era obsession with scrutinizing women's sexual behavior and classifying all those who stray from chastity and monogamy as "aberrant, sexually unchaste, outside of respectable society, socially ill, criminally dangerous, or sexually unbound," as Mitra discusses (2020, 6). Since then, the Indian nation state has constantly endorsed and reinforced these hegemonic codes of female sexuality (Puri 1999). This ethical dilemma seems particularly prevalent among Dalits seeking social mobility and respectability, and conversely among non-Dalits experiencing social downgrading. Pushpurani (a Dalit) and Raika (a non-Dalit) illustrate these two cases.

Compared to other indebted women, the indebted woman in love engages in even more intense relational and emotional work to protect both her reputation and her self-esteem. Framing the transaction with her lover as a debt, and not as a payment or a gift, is part of this relational work. By becoming indebted to this man, she seeks to escape the stigma of the prostitute or the adulterer and lover. Paradoxically, debt emerges as an opportunity that the indebted woman seizes to escape, at least partially and temporarily, from the norms of passive sexuality. This loophole is fleeting, however, and the specter of guilt over sexual pleasure is all-pervasive. The indebted woman in love compensates for such guilt by taking on even more family obligations and debts, in an endless cycle. Sexuality and its oppression make the debt both infinite and unpayable. Whatever women pay back, both monetarily and by fulfilling manifold obligations as mothers, wives, or daughters-in-law, the debt seems impossible to expunge. Unpayable debt is above all an obligation, a moral debt contracted toward society as a whole, simply because of their status as women. Womanhood implies both deprivation of financial and sexual autonomy and obligation toward the social reproduction of the family. This in turn makes deviant sexuality necessary, as the only means of accessing both material resources and the care and love women are deprived of. This contradictory imperative generates an unpayable debt.

The Fabric of Love

Returning to Pushpurani's first disclosures, we learned that she met Ramesh in the early 2010s. At the time she was struggling because her son was suffering from a rare disease. After years of visits and consultations with medical services, doctors, and hospitals, she had finally found him treatment. Then her daughter, a young teenager at the time, was wrongly accused of theft and had to go to court. It took over four years for her daughter to be exonerated. During this time she met Ramesh. In her own words, he was her only source of support; her husband, Kandan, didn't seem to care. He had had an affair very soon after they got married. Given that their marriage was a love match, not arranged as was the custom, the affair was a severe blow to her pride and sense of emotional security.

Meanwhile, her love marriage had seriously weakened her relations with her kinship group. The fact that her husband seemed to be losing interest in his own children reinforced her feeling of isolation and desire for affection. Ramesh was one of the only people to care and encourage her to keep fighting. He was very supportive in negotiating with the local government, including through the legal system, and started lending her money to pay for a lawyer. Since then, he had always been there for her, both emotionally and financially.

She remembered the first time Ramesh loaned her money, in 2011, as the turning point in their relationship. She called Santosh to discuss it. She felt obligated to give Ramesh "compensation," as she put it. Offering her body, she thought, was the only possible option. She confided her doubts to Santosh, as she did not know what to do. She finally gave in. Ten years later, she was still seeing Ramesh and still confiding her doubts to Santosh. Several times, she wondered about ending the relationship. Her daughter was growing up; she had to preserve her reputation. Her son was increasingly asking questions. At the same time, she felt stuck. As soon as she took some distance, Ramesh would reproach her for only being interested in his money, which exacerbated her guilt. The early days of the relationship were a source of painful tension since she felt she was doing something dirty, reprehensible, and immoral by selling her body.

As time went by, her comments about Ramesh changed. While her initial dilemma had seemed to suggest a lack of choice—refusing sex would have meant the end of Ramesh's support—Pushpurani increasingly mentioned a relationship of mutual support and affection, something that could be described as romantic love. The moments she spent with Ramesh were precious. She could express things she could not at home. She shared her state of mind, her chronic fatigue from her multiple obligations, and the lack of recognition from her husband, in-laws, brothers, and even children. Ramesh took care of her, cared about her health, and smiled at her. With him, she said, "I feel like a person. . . . I realize I'm a woman, and he sees me as a woman."

Her tension did not go away over time but shifted. In discussions with Santosh, she would always justify herself and bring up issues of "morality." Santosh was careful not to pass judgment; he just tried to help her express her feelings and doubts. She would constantly wonder whether she was doing something "wrong" to her family and her parents. But she tried to convince herself that she was entitled to a relationship that validated her as a person. "I know my values, I know my situation [here she referred to the fact that her family had, to some degree, climbed the social ladder and aspired to respectability]. How am I supposed to face my brothers? I have my mother, my father, my kids, my brothers, but do I have anything for myself?" This is how she explained her decision to cross what she called "the frontiers of morality."

Pushpurani, let us recall, was the one who fully managed the family's finances, with energy and efficiency. She had found (and financed) a permanent job for her husband, financed the education of her two children, renovated their house—which became the most prestigious in the neighborhood—and married off her son with great fanfare. The family is a typical case of Dalit social mobility, as relative as such mobility remains. They still live in the Dalit neighborhood, only associate with Dalits, and when they interact with non-Dalits, they are frequently reminded of their Dalit status. Yet Pushpurani's social rise exposed her even more to rumor and harsh criticism. This not only occurred because respectability required compliance with morality codes but also because Dalit social mobility has always been subject to suspicion for immoral behavior, such as sex for money. Her husband acknowledged her effectiveness, saying that without her they would never have reached their current situation. But, Pushpurani said, he didn't see "me as a person who has her own needs." Ramesh, by contrast, regularly complimented her and she existed to him as a person. To compare the two men, Pushpurani evoked the image of a successful chicken curry: the exquisite taste comes mainly from small, seemingly insignificant yet essential details in the recipe. As time went by, she rejected the idea that her relationship with Ramesh was only motivated by material matters. She sarcastically argued that if this were the case, she would have chosen a much wealthier man. She also saw her extramarital relationship as ultimately decisive in helping her to respect family values since it brought her material security. "Maybe it's stupid, I have a marital value but in my own sense; marriage is something to support us, to take care about us, to be a security for us; but these three things don't happen in many marriages; the *thali* gives you an identity of a married woman but no security. . . . With him [her lover], I have the security."

Raika, meanwhile, is a Vanniyar, a caste just above the Dalits in the local social hierarchy. Over the past fifty years, the Vanniyars have grown dominant through control of the land, involvement in multiple nonfarming activities such as transportation and finance, and political engagement. But not all Vanniyars fare so well. Raika's family, for example, was struggling to cope with the decline of an ancestral occupation, handloom weaving.

As we saw earlier, Raika set up a business center in 2004, initially on the advice of an NGO, which she soon left after a conflict arose. She had known her lover, Anand, since the outset of her business because he regularly loaned money to traders. She was imbued with a very conservative morality and kept her distance from men. During the early years of her business, she took advantage of the use of a very cheap room from the municipality. The contract ended in 2008, and she had to pay a much higher rent and an advance to the owner. Anand found out that she needed money and offered to help her. She needed 2 lakhs, or about two years of her net sales. He offered to lend her the amount the next day, without asking for any guarantee. When she asked him about the lack of collateral, he replied that he trusted her. While she had always been on her guard, she admitted that "these words made me move a little closer because I never heard that from my husband. My husband never believed me." Anand offered her a fancy saree and took her to visit a temple. Her husband never took the trouble. Her dilemma began, which was when she called Santosh in tears. Anand certainly expected sex from her, she thought. If she refused, she would put her business at risk. And she admitted that this man was kind and considerate. Closing her business would mean going back to "the kitchen," which she categorically refused to do. She finally gave in to Anand's advances. He then became a regular lover and an essential support for her business, whether for short-term credit when she was low on cash, for investment credits to buy new machines, or for helping her get in touch with public administrations for orders.

Like Pushpurani, Raika had a constant sense of guilt and, as we will see in the following section, she employed endless tactics to remain discreet. She kept saying: "I know this is not good, but I am also a woman, right?" When Santosh asked her for clarification, she explained that she was a woman with feelings, which her husband did not understand, nor did he want to. Her lover saw her as a "boss," she said, constantly motivating her to get ahead in her work. He would hold her hand to comfort her. Through his eyes, she felt both "strong" and "young."

Chandran, whom we also met earlier and who felt crushed by his obligations as an older brother with three sisters, had an affair with another Dalit woman, Rajamma, for several years. She greatly helped him financially by regularly lending him money. In the first few years of our discussions, he stressed his obligations as an older brother since he was in charge of financing his sisters' marriages. Unlike Pushpurani and Raika, he did not feel guilty because extramarital relationships were allowed and accepted for men. As his own wife had come without a dowry, he felt free to have another relationship. When the pandemic broke out in 2020, he seemed in a very bad way, both physically and morally. At that moment, it was his breadwinner status that was undermined. He had needed an operation a few months earlier, at a cost of INR 80,000 (USD 1,250) (almost the equivalent of one year's average income for a Dalit family), and Rajamma had loaned him the necessary sum. His income had always fluctuated due to his unstable position as a social worker. He earned nothing for several months as a result of his surgery, losing all consideration from his wife. "Only if you bring something home are you respected as a husband," he said, contrasting this to Rajamma, who supported and respected him without him contributing anything. Rajamma does "all this only because of me, without any obligation, without any recognition, without any future . . . society's bad name, morality and all that, does not matter compared to this . . . there is only one person who wants me to be happy."

What can we learn from these three cases? We can first note, in an echo of various feminist works and running against common stereotypes, that the

bodies of subaltern women are not just a vehicle of oppression and exploitation, and that love and sexual passion are not just the privilege of upper or
Western classes (Illouz 1998; Hirsch 2003).[1] Indebted women use their bodies
for economic gain, to fulfill their obligations, and to improve their children's
chances in life. But they also use their bodies for recognition, attention, love,
pleasure, and as a form of self-accomplishment. And the same is true of men
in debt, as the case of Chandran shows.

Here again, echoing feminist research, love proves to be a social construct.
Feminist approaches argue that the understanding of private and intimate
life, of sexuality and feelings, cannot be left only to psychology. People, who-
ever they are, do feel and embody affects, impulses, and emotions. But these
emerge out of specific political, social, and cultural economies.[2] In the same
vein, the psychological predispositions of individuals, women or men, cannot
explain desire, love, and their intertwining with money and the market. They
are shaped by and constitutive of a broad set of social and political structures.
The spheres of public and private, and of intimacy and the market, interpene-
trate and mutually transform each other, both in terms of interpersonal relations and the broader structures into which interpersonal relations are inter-
woven (Zelizer 2005).

In other words, desire and amorous feelings are both related to and reveal
processes of social differentiation. In Japan, migrant Filipina bar hostesses
looking for protection fall in love with their lonely rural Japanese clients (Faier
2007). In Vietnam, middle-aged European businessmen on the decline are
charmed by young dark-skinned female villagers in need of help; Vietnamese
businessmen on the social rise are proud to pay for high-class light-skinned
sex workers (Hoang 2015). In Europe and the United States, upper-class young
men and women, freed from the rules of marriage and focused on their own
freedom and autonomy, are increasingly using the marketplace as their primary form of sexual encounter, be it as paid sex or online dating platforms
(Bernstein 2007; Illouz 2019). These various examples point to changing political economies of desire and love. They are based on new forms of markets
and capital flows and reflect profound changes in the way the family, groups
of belonging, and national ideals are represented. In turn, these political economies of desire and love actively contribute to the production of social differentiation, whether of gender, class, or race, from the local to the global level.

In Tamil Nadu, anthropologist S. Anandhi and her colleagues (2002) have
explored the contemporary political economics of desire and love among

young Tamil Dalit men in the early 2000s. The seduction of non-Dalit girls, together with new forms of consumption and public displays of violence, are expressive of new forms of masculinity. These have stemmed from the decline of agriculture and high-caste control, which was historically based on land-ownership. At the same time, young Dalits are exercising increasing control over the sexuality of their own wives, sisters, and daughters, both as an expression of their own power and in reaction to the increasing mobility of young girls, who are now employed as manual laborers in nearby industries.

It is certainly no accident in South Arcot that some women fall in love with their (mostly same-caste) male lenders, as the case with Pushpurani and Raika. The converse can also happen, as with Chandran, although this is probably less common. Our goal here is not to question the authenticity of their feelings, or those of their lovers; nor is it to give in to absolute social determinism. Our goal is rather to highlight the material aspects of desire and love, and, following anthropologist Lieba Faier, both to explore "the conditions of possibility for, and introduced by, love in these women's lives" (2007, 150) and to approach love as one of the "techniques of the self" as Foucault conceived of it. Foucault's techniques of the self refer to historically constructed techniques through which people model their bodies, their "souls," their "thoughts," and their "behaviors" according to moral imperatives and their own sense of ethics (2004, 794). In our case, the love and affection that indebted women develop over time toward their lenders at the same time secure their access to credit, give ethical meaning to their lives, and distinguish them from the repulsive, terrifying, stigmatizing image of the prostitute. We return to this point next.

Managing Risks and Ethics

Having an affair requires real risk management skills, Pushpurani once told us. Since we often discussed debt and credit, she interjected that the risks of credit were nothing compared to the risks of "affairs." Every meeting requires careful planning—"You spend ten times as much time planning as you spend with the man." A story is needed, as are excuses if someone sees her where she shouldn't be, and the support of people around her if there is any doubt, as well as friends who can testify that she had good reason to be where she said she was. She also needs a convincing way of answering questions and steady emotional control. For example, if someone in the village sees her with her lover on the bus, before any rumor starts spreading, she will announce that she met him by chance and give some news about him. Over the past few years, Pushpurani had most feared her son's questions, especially since he got married and moved home with his wife.

The women most at risk of exposure are those whose husbands or brothers are weak, in the sense that they have little local respect. Male and female neighbors do not hesitate to make fun of a woman accused of using her sexual freedom, mocking the husband by extension as incapable of controlling his wife. Pushpurani gave the example of her neighbor Geeta, who went to the cinema with her lover. Unfortunately, an old man from the village was also in the room. He didn't say anything to her husband but would implicitly threaten Geeta by publicly joking with other men as soon as she walked by, asking her if she enjoyed the movie, what her favorite scene was, and so on. Geeta lived in terror that her husband would finally understand. But because of their social standing, no one made this kind of joke around Pushpurani or her husband.

Raika compared her situation to a sheep in a butcher's stall with a knife at her throat. The slightest mistake would plunge her into conflict and disgrace. "Here," she said, "women have to deal with two major pressures: financial pressure and moral pressure. There are some women who manage financially but get their morality spoiled. Others are unable to sell a thing but keep their reputation. The biggest challenge is to combine the two." She was referring here to women traders who had regular business interactions with male suppliers, customers, lenders, and government officials. Simply being in contact with men could easily earn women a reputation as "easy." Raika, too, had to regularly interact with men. She exercised strict emotional control, feigning a calculated coldness, and kept her saree very neat. It was a constant effort.

Paradoxically, although the need for debt had been the starting point for these extramarital relationships, the debt was also taken as an opportunity to give ethical meaning to their transgressive sexuality. To cope with their dilemmas, the women do a meticulous job of "earmarking" their monetary transactions, to use Zelizer's expression (1994, 21–25). As Zelizer demonstrates, money neither withers nor corrupts intimate relations but reveals their nature. In order to match up their monetary practices to their social relationships (whether experienced, imagined, or projected), men and women constantly perform what Zelizer calls "good matches," adjusting their transactions—the medium used and how it is framed—to expectations of the relationship (2005, 27–28).

In this example, the women strive to find arrangements and means of compensation that are a good match for the relationships they want to develop, sustain, or circumvent, and to "maintain boundaries between intimate relations that could easily become confused" (Zelizer 2005, 28). Earmarking—using money for specific purposes—is one such form of matching work. Sex-for-debt money is put toward essential, "respectable" expenses such as children's education, domestic expenditures, and debt repayment. The women reason that using sex for cash is morally acceptable if husbands fail to meet their obligations. The so-called cheap women are the ones who use sex to buy sarees or jewels for themselves. Pushpurani insisted that the money she asked her lover for was a "last hope" as she tried to keep the requests to a minimum, and in no circumstances was the money for her own needs: "at no cost." As such, the indebted woman transgresses sexual prohibition but not the rule against owning her own resources. This probably explains why the men, who are not completely fooled, turn a blind eye (see also chapter 5).

Framing the exchange as a debt to be repaid rather than a service with a fixed price (as with prostitution) or a lover's gift is another example of "matching" being used to clearly differentiate the exchange from prostitution or love. It is the women themselves who insist that the exchange should take the form of a debt to be repaid. Accepting gifts, we were often told, "morally" discredits a woman. Being in debt instead of receiving a gift preserves both her and her lover's honor: "If she accepts help as a gift, her value to him will go way down," explained Praba, describing the love relationships that many women in her neighborhood had with their lenders. Pushpurani repaid every *paisa* to Ramesh, and the same was true for Raika and Anand. The debt emerged as a kind of middle ground, between payment and gift, distancing both parties from the specter of prostitution, the ultimate degradation, and from love outside marriage, which is strictly forbidden to them. This framing and matching work therefore decisively shapes how women legitimize their practices, for themselves, their lovers, and their community. Framing the exchange as a debt distances the exchange from payment and hence from prostitution but also from giving and therefore from love. This, however, is not enough.

The Specter of Prostitution

"Am I a whore?" Ever since the early days of her relationship with her "friend" and still fifteen years later, Raika kept asking Santosh this question. Raika's fixation probably reflected the Indian obsession with the image and definition of the prostitute. As Mitra (2020) argues, throughout the last two centuries, intellectuals, scientists, and politicians have constantly debated the definitions and delineations of the female prostitute, with a crucial political stake. Because prostitution is emblematic of sexual degeneration (far more than homosexuality), it has been equated with social inferiority. Defining it makes it possible not only to describe and explain it but also to enforce social hierarchical ideologies, notably concerning caste, religion, and class. Is the prostitute someone who is forced to sell her body for money? A being with inherent sexual proclivities and unable to contain her desires? Or simply a woman who does not conform to monogamous marriage? Beyond women monetizing their bodies, any practice that falls outside the chastity of monogamous Hindu marriage is suspect. People in lower castes and Muslims, whose marriage practices are more diverse, are stigmatized as sexually deviant and therefore inferior, owing to their inability to channel their wives' sexual promiscuity.

Still today, as discussed earlier in the book, debates over deviant female sexuality remain heated. In South Arcot, the arguments are fueled by the ultraconservative politics of the ruling party, by public agendas that construct women as weak entities that need to be protected, and by men in Dalit parties and movements seeking to reclaim their masculinity. In the public arena, the moral denunciation of "bad" women and attacks on interreligious and intercaste marriages are widespread. Monogamous patriarchal marriage and the repression of female desires are emerging as the only legitimate norm. More than ever, the control of women's bodies and desires is a social differentiation issue, which women and their children also contribute to.

Raika's husband, Kothandan, had always opposed his wife's professional activities. The mere fact that she ran her own business and had to deal with men outside the family was morally reprehensible. He would constantly repeat that it went against "family norms." In this historically wealthy, well-respected Vanniyar family in the village, adherence to caste and gender norms had always been strict. In 2015, Raika and Kothandan were in open conflict. He had forbidden her to continue her business, so she had gone back to her parents. He had sought advice from Santosh, and they met in a bar. Kothandan came across as highly emotionally fragile. He talked about his own shame, as he had been unable to live up to family ethics. His own mother constantly reproached him for his laxity: "What sort of man are you? If it were your father, he would have killed me, that's very sure," he quoted her as saying. He said he had turned into a "security guard," checking all of Raika's comings and goings and her phone. He had noted that she lied regularly. "She thinks only about the business, Xerox, computers, etc. She comes home at 9:30, and still she makes calls. I feel like I'm taking care of the home and she is the one outside. She lost the home attitude. . . . What's the meaning of all this? What sort of life is it?" he asked Santosh shakily, visibly dismayed, unhappy, and humiliated. His own professional setbacks certainly did not help. He had been an artisan weaver, like his father before him. This craft was under severe threat in the region, and he was not coping well. Over the years, Raika had been the main breadwinner and had made the important financial decisions. She was the one who wanted to pay for expensive private schools for her two sons. When Kothandan objected that this was not necessary, she retorted that she didn't want her sons to "end up like him," to miss out on their professional lives by clinging to a craft with no future.

Raika had little esteem for her husband and found him incapable. But she felt indebted to her own family. As discussed earlier, her marriage was a "traditional" one since her husband was her cousin, and she had been given a generous dowry. Rather than being a sign of her value, she felt that the dowry trapped her, forcing her to play along for the sake of family harmony. Beyond her own family's judgment, Raika judged herself, obsessively wondering: "Am I a good wife and especially a good mother (nalla amma)?" Her tensions were clearly increasing as her sons grew up and needed more and more money for their education. At the same time, there was no way she would close her business. It allowed her to breathe, to exist, and to maintain her relationship with her lover. She needed Anand both emotionally and economically, as he financed her business but also regularly loaned her money for her two sons' private schooling. Every time she talked to Santosh, she would share her ethical dilemma. It seems she was condemned to live with it, in a kind of unpayable debt.

Pushpurani illustrates another case of unpayable debt. She paid money back to her lover, but his trust in her, and his moral and material support, created a feeling of infinite gratitude. Pushpurani herself described this as a debt. A few years ago, she thought she would end her affair when her daughter reached puberty—"I should be a better role model," she told us at the time, but she gradually found herself stuck. She attempted to meet Ramesh less often, but then he started accusing her: "Now you are better off, you don't need me anymore," she recalled him saying. "You are only interested in money." This made her feel even guiltier since it made her a "prostitute." She could not handle his criticism and feared he would make their relationship public.

Santosh and Isabelle tried to help her make sense of her feelings. Did she feel she was in love? Did she feel obligated? Did she feel dependent or even trapped? We had this discussion many times, and she was always confused. But one thing was clear. She repeatedly said she felt in "debt" (*kadan*). As previously discussed (see chapter 1), the term *kadan* refers to both financial debt and moral obligation and is rarely used. "Exchange of money" and "help" are used more often, conveying the idea of interpersonal relations, trust, and negotiability. *Kadan* is limited to transactions involving some sort of moral commitment and obligation. Pushpurani regularly justified herself, saying that the money was for the household, not her personal needs. This earmarking clearly helped her feel less guilty.

Over time, as noted earlier, she tried to convince herself that she deserved a relationship with someone who recognized her as a person and not just as an "ATM machine," as she often put it. In addition to her ongoing tug of war over family ethics, another sense of guilt stemmed from the sexual pleasure she experienced with her lover. Her husband would simply ejaculate and did not care about her sexual pleasure at all. She felt "dirty" wanting pleasure, but Ramesh allowed her to dispose of her "garbage" (her sexual desire) at his place. Ultimately, she owed him something. She was not just financially indebted to him but *obligated*.

Of course, we are all obligated to our loved ones. But there was more to it than that: the flow of exchanges defined Pushpurani as a wife, mother, daughter-in-law, and lover, and these exchanges intertwined obligation with financial debt. Pushpurani borrowed to meet her obligations to her relatives, especially since she had not respected the rules of kinship exchanges. This financial debt was profoundly ambivalent. It gave her value as a "good woman," enabled her to meet her social mobility aspirations, and served as a pretext for maintaining her relationship with Ramesh, who was the only one to recognize her as a person. But that same debt crushed her, materially and morally.

There were days when the stress and lack of recognition made her wish she were dead. Pushpurani felt "like a railway track, which everyone [her family] travels on [to meet their financial needs] when she never travels." *Kadan* was always there but never for her own needs. She said she was seen merely as a machine, devoid of desire and emotion. In an environment of domesticated female sexuality, her sexual pleasure deepened her sense of debt, with feelings of fault and culpability that she constantly sought to offset this by further satisfying the financial needs and desires of her family circle. What was Pushpurani's debt, if not an incommensurable and hence unpayable one, toward both her lover and society as a whole? None of the time she spent with Ramesh, the sexual pleasure she gave him, or the money she paid back relieved her debt, and she constantly felt obligated to give something back, both sexually and financially.

Unpayable Patriarchal Debt

A major advance in feminist studies is the recognition that economics, kinship, and sexuality cannot be studied in isolation from one another. The rules of kinship determine the rights and obligations of women and men and in turn property rights and the sexual division of labor. In many situations, as in South Arcot, this system of rights and obligations is deeply and increasingly asymmetrical, especially for Dalit women. The rules of kinship also determine the right to sexuality, which is now limited to an eminently passive sexuality. Although this was not always the case among Dalits, today women's passive sexuality is a condition for social respectability.

The indebted woman is an illustration of this intertwining of economics, kinship, and sexuality. Deprived of economic and sexual autonomy, women are forced into debt to regain their value and fulfill their obligations. Some of them also engage in transgressive sex, both to access resources, ensuring the social reproduction of their family, and to resist the norms of passive sexuality. This in turn is a source of guilt. They are thus caught up in an endless spiral, a source of unpayable debt. This "state of mind," as discussed in previous chapters, not only involves complex financial calculations, and constant relational and emotional work with lenders, but it also includes a sense of guilt that seems to eat away at them from within. In 2018, after lavishly marrying off her son, Pushpurani seemed relieved, as though she had paid off a large chunk of her debt. At the time of writing three years later, her debt burden seemed as heavy as ever due to various contingencies. These included the COVID-19 pandemic crisis and especially the successive lockdowns. It would only end when "I go under the earth," she told Santosh.

She worried about her son, who had no paid job since the COVID crisis. As we saw earlier (see chapter 2), the precariousness of the labor market for young male graduates weighs heavily on young women. Their in-laws demand exorbitant dowries from the bride's family to compensate for their risky investment in their sons' education. The instability of the labor market also weighs heavily on mothers, who try by every possible means to protect the dignity of their husbands, and subsequently of their sons. But the need for resources leads them to transgress the norms of passive sexuality, confronting them with contradictory imperatives.

In the end, the indebted woman keeps on paying her debts and fulfilling her obligations but without ever managing to completely repay or honor them. As we also saw earlier, the primary debt of the indebted woman is one of kinship. By being born female, she incurs an obligation as wife, mother, and daughter-in-law, as if femininity were a definitive condition of primordial debt. She incurs financial debt to ensure her status as a housewife responsible for balancing income and expenses, to prove her economic worth, and to improve her children's chances in life. This is a chronic financial debt since she lacks income and constantly needs new debt to pay off old ones. She also needs to engage in transgressive sex to build and maintain her creditworthiness, and sometimes falls in love with her lender, as happened with Pushpurani and Raika. In addition to the financial pressure to repay, there is also the shame and guilt of transgressive sex, of forbidden love and pleasure.

Contemporary debates on debt and unpayable debt highlight the hold of neoliberalism on individual subjectivities and how people, the poor in particular, live and experience their condition of indebted poverty. Neoliberal subjectivity, Lazzarato (2012) argues, produces a subjectivity of guilt and individual responsibility. Not only is the poor person constantly in debt to make ends meet, and must manage to repay, but the very condition of being in debt forges a morality of responsibility and guilt. The citizen, transformed into a debtor, repays not only in money but in behavior, constantly demonstrating that he or she is the deserving poor, submitting to whatever is imposed on him or her. This criticism is very accurate, but it only covers part of the problem. For the indebted woman in South Arcot, the subjectivity of debt is first and foremost imbued with the obligations of kinship, caste, and sexuality. Kinship obligations are in turn shaped by the transformations of the economy, both in terms of the men's increasing hold over paid employment and the extreme volatility of labor markets. These are also shaped by social policies that construct women as vulnerable mothers and wives in need of protection while failing to provide real social protection. Finally, they are shaped by ultraconservative and ultrarepressive ideologies on women's sexuality. These processes are intertwined and difficult to dissociate.

7

Human Debts

IN JULY 2018, VENKATA met up with Danam, who looked very worried. She was short of cash herself but desperate to find money for her friend Parvati, who she knew would have trouble paying back her microloan. "She's my friend, I owe her this," she said. Venkata saw Danam again in the evening after she had spent the day soliciting friends, relatives, and various acquaintances and had finally found some cash.

In May 2012, a group of women from a microcredit NGO had just attended an awareness-raising training session on sex education, contraception, and the need to encourage men to use condoms. Once the trainer had left, the women stayed back among themselves, commenting on the session's content, which had been far removed from their own concerns. The discussion strayed into their sexual practices, and the women tried to outdo each other in talking about the most salacious of sexual experiences, real or imagined. The group discussion gradually turned somehow delirious with the women crying with laughter, slapping each other on the thighs, and peppering their jokes with songs but also offering each other suggestions and advice.

The indebted woman reflects and reproduces the way in which kinship, sexuality, and capitalism intertwine. But she also constantly tries to extricate herself from this unpayable debt. She does not radically oppose capitalism and patriarchy but juggles different types of exchange. She develops her own circuits based on reciprocity, sharing, and caring, which vary along the lines of kinship positions, class, and caste affiliations and aspirations.

We have already discussed how the finance industry uses female bodies as collateral, and in the same way, female reciprocity primarily serves the interests of the finance industry. It serves as an "asset," to use the terminology of anthropologist Susana Narotzky (2015, 179). Clearly, this is the case within our study. But it is instructive to explore the ambivalences of market and capitalist relations. James argues that we should look beyond old oppositions between "mutuality" and "commodity," between "capitalist" and "non-capitalist debt." She observes that capitalist debt, in South Africa but in other settings, too, can prove essential to "creating productive relationships" (2021, 40).[1] We have already seen how the indebted woman seizes on market debt in the hope of escaping from caste debt. And, as we will see here, she tries to use female reciprocity as a way of bypassing the financial industry. Debts must certainly be repaid, often at a high cost. But they also have much to tell about debtors' constraints, aspirations and hopes, and perhaps their potential pathways to emancipation.

As Danam's case reflects, the indebted woman invests the tiniest of surpluses into female sociality circuits. She can rely on these in the future and avoid banking circuits, which are experienced more as dispossession than as a place to deposit value. To echo the incisive observations of Karunakaran on another region of Tamil Nadu, female reciprocity is also used as an opportunity for "learning the state," and to gain access to small pieces of state protection (2017, 167, chap. 7). In other words, the indebted woman seeks to navigate between reciprocity and market and public redistribution as best she can.

Finally, female circuits are more than something financial or material. The indebted woman urgently needs cash and credibility. But she also desperately needs recognition, care, and affection, as we all do. This is precisely what some of these women's circuits offer. These are spaces where the indebted woman can, at least fleetingly, receive care, which is something that she constantly provides to others while being deprived herself. In these spaces, the indebted woman can free her speech and her body and escape omnipresent control over her every move and word, as the second opening vignette illustrates. Ultimately, she uses circuits of female reciprocity to reconfigure the webs of interdependence within which she is embedded, juggling different spheres of value and deriving "marginal gains" from them (Guyer 2004, 25). She also uses circuits of female reciprocity to support her own emancipatory aspirations, "inhabiting" and "enduring" oppression rather than radically challenging it (Mahmood 2005, 32). These are only interstices, and the unpayable debt does not go away. But they offer various lessons for thinking about human debts—namely, those debts that can be a source of solidarity and interdependence based on equality, as opposed to unilateral power, exploitation, and guilt. As we will see at the end of this chapter, and following philosopher Nancy Fraser (2013), revisiting the lessons of economist Karl Polanyi (and anthropologist Marcel Mauss) from a feminist perspective can help us move forward in this direction.

Caring and Sharing

South Arcot's economy is founded on financial predation and exploitation, as we have seen throughout this book. Yet there is also a moral economy of caring and sharing, as is often observed in contexts of great precarity.[2] Those in need are loaned even the smallest of surpluses, whether in cash or in kind. This is both to demonstrate empathy and care and to anticipate future help in return. "Care" is used here in its broad sense, referring not just to raising children or caring for the elderly or disabled but also to adopting an attitude of kindness, attention, and love. The recipients of such help cannot refuse to help in return. These practices are also a way of avoiding unnecessary expenses, or solicitations from husbands, in-laws, or parents. Helping and lending is indeed a form of saving, in the economic sense of putting value aside in case of need. The poorest people may rarely have enough to lend, but many of them, not just the richest, are creditors too.

Sharing and showing concern for others is not about poor women having a naturally caring instinct. They simply have no choice. Life in close quarters complicates any form of privacy, including financial privacy, and encourages sharing practices. Women's two main employment sources, daily agricultural wage labor and the public employment program, are collectively negotiated, so everyone knows everybody else's incomes. Most Dalit women still cook on the ground outside their doorsteps, showing and sharing what they can afford to cook. In the early morning or at dusk, most go to the fields in small groups to gather wood and take care of their natural needs. This is sometimes the opportunity to share personal confidences. Children come and go while adults, sometimes including men, look on. Far from being harmonious, this spatial and social proximity is peppered with permanent conflicts. Many of these are settled in the street, in full view of everyone, in what amounts to constant, omnipresent mutual surveillance. The women do help each other out in many ways. For example, they may threaten or publicly insult a husband who beats his wife too badly, or feed another's children who have missed several meals. But at the same time, they watch and spy on each other, judge, criticize, and mock each other. The slightest movement is scrutinized, commented on, and judged.

There is nothing new in this moral economy of caring and sharing between Dalit women (Racine and Racine 1995). But what has changed is that cash now makes up the bulk of transactions, which formerly consisted of many other goods and services such as cereals, vegetables, soap, betel nuts, incense, subsidized food cards, and childcare. The amounts owed heighten the interdependency, leading to new forms of obligation. This echoes Danam in the opening vignette; she always tried to keep cash on her to help out her neighbors when loan officers or door-to-door lenders came around. One must lend when called on, of course, even if it means getting into debt elsewhere. But when microcredit payments are due, one should also set aside money for others who may struggle with repaying, to maintain good terms. Women may also have to join a microcredit group even if they don't need its services, simply to enable other borrowers to be eligible; this not only means being a guarantor but borrowing as well. Jewelry also circulates at an intense rate, either for ceremonies, as it would be inconceivable to attend with "empty ears" (N. Joseph 2018, 208), or to pledge for cash.

In this moral sharing-based economy, it makes little sense to tie up cash in a bank account. Due to active financial inclusion policies that encourage rural populations to deposit their savings in the bank, almost all women now have at least one bank account, and some have more. It is now a prerequisite for receiving state cash transfers, so they have no choice but to have an account. But very few women use the bank for savings, and neither do men. "It's useless," they often say. Most of these accounts are dormant, in the sense that the money is withdrawn as soon as it is deposited, simply because it makes much more sense to circulate the money within local networks. According to our quantitative data, 76 percent of women and 77 percent of men had a bank account in their own name or jointly (and 95 percent of households) in 2016–17. Bank savings remained negligible (average and median amounts were INR 500 [USD 8]) and had not increased since 2010, when our first survey was conducted (Guérin et al. 2017). Women prefer to invest in their own circuits rather than to lock up their assets in the bank. Bank saving is seen as something that dispossesses them of control over their wealth. Bank savings mediate and circulate wealth in the service of social groups, entities, temporalities, spaces, and objectives that elude poor savers.[3] Again, tactical choices of Tamil Dalit women (and men) are not unusual. Distrust in and resistance to the banking system and a preference for investing in people prevail in contexts of weak state social protection and a blurred division between economic practices and sociality.[4]

These circuits and support networks play a crucial role on a daily basis and even more so in times of crisis. Over the course of our two decades of investigation, South Arcot has experienced regular crises, such as cyclones,[5] the 2016 demonetization,[6] and the COVID-19 pandemic. For each event, and as is often the case in times of acute crisis, female mobilization was instrumental in ensuring family and neighborhood survival. This was especially clear during the first pandemic lockdown. The lockdown was imposed brutally and severely between March and September 2020, bringing a very large part of the economy to a halt. After a period of stupefaction, due to the intensity of the shock, women organized themselves to ask farmers to return to manual and therefore more labor-intensive techniques, whether for irrigation, ploughing, or harvesting. They also organized themselves to share the work, the food, and the little cash that was in circulation. Mutual aid followed the lines of preestablished savings and credit circuits. Men also have their own networks, more often built on their workplaces and outside the village and sometimes during their schooling for those who have studied.

Marginal Gains

Women's socialization is largely articulated around debt and is an integral part of debt work. It involves monitoring who has received what, who owes how much to whom, who is in need, and who can offer help. This in turn feeds into opportunities to help or receive help. Such constant attention is a further facet of debt as a state of mind (see chapter 4). Small sums circulate "from hand to hand" (*kai mathu*), without interest being paid. The implicit agreement is to pay it back quickly, within a few days, or as soon as the lender is in need herself. Past that point, interest is usually charged, even if the loan is still called "help." It is common for women in desperate need of cash to propose to pay interest, to help persuade their creditor. This constant circulation of debt and credit comprises a delicate, inseparable mix of care and financial calculation. The slightest financial interaction is seen as an opportunity for what anthropologist Jane Guyer calls "marginal gain" (2004, 25). This consists of making small profits of a social or financial nature, or sometimes both, by juggling different spheres of value. The indebted woman juggles values of caring and sharing with values that are strictly financial, borrowing cash at a lower cost or making a surplus through lending.

Consider the case of Devaki, who came to her neighbor's rescue when she was unable to pay off her microcredit installment. The loan officer was yelling outside the neighbor's house so the whole neighborhood could hear that this woman had defaulted. Devaki ran over and loaned her the 700 rupees (USD 11) needed for the installment. In the days leading up to the repayment date, this neighbor had repeatedly asked her for help before the deadline, and Devaki had refused. Later, after the loan officer had left, she explained to Venkata that she had deliberately waited for a public opportunity to help her neighbor and "save her prestige" in front of the loan officer, the members of the microcredit group, and her neighborhood. This put Devaki in a good light, as a generous, helpful neighbor. This premeditated move served a specific purpose, as she needed her neighbor to introduce her to another lender and act as a guarantor. Now the neighbor would not be able to refuse. Yet Devaki also very much cared about her neighbor, with whom she shared her daily meals, childcare, worries, and moods.

Beyond Devaki's marginal gain from this performance, this example highlights the importance of protecting the creditworthiness of people one cares about, as well as one's own creditworthiness.[7] While debt is fully part of an ontological condition, loss of creditworthiness is supposed be avoided at all costs, in a process Chu refers to as "creditability" (2010, 122). Debt work is a constant effort to maintain one's own creditworthiness and that of the people one cares about and seeks to help.

Parvati's case is also common. She repeatedly felt under pressure to join Danam's group and take out microloans because it was one member short. She agreed out of loyalty and friendship for Danam as the group's leader. But this did not stop her from lending out the sum she borrowed at a higher rate, dividing it into small amounts to limit the risk and multiply the "help." Charging interest is commonplace and is not necessarily synonymous with selfishness or greed. Dalit women prefer to pay interest rather than doing drudge work for high-caste women—cleaning barnyards or doing the dishes, as was long the case and sometimes still is—or, worse, satisfying the sexual desires of high-caste women's husbands. Paying interest may also be considered fair compensation for the effort and risk taken by a lender who is not very well-off. Sometimes debtors pay interest in kind, through personalized thank-you gifts to the lender. This was the case with Geeta, who paid interest in the form of vegetables from her own garden. Saraswathi would give half a liter of milk every day to her lender, who had young children, or ask her rickshaw driver son to offer a discounted fare to her lender.

Savings clubs (called *chit funds* or *seetu* ["ethics" or "trust"]) were historically very popular with men and women across all caste groups. The basic rule was to make regular, often monthly deposits as part of a fixed group over a set period, often a year. Each member would take turns using the full amount saved in each round. As has been observed in various parts of the world, savings clubs serve primarily as a form of discipline for saving. The simple fact that you have to make regular deposits forces you to have self-discipline and set the money aside, sometimes with a specific purpose in mind. In South Arcot, this could be expenditure on jewelry or on an upcoming religious festival, which mainly concerns women, or on a pilgrimage, which chiefly concerns men. The speed with which savings clubs have all but disappeared, being mostly replaced by market credit, is fascinating. In 2010, about half of all families belonged to at least one savings club. Six years on, no more than 10 percent did. Credit as a form of discipline has replaced the savings clubs. This process resembles what anthropologist Hadrien Saiag (2020b) has observed in the industrial city of Rosario in Argentina. In just a few years, at the turn of the 2010s, the mass-scale entry of financial companies supplanted the old savings and self-help practices.[8] It should be noted here that savings groups often had scattered members who were not bound by reciprocal obligations. The discipline of payment was based primarily on the authority and charisma of the organizer. Many people lost money and trust in the savings clubs, whether as members or organizers, and preferred to turn to the market. Various massive scandals certainly explain the collapse of trust in chit funds (Radhakrishnan 2022, 75), but the women also say that the ease with which microloans can be granted without prior savings has made them more attractive.

Prior to microcredit, Pushpurani regularly ran savings clubs, for example, and while they had brought in a regular cash flow, she had often lost money to unreliable members. She then turned to microcredit groups. Her role as group leader gave her priority for loans, and she was able to obtain fictitious loans for her sisters-in-law and close friends. Members rarely defaulted because that would have meant losing access to market credit, which was something to be avoided at all costs. Meanwhile, Pushpurani used the discipline of the market to support her own financial juggling.

Ceremonial gifts are also potential opportunities for marginal gains. Marrying off a female is bound to be a "financial loss" owing to the dowry.[9] But organizers often hope to make a "profit" (they use the English term) from other ceremonies, such that the value of the gifts received at the ceremony exceeds the expenses incurred, as well as gifts the organizer has given in the past. This, too, requires specific work, which mainly women carry out, such as choosing an appropriate day for the ceremony that is both auspicious and compatible with local calendars; carefully selecting the names of the relatives who appear on the invitation, and the gifts that will be given to them; following up regularly; visiting the guests in the weeks or even months before the event to hand-deliver the invitations; and arranging transportation and accommodation for those coming from far away.

Pushpurani held a housewarming party in 2016 after completing the second floor of her home. This event served various purposes. The first was to bring together family, friends, and local personalities, including her trusted moneylenders. She also planned to use the guests' gifts to help pay off some of the debt on the house. The event cost about INR 100,000 (USD 1,560), or over a year's average annual income for a Dalit family. She received INR 188,365 in gifts of cash and gold and kept an accurate account book down to the nearest rupee. This left a surplus of about INR 88,000 (USD 1,300), which would allow her to pay off a small proportion of her housing debt. She had hoped for more, however. Like most women, she kept track not only of what she received but also of what she gave, and over the years she had gone into INR 126,000 (USD 1,880) of debt. The INR 88,000 surplus was just a partial offset of her own entitlements. For her son's wedding in 2018, she did not seek to make a "profit." Not only had she agreed for her son to marry her brother's daughter—in other words, her niece—as a sign of her attachment to her brother and without expecting a large dowry, but she wanted to hold a grand ceremony, no matter the cost. She spent about INR 800,000 (USD 12,500) and got back exactly INR 657,724 (USD 10,300). Part of this was in cash, which helped her to pay off the debts from the ceremony. The rest consisted of gold and furniture for the newlyweds, although they were moving in with her.

Ceremonial debts and claims are arguably a form of circulating wealth. They go unnoticed by statisticians and development experts yet offer a completely different view of the material and social wealth of families. "I'm in debt, but no rope around my neck because I have everything outside," Danam told Venkata, regarding the multiple contributions she had made at ceremonies in recent years and that she would get back the day she held her own event, presumably her eldest son's wedding. When women are asked whether they have savings, many women reply in terms of ceremonial gifts.[10]

On the basis of a standard accounting analysis, we can see that Danam was in debt to the tune of approximately INR 280,000 (USD 4,400). Taking into account the various entitlements she had accumulated over the past few years by contributing to numerous ceremonies, her net financial wealth was positive (INR 5,000 [USD 80]). Devaki, Rani, and Yoganathan were heavily indebted but were also creditors by way of ceremonial expenses, to the sum of around INR 100,000 (USD 1,560). But their claim to repayment was conditional on their own children getting married. Their first son chose a love marriage, forbidding any ceremony, which broke the cycle of exchange. They were counting on the next two sons to have proper weddings and to thus restart the cycle of exchange. If we take their ceremonial balance into account, their debt drops by half (from INR 227,600 to INR 105,300 [USD 3,560 to USD 1,650]). As a young couple with young children, Parvati and Abinesh still had limited ceremonial wealth and a positive balance of INR 5,900 (USD 92). By contrast, Pushpurani accrued a heavy ceremonial debt from her son's wedding, which compounded her monetary debt and her mental stress. She talked about sleepless nights spent thinking about the list of her creditors, upcoming ceremonies, and the endless race to find money.

As such, the opportunities for making marginal gains by way of female financial circuits vary greatly. In chapter 5, we have already discussed how seduction and body techniques are unequal in their potentialities and their deployed tactics. Some women seek to diversify the circuits they use, while others look to protect themselves from them. Some are more likely to be creditors and others are more likely to be debtors, this in response to kinship positions, class and caste affiliations, and aspirations.

Let's start with Danam. As discussed in the previous chapter, she was the daughter of a bonded laborer, like her husband. They had broken free of this status, and she hoped to make further progress on the back of their sons' education and marriages. Danam had a strong network since she married within her own neighborhood. She efficiently managed several microcredit groups while acting as a "local bank" herself, as the neighbors who regularly borrowed money from her put it. She worked hard to constantly densify and expand her network of connections—within the Dalit neighborhood, the non-Dalit village, and beyond. Her active role in organizing prayers and religious festivals greatly helped. One Sunday morning in late October 2019, as the auspicious wedding season was coming to an end, Venkata ran into Danam. She was about to leave and had six wedding invitation cards in her hand, all from Dalits. These were not relatives or friends but "acquaintances" she had recently met: a moneylender, a veterinary assistant, a fertilizer salesman, the son of the chairman of the nearby village, a local leader, and a business correspondent—namely, a bank officer who carried out banking transactions in the village on behalf of the bank. She had met these people a couple of times, they had given her a wedding invitation, and she would be going in person. Venkata was surprised since she barely knew them. She could always have sent someone in her place, or just refused the invitation. But Danam explained that she would make the effort to honor the invitation and go in person, that she had gained their trust, and that she could certainly borrow from them in the future or ask for a favor. During the first pandemic lockdown, she spent her time on the phone checking in with her large network of acquaintances, including her husband's networks. She didn't want to "lose touch."

Parvati had adopted the completely opposite tactic. When Venkata first met her in 2016, she had been married for a few years. She was from a different village, from "outside," and therefore had few contacts in the neighborhood. Her circle of debt and loans was small. She mostly relied on her sister, who lived in a neighboring town about fifty kilometers away and whose house she regularly visited at the weekends, and she had a few friends on the street. Here again, her position within the family was key. Like other cases throughout this book, she had not "brought" what she was supposed to as a dowry when she married, and expectations of her were still high. The pressure was constant. But it was roughly understood that she intended to resist and to put money aside for her own projects, starting with renovating her house, and then supporting her children's education. Regardless of her secretive nature, keeping to a small circle was certainly a strategy. Her husband regularly migrated to Kerala and sent significant amounts of remittances. If she established multiple relationships, she would feel compelled to redistribute this money. At the same time, she nurtured close ties with a few friends on the same street including Danam, with whom she shared not only money but food. This was also why she saved money in the bank, which remains very rare. Depositing money in the bank, immobilizing it, means extracting it from local sociability.

She also saved in a savings club run by a friend of her sister, in the city and out of sight. Both the bank and the savings club were deliberate choices to protect herself from local solicitations. But rumors were running wild, and she was being called selfish, like her parents who neglected her dowry. It was not certain whether she would be able to keep from circulating her wealth locally much longer. At the time of the first pandemic-related lockdown, she tried to start a local fish business but was plagued with defaults. Rumor has it that she was paying the price for her greed.

As discussed in chapter 3, debt is just as much a marker of social hierarchy as of commensality or endogamy. Pushpurani, whose story we have returned to throughout this book, was certainly the most successful of all the women we met in terms of social mobility, although she was paying a high price in terms of her mental health. She was motivated, let it be remembered, by the idea of "proving herself" to her in-laws because she had arrived dowryless, "empty-handed," and then gone back to live in her native village with her husband. Her gamble had paid off and she had built one of the most beautiful houses in the village. Her status was made very clear in her position as a creditor in the neighborhood, while being very heavily indebted outside of it. She lived close to her two brothers, who were constantly going into debt with one other. They stuck to a clear principle that they would lend to, but never borrow from, others in the neighborhood. "If my brother asks for money in the village, what will people think? I lend to others and I'm not even able to lend to my own brother?" she said. Being a net creditor in the neighborhood is a clear way of marking status. Among non-Dalits, it is common to talk about borrowing only from within one's caste, to maintain one's status. Both men and women constantly seek financial autonomy within their caste so as to maintain their social standing, or, in the case of Dalits, to improve it. At the time of the first lockdown, Pushpurani agreed to lend to a neighbor, pawning her stepdaughter's jewelry to do so, which sent her son into a rage. Although she was very saddened by her son's fury, she had no regrets: she "had to help," she told Santosh. This reflects another aspect of the marginal gains processes that Guyer (2004) discusses: far beyond profits and sums of money, gains must be assessed in terms of the social positioning and recognition of lenders and borrowers on a local scale of value.[11]

Whether social or monetary, these gains remain marginal, however. With very few exceptions, women struggle to be lenders on any kind of large scale.[12] Besides a lack of capital, discrimination, limited mobility, and morality restrictions are barriers. Pushpurani only lends to Dalit women in her neigh-borhood, which hinders her. Most Dalit women face the same constraints. In South Arcot, as noted in chapter 3, "you don't lend to anyone lower than you are," even if there are exceptions.[13] Beyond caste barriers, there is the issue of patriarchal control over women's bodies, particularly for non-Dalit women but increasingly for Dalit women as well. This unavoidably restricts their movement and the size of their clientele. Just as importantly, a woman who gets rich is always going to raise suspicion. Gossips will start asking questions about what she has been doing with her body. For the great majority of women, lending is not a source of income but a means of storing their meager surplus in a safe place, thus playing with time and maintaining or consolidating rela-tionships of loyalty and friendship. High-caste women lenders, of whom there are usually one or a few per village, follow distinct social norms. Their status limits suspicion, and their lending is often seen as a duty and service to the community. Historically, they would only lend to their labor force, which was considered "help." Over time, their dependency on workers has weakened and their lending has expanded to a much broader clientele. Moreover, while the women manage the relationship with the debtors, the money accumulated is not theirs but goes to their family. Whatever their caste or wealth, women do not own their own money.

If we make a comparison over time and space, it seems that women can only lend on any significant scale if kinship rules and associated property rights permit. In West Africa, for example, the family unit is often organized around the mother and her children. Mothers historically had usership over their lineage's fields and production, and as such had their own resources, based on the custom of "separate purses" (Guérin 2008, 62). At the end of the 1990s in Senegal, Isabelle had met some women who loaned money to their husbands, at interest rates that would make the most rapacious private lenders pale. Accumulation was still frowned on. Although women enjoyed freedom of movement, across most Senegalese social groups, becoming rich would still meet with suspicion over the use of their bodies. But the rules of kinship and ownership meant the idea of owning their own money was legitimate, which is a huge difference from the Dalit women we discuss here. It may also explain why in some regions of Senegal, women could adopt microcredit to develop large-scale moneylending practices (Perry 2002). Elsewhere in the world, women's ownership of and ability to draw on their dowry has not only brought them financial autonomy but creditor status. And, as discussed elsewhere in this book, history can also be instructive. In preindustrial Europe, as feminist history has clearly shown, women's position in debt and credit networks was closely related to the diversity of de jure and de facto kinship rules and associated property rights (Fontaine 2008, chap. 5; Dermineur 2018). In premodern Italy, the Roman tradition allowed women to use their own dowry, so even if it was small, they could become "quintessential creditors" in local economies (Shaw 2018, 192). In contemporary Taiwan, the family code allows women to manage their own assets, including their dowries, as a personal "cash box" (Pairault 2004). Despite various other strong limits to their emancipation, they can enjoy financial autonomy and are active lenders.

Division and Exclusion

Debt cements friendships and, as Danam's husband told us, "multiplies friendship." He observed his wife coming and going around the neighborhood, as she was ever on the lookout for people to help or solicit. But debt also divides and excludes. As Roberts discussed in his ethnography of a Chennai slum, female debt is both the essence of moral community and "the biggest threat to it" (N. Roberts 2016, 83). Pushpurani had fallen out with her best friend over an unpaid loan, and they had not seen each other for many years. "As long as it is pending, you are standing on fire," Danam told us about her multiple bonds of debt and entitlement within her neighborhood and beyond.

Division and exclusion are equally inherent to market-based credit. Microcredit providers mostly target Dalit women, while non-Dalits try to stick to SHGs, which are less expensive and less socially stigmatizing (see chapter 3). Raika, as we saw earlier, now refuses microcredit because it is humiliating and degrading, as do many non-Dalit women. And not all Dalit women are eligible for microcredit. Women who prove unreliable at repayment, perhaps due to absent, irresponsible, lazy, or alcoholic husbands, or because their networks are too limited, are excluded. The primary reason for good repayment, however, is having the ability to borrow elsewhere, rather than the loyalty of husbands or sons. Women who live under the thumb of their mothers- or sisters-in-law, with no financial responsibilities, are excluded. So, too, are women who are unable to hold their tongues and who have a reputation for spreading rumors about others' morality. The women themselves are the ones doing the excluding since they are often in charge of screening clients. Danam reigns supreme over her microcredit groups, and anyone speaking ill of her or criticizing her behind her back would need to watch out for themselves. A woman called Leila had this misfortune, accusing Danam of greed and self-ishness. Since then, Danam has been successfully deterring every single loan officer from lending her money.

Interstices

In March 2006, an NGO invited the three of us to its exhibition of microcredit group members' handmade products. The NGO manager told us to come at noon. Some women had been there since nine and had gotten up at dawn so as not to be late. Some had walked, others had taken one or more buses, owing to the distance. They stood there waiting in the sun for the distinguished guests to start the inauguration. Wooden toys, dolls and cloth bags, candles, clothes, coconut ropes, cleaning products and cosmetics items, and processed food such as jam, pickles, or snacks were on display. Besides the NGO and the district collector, representatives of various public administrations in the fields of rural development, social affairs, and family were attending. Each distinguished guest was invited to speak and share his or her opinion—most of them were men—on "women's empowerment." The women listened along. They were tired of seeing "always the same faces," as one of them put it. As was often the case, the exhibition drew few people, and most of the women left without selling anything.

There are countless examples like these. Besides the craft fairs, women are asked to take part in numerous training courses. These are reminiscent of campaigns to educate the poor during the industrialization of Europe and North America, explaining favored topics such as hygiene, family planning, sewing, and financial education. Alongside these are subjects dear to contemporary neoliberalism, such as entrepreneurship, which has proved a failure, and leadership, which has never gone beyond the microcredit group management.

Over several years, we followed these women and shared their criticism and dismay as to the absurd, sometimes grotesque, projects for women's "empowerment." But how can we explain why women still willingly submit to all these programs? Karunakaran (2017) has proposed one explanation, based on an ethnography of a neighboring Tamil region. In a context where access to public resources remains conditional on participation in power networks, microcredit groups have become favored links in the local patronage system.

Many microcredit groups have used NGOs' support to "learn the state," to quote Karunakaran, in the sense that they have learned the tactics, strategies, and practical know-how and know-how-to-be to approach the state (2017, 172, chap. 7). They use these abilities to gain access to public programs, take part in local municipality meetings, and voice requests for basic public services like electrification, domestic water, and sanitation. In other words, microcredit groups serve as access platforms to state government-sponsored programs, which gives the NGOs appeal. Some of these collectives become successful at political campaigning, demanding and receiving police support in the event of domestic violence or marital abuse, challenging harassment and violence against women in public spaces, and denouncing the waste or misappropriation of public resources. State redistribution remains haphazard, uncertain, and discriminatory toward Dalits, being rooted in populist politics and conditional on local patronage networks, which now include microcredit groups. It does, however, offer some tokens of protection, which women constantly try to grasp. These include distributions of subsidized food, gas, appliances, and bicycles, as well as the development of employment programs, pensions for widowed women, and various subsidies for housing, education, women's marriages, and small livestock breeding.

It took us some time to grasp a much less visible, yet integral part to any emancipation process. At least some women sometimes use the spaces NGOs make available to create interstices and microspaces of care, for sharing but also for the liberation of bodies and speech.

Activists in pioneering empowering movements by and for subaltern groups, including Black feminism, American community organizing, and Latin American liberation theology, have well understood the importance of the body, speech, and affects in the acquisition of self-esteem, inner power, and critical consciousness as the first steps to any emancipation process. Contemporary rural development and microcredit programs, imbued with a neoliberal ideology that limits emancipation to a process of individual responsibility, have been blind to these bodily and emotional aspects. Yet Dalit women seek to reclaim NGOs' actions on those very terms.

Now that the golden age of Tamil NGOs is over, some women look back regretfully to the days of the groups, meetings, and multiple solicitations. They talk about the "social demand" from the government, political parties, temples, and festivals. "The *panchayat* leader [village mayor] would be waiting for us, political leaders, religious leaders would come and look for us on our doorstep," Praba recalls. Being part of an SHG was like an "identity card," we were told several times, in the sense of the recognition of their role in local communities. NGO program membership involved participation in many rallies, such as marches for women's and minority rights, protesting the war in Iraq, dowries, supporting the Tamil community in Sri Lanka, marking women's day, AIDS day, environment day, and attending political rallies, the inauguration of government programs, and awareness raising and prevention campaigns on various diseases. For Dalit women, this was often the price to pay for eligibility to credit. Many NGOs formed alliances with political parties and pledged to boost numbers at political rallies in exchange for funding, or simply to be allowed to operate in the villages. Dalit women, more docile and with greater freedom of movement than non-Dalit women, were the prime targets for these mass events (see chapter 5).

The women were often crammed into small rooms and tents. There were sporadic formal speeches from officials and VIPs, as in the scene described earlier. But when some of the women took to the stage to give testimony or to sing, and the other women joined in the songs in chorus, it created an electric atmosphere, with a sense of exuberance and euphoria. Those women who went onto the stage felt galvanized, as did those who applauded. Some of them, like Pushpurani and Danam, still speak about it with tears in their eyes. In that moment, the women were carried along by the "collective effervescence" of the crowd, in what sociologist Émile Durkheim termed an essential ritual in the construction of a collective belonging (1912, 211).[14] This exuberance is certainly even more prevalent in smaller groups, where women feel free to speak, gesticulate, and to loosen the shackles around their words and their bodies on a daily basis. In this chapter's opening vignette, the women go into a sort of collective delirium thanks to a barrage of salacious jokes about their husbands. At the time, Santosh was in the next room and listened discreetly.[15]

Some women have less freedom than others. This may stem from family pressure. This is the case of Mandi, whose father-in-law was the village mayor at the time of her interview (2010–12). Her in-laws constantly pointed out that she spoke "a lot and loudly" and that she had to make an effort to honour her father-in-law's status. Curtailed freedom may also stem from self-censorship in a bid for respectability and social ascension. When Santosh visited Pushpurani in August 2021, after two years of absence due to the pandemic, Geeta, whom Santosh knows well, made fun of him: she pointed out that he was getting old, had lost some of his hair, and asked him with a smirk if he was losing it "elsewhere." Pushpurani was present, but the joke did not seem to amuse her, whereas all the other women laughed. A few months previously, Isabelle and Santosh had caught up with Pushpurani's mother on Skype. As usual, Pushpurani's mother had been laughing loudly, and incidentally lamented about her daughter. Pushpurani was so worried about her debt that she would only meet up with lenders, and she "can't even laugh anymore." Pushpurani was indeed often stressed, tormented and distressed by the debts she constantly juggled. She confided to us that it was also a matter of reputation: to honor her status as a respectable woman, she forbade herself any form of bodily or verbal extravagance in public, even in front of her neighbors. Pushpurani's self-discipline was a simple reflection of the morals that Miss Mary had always instilled in them. Some women transgressed Miss Mary's injunctions by reappropriating NGO events, creating the very complicity that is now forbidden to them in their own village, while others, like Pushpurani, sought to conform at all costs.

Complicity between women concerning their intimate and sexual lives is another facet of the interstices of female sociality. In June 2010, Santosh was at the premises of Miss Mary's NGO. Reetabai's husband arrived, looking for his wife. Miss Mary told him that she had gone to the bank. Once the man had left, visibly reassured, the other women made fun of Miss Mary, saying that she was acting like a "pimp." Of the five or six women present, all were aware that Reetabai was having an "affair" with another man, but they were united in not disclosing anything.

As we have seen many times throughout this book, the indebted woman is constantly fighting the world but also herself. Simply having an occasion to open up, to share her own ethical dilemmas and suffering, comes as a relief. These women's spaces for letting go, for relaxation, excitement, and euphoria, are places where women can let their guard down, in both words and gestures, often unbeknownst to the NGOs that provide the spaces. They can sing, dance, and make jokes about themselves and the world around them, and especially about men, but also about other women they consider oppressive; they can shout, give each other standing ovations, or sometimes become delirious. Being condemned in their everyday spaces of existence to keeping their voices down and to self-surveillance, caught up in prescriptions and prohibitions that restrain and censor them, their every word and gesture straitjacketed, be it their sexuality or their appearance, they can briefly free themselves from this power over their bodies and their words.

Spaces also exist where women can discuss, chat, express themselves, and listen to each other; in doing so, they take care of each other. In her essay on the ethics of care, political scientist Joan Tronto argues that care is universal—each of us is vulnerable and interdependent—but also "tragic" (1993, xx). Often, those who are responsible for providing care to others do not receive it themselves. When indebted women share about their suffering, helplessness, and fatigue, they repeatedly stress this fundamental injustice. They spend their time caring for others, without anyone ever caring about them, their health, their fatigue, or simply their well-being. "Who cares about me?" Pushpurani and Raika kept wondering when they spoke to Santosh about their ethical dilemmas. "I am considered as god when I help, but when I ask for help, I am treated like a dog," Raika once said.

Debt, Emancipation, and the Human Economy

Whether with her women friends or her lovers, the indebted woman is constantly seeking to build and strengthen circuits at the margins of kinship and capitalism. There she finds material support but also comfort, attention, care, affection, and love. Of course, this does not challenge the patriarchal or capitalist order, and a radical feminist reading would be tempted to conclude that these are acts of resistance incapable of true transgression. While this is true, there are nevertheless a few lessons to be learned. The first concerns emancipatory aspirations. Not only does the indebted woman strive to meet her obligations, to build a better future for her children, and to get recognition, but she also seeks to liberate her body, to express her feelings and her affects, and to receive care. Widespread references to the emancipatory politics of subaltern women too often neglect the eminently political dimension of the body, of care, and emotions (Jolly, Cornwall, and Hawkins 2013; Harcourt 2009). By emancipation, here we mean a process that enables people to free themselves from oppressive bonds that deprive them of their social relations, their time, their bodies, and their space. Such emancipation does not mean cutting oneself off from all relationships, as a liberal definition would have it, but rather negotiating the bonds of interdependence, in a constant quest amid needs for protection, and aspirations for recognition and emancipation (Fraser 2013, 125).

The second lesson concerns noncapitalist financial circuits. While capitalist finance has been remarkably successful in capturing female clients for credit, this has not been the case for savings, which continue to circulate on the margins of the financial industry. Significant sums of money continue to escape the grip of the market, be it due to ceremonial spending or mutual aid networks. To some extent, the indebted woman in South Arcot ultimately has more control over her savings than Isabelle, Santosh, and Venkata, and probably most of the readers of this book, since the three of us deposit our (meager) assets into a bank account, without knowing what it will be used for. Unbeknownst to us, we are probably helping to fund armaments and war, child labor, extractivism, or some other kind of activity we completely oppose.

While the indebted woman has largely been captured by the financial industry, in both body and mind, she has nonetheless managed to preserve parallel circuits, which can serve as inspiration for thinking about the future of debt and finance. Of course, the idea of having alternative circuits to mainstream finance is nothing new. History is littered with all kinds of experiments aiming to enable the poor to mutually support each other and to get organized to save and borrow. India is no exception to this. As far back as the colonial period, British officials, social reformers, and churches encouraged the poor to form cooperatives as a way to break free from high-caste moneylenders.[16] In preindustrial Europe, some experimental programs explicitly targeted working-class women (Lemire, Campbell, and Pearson 2001). Federici (2013) sees women-led communing initiatives, such as communal kitchens or women's cooperatives for production or the daily management of social reproduction, as concrete forms of powerful political resistance to women's indebtedness. Cavallero and Gago, in a feminist essay on debt, call for "financial disobedience" and advocate for the multiplication of autonomous women's savings and credit groups (2021, 54). In his anthology of debt, Graeber calls for a specific form of "communism," whereby each person would exchange and share based on his or her capacity to do so, and receive according to his or her needs (2011, 94). As in precapitalist societies, people would switch between the role of debtor and creditor. Reciprocity, rather than market or hierarchy, would drive exchanges and relationships.

But where does reciprocity come from? Graeber's plea stems from an anarchist perspective that would wipe out the state as well as the money. There is no evidence, however, that women would have it any better. It seems that patriarchy has a longer history than the state or modern money. A common misconception about solidarity and cooperativism is to underestimate the institutional conditions that allow reciprocity to become solidarity, in the sense of interdependency based on equality rather than on asymmetry (Servet 2007; Hillenkamp and Laville 2013).

After World War I, Mauss (1993a) wrote his famous essay on *The Gift*, which he considered the essence of human societies. Social justice was his primary concern: How does one set up a gift system that is not asymmetrical but a source of solidarity and therefore of equality? Almsgiving and charity were very popular at the time, which Mauss primarily viewed as the humiliation of the poor, assigned to a status of permanent debtors. Mauss called for the inversion of debt and the establishment of social rights, defined not as charity and almsgiving but as rights (1993a, 222). He argued that such rights would transform citizens into creditors of the state, which would henceforth hold something that could be called a "social debt." Once citizens became creditors and not debtors and enjoyed the protection of the social debt of the state, they would be able to engage in reciprocal giving, as a source of solidarity.

Polanyi called for the same during World War II after observing the decay of human reciprocity, destroyed in the grip of the self-regulated market in the runup to fascism, and the totalitarian state that preceded Stalinism (2001, chap. 21). He pleaded for a reembedding of the market and the redistributive state within relationships of reciprocity, arguing that these were the only ones capable of ensuring protection while creating a sense of belonging and dignity. This is what happened in Europe and North America after World War II in what Polanyi called the "great transformation." The devastation of war was so great that it led to a consensus among a wide variety of forces, including conservatives, to protect society from the ravages of the self-regulating market and totalitarian states. This process was driven by multiple citizen initiatives such as mutuals or cooperatives, seeking to protect themselves from the ravages of the market. Social states stem from this combination of forces. For a short period in history, and in a limited part of the world, citizens were recognized as creditors and enjoyed unprecedented social, economic, and political rights. But the focus here was mostly on men.

Today, the hold of the market, private capital, and authoritarianism are back. Exploding inequalities are threatening the very survival of the planet. The COVID-19 pandemic is a striking example. There are, however, many citizen initiatives attempting to reembed the market, which some researchers have called the "human economy" (Hart, Laville, and Cattani 2010, 7–11).[17] These initiatives all seek to bring together Polanyi's various principles—redistribution, market, and reciprocity—with the primary objective of encouraging solidarity over individual (or group) profit- and rent-seeking be-havior, now and for the future generations (Laville 2016). In keeping with this line of thought, one can conceive of the possibility of "human" debts, inspired by the logic of care and recognition described here, benefiting from the advan-tages of both the market (greater resources) and public redistribution (greater solidarity). The key challenge is to find the right balance between market, rec-iprocity, and redistribution, to avert the market's constant tendency to cap-ture or collateralize reciprocity and redistribution for its own benefits. Fraser, revisiting Polanyi's great transformation from a feminist perspective, warns of the risks of fetishizing the market, reciprocity, and redistribution. "Each of [these] three constituent poles is inherently ambivalent . . . each term has both a telos of its own and a potential for ambivalence which unfolds through its interaction with the other two terms" (2013, 129). As we have seen throughout this book, no particular type of debt serves to dominate, protect, or deliver recognition or emancipation. There is no "good" or "bad" debt.[18] The way a particular debt relationship is articulated with other forms of interdepen-dence is what can tell us about its exploitative or emancipatory dimensions.

As a final note, one may wonder why a new "great transformation" has not emerged. As Fraser (2017) has argued, the explanation mostly lies in the hold of financial capital, which weighs on both populations and states that are now disciplined by finance. A new great transformation would require breaking the hold of the creditors. For this to be feminist, it would also require a com-plete inversion of the ontology of debt, turning women, particularly the most disadvantaged ones, into true creditors, not only to the state but also to their kinship group and to society as a whole.

8

What Does the Future Hold?

THE INDEBTED WOMAN IS a crucial cog in contemporary financialized capitalism. Feminist research has regularly highlighted the key, yet invisibilized, role of women in supporting the emergence and prosperity of capitalism, including as the producers of workers, in their domestic and unpaid care work, as disciplined and cheap paid workers, as primary consumers of goods and services, and as meticulous family budget managers.

This book has shed light on another facet of capitalism: women's crucial role as household debt managers. Debt work emerges as a new form of unpaid yet eminently productive labor. Women's debt work is not only a matter of producing workers but of producing solvent families capable of paying their debts and borrowing again since debt now conditions the social reproduction of workers. Managing debt constitutes a domestic task, alongside childcare, cooking, and cleaning the house.

Feminists have gone to great lengths to prove that producing and reproducing people amounts to real work. This work encompasses all the activities, behaviors, relationships, responsibilities, and obligations deployed to maintain life and dignity, both on a daily basis and intergenerationally. These include giving birth, breastfeeding, childcare and care for everyone in the home, providing sexual pleasure, preparing meals, cleaning, changing clothes and linen, collecting water and wood, welcoming guests, organizing ceremonies, and reciting prayers for supposed good fortune, or at least protection. With the growing dependency on the market and the state, the production of people also necessitates work such as household budgeting, food shopping, and filling out paperwork for social benefits.

In South India's unstable, increasingly male-dominated and debt-based market economy, producing people requires constant borrowing, repaying, saving, and lending work. For the Dalit families in this book, this is intense, mainly female work. These various financial tasks in turn entail negotiating with a wide range of lenders and acquaintances over amounts, prices, and repayment deadlines. It involves regularly negotiating and rescheduling repayment plans, to make them better suited to income irregularity and unpredictability. It involves juggling five, ten, fifteen, or even more loans at once, and keeping track of these webs of debt by way of incessant mental gymnastics. It requires complex calculations based on the criteria of both price and feelings. It also entails handling derogatory or contemptuous comments and insults while keeping calm. It necessitates paying attention to one's appearance, dress, posture, and attitude, to come across as a strong, determined woman capable of paying off her debts. If material resources are lacking, it means monetizing one's body and entering into a myriad of sex-for-debt exchanges, from smiling and touching to penetration. Yet it also requires that women sustain a reputation as chaste and respectable. These contradictory imperatives are a source of endless ethical turmoil and moral conflict. In the Tamil context, where labor market instability collides with the rise of patriarchal conservatism, the indebted woman must observe an unassailable discipline that is at once financial, corporal, and sexual.

The indebted woman must equally display an impeccable repayment ethic, to prove her worth as a wife and mother. She works hard to build and maintain her creditworthiness and respectability, which requires cognitive, relational, emotional, and sexual skills among others. Husbands and sons help out, but repayment has become a woman's responsibility, condemning her to an endless race to repay by taking on debt elsewhere. Beyond financial pressure, the indebted woman is caught in feelings of guilt that no repayment can extinguish. This incites her to constantly take on new obligations in an endless blending of financial and moral obligations. This specifically female debt is thus unpayable.

As feminist research has shown, womanhood manifests itself less in terms of biological sex than as an ontological condition—namely, that of the obliger personality. Merely being a woman entails the obligation to dedicate one's sexuality to the reproduction of one's lineage, to take care of children, elders, and others in the household, to uphold the reputation and honor of the family, the lineage, and indeed the nation. India has had a long history of projecting womanhood as maternal devotion, sexual availability, and social inferiority, albeit with considerable variation across social groups and periods of history. In South Arcot, the recent constitution of Dalit women as dependent, useless, unproductive, and sexually passive has reinforced such a subjectivity of debt and guilt. As a growing model, it is symptomatic of the male breadwinner family model of early capitalism in Europe and North America. It is fueled both by reactionary nationalist policies and by Dalit men's pursuit of respect and honor.

Financial debt is both shaped by and constitutive of feminine feelings of obligation. The feminine repayment ethic, which credit organizations have understood so well, draws on the ontological condition of womanhood as an obligated personality. The very fact of being in debt and unable to make ends meet, facing constant repayment difficulties, and the transgressive sex that the indebted woman has to deploy, reinforce feelings of obligation and guilt.

The indebted woman is also ambivalent, torn between conflicting constraints and aspirations. Debt is above all a credit, a source of hope, a plan for the future and potentially for social ascendancy, especially in contexts where employment offers little opportunity for mobility. The indebted woman does not simply use debt because she has mouths to feed, or give in to easy credit offers because she wants more for herself. In many cases, she tirelessly seeks to improve her children's chances in life and to further their social mobility, or at least their social integration. She is designated to a passive form of sexuality that confines her to chastity and conjugal sexuality. Yet it can happen that she falls in love with her favorite lender, who becomes her lover. Framing this love and sexual relationship as a monetary debt is the only way for her to overcome the internal ethical conflicts she faces. As James argues, it is crucial to explore the "complicity" of the indebted in the processes of financialization of everyday life and intimacy if we are to truly consider the future of debt (2021, 38). Following Bear and her colleagues, we have attempted to "understand the complicit and intimate ways in which inequality is propagated, recognizing that without tracing these realities, *we can neither comprehend nor challenge them*" (Bear et al., 2015, our emphasis).

A Global Analysis of the Gender of Debt

Far beyond our South Arcot Tamil case, women from the working class and other disadvantaged groups have consistently specialized in expensive, degrading, and emasculating debts refused by men under the rise of capitalist societies. Feminist history, alongside many contemporary analyses, has highlighted the existence of a sexual division of debt, which serves both as a marker and as a revealer of gender hierarchies. Going into debt to make ends meet and to ensure the social reproduction of the family is a female responsibility. In contemporary India, as it was in Victorian England, men leave this task to women since it threatens their supposed breadwinner role. There is, however, a central difference between the contemporary indebted woman and the indebted woman under the Industrial Revolution. At that time, policy makers, reformists, and charities focused on financial education and saving, which they considered a liberal virtue par excellence (Zelizer 1994, chap. 4). Today's capitalism is driven by financial speculation. Social and development policies are often complicit in the financial industry's push for expansion, and poor women face contradictory imperatives. They are supposed to be frugal, prudent, and good managers—debt remains morally degrading and a sign of profligacy and improvidence—yet they are constantly flooded with credit proposals.

A comprehensive analysis and history of the gender of debt remains to be done. However, we can already point to some similarities and dissimilarities between the indebted women of South Arcot and other indebted women figures.

In today's United States, where the working classes now face considerable financial stress, debt work remains a female task, bringing considerable strain and mental distress. The indebted woman spends her time arbitrating between various forms of penalties such as fees, significantly higher interest rates, collection calls, cancellation and disconnection notices, lawsuits, wage garnishments, falling credit scores, property repossession, eviction, and foreclosure notices (Thorne 2010). She gets called a "loser"; in addition to financial stress and material dispossession, there is the humiliation of contempt and a loss of dignity (Wherry, Seefeldt, and Alvarez 2019, 10). Indebted women of color lose their homes more frequently than others, as they are the prime target for aggressive subprime mortgages, defined by some bankers as "ghetto loans" for "mud people" (Appel, Whitley, and Kline 2019, 20). More often than others, the indebted woman of color must pay off her husband's, son's, or partner's criminal legal debt, to avoid rearrest and to prevent her being cut off from social benefits (2019, 30).

In the suburbs of Barcelona in Spain, the indebted woman is often a Latino migrant from Honduras or the Dominican Republic, two countries ravaged by decades of structural adjustment policies (Palomera 2014a, 2014b; Suarez 2022). Men are also debtors, but the responsibility for debt management rests largely on women's shoulders. Motives for taking out a mortgage are also gendered. The indebted woman fled misery but also sexual oppression and has taken out a subprime loan to become a homeowner, "hoping for economic advancement but also as a way of 'making up' for (her) children's 'abandonment'" (Suarez 2022, 134). After the 2008 global financial crisis, crushed by a debt of several hundred thousand euros, she sublet rooms to illegal migrants that she had to both supervise and help, found multiple odd jobs, and saved every penny on water and heating. Because she left her children behind, "gendered sentiments of guilt constitute the backdrop of (her) engagement with subprime lending and later with mortgage default and foreclosure" (2022, 134). She strives at all costs to avoid eviction and prevent the collapse of a family's lifelong dream. This includes family that stayed behind in the country of origin and for whom the indebted woman is also responsible.

In contemporary France, the credit market remains highly regulated, and redistributive social measures mitigate the need for consumer credit (Lazarus 2022). Working-class debt mainly takes the form of rent and utility bill arrears, although personal bankruptcy has been on the rise since the 2008 financial crisis. In both examples, women are on the frontlines (Perrin-Heredia 2018). The indebted single mother, beyond the guilt of being seen as a bad mother and transgressing family ideals, is humiliated by social workers and bankers who often accuse her of bad management. She feels both ashamed and guilty, and sometimes hides at home to avoid judgment and scorn (Guérin 2003, 113). If she lives with a husband or partner, she risks the humiliation of bailiffs, who often see indebtedness as a reflection of her failed responsibility as a wife and mother (François 2018, 43).

In the industrial wastelands of Buenos Aires, inhabitants are still suffering from the deindustrialization of the military dictatorship era and repeated hyperinflationary crises, which were poorly compensated for by welfare policies partly financed by the Inter-American Development Bank and the World Bank (Wilkis 2018). Consumer credit exploded in the 2010s, partly due to the inclusion of the poor in a formal welfare system that makes them creditworthy (Saiag 2020b). The indebted woman is often a grandmother who juggles debts incurred from relatives, neighbors, shopkeepers, patronage ties, and bank cards (Schijman 2019). With the economic crisis depriving men of stable work and emasculating them, the indebted woman, with a pension and a home, is the main solvent figure in the house. She spends a lot of time claiming for her rights, such as aid from the health center, her church, the housing institute, the canteen, or the post office, affirming her status as a respectable mother or grandmother. She stores, recycles, reinvests, sells, and exchanges goods. She works for free for the condominium collecting garbage, cleaning the stairs, and delivering the mail to pay her rent. She houses fictitious relatives, so that they contribute to the common fund. She puts considerable energy into taking care of her reputation, which entails watching how she presents herself, and, above all, she takes care of others.

The peasants of Fuzhou province in post-Mao rural China aspire to emerge from underdeveloped rurality into transnational modernity, despite facing many risks and sometimes insurmountable financial debt (Chu 2010). Rural Fuzhouneze suffer from "a nested set of inferiority complexes," the result of unevenly distributed central policies and economic investment, coupled with biases that discriminate between urban and rural areas, subregions, and a South portrayed as "uncouth and mongrel" in contrast to a supposedly "more civilized and purified" North (2010, 27). Since the voluntarist post-Mao policies of the 1980s for transforming the provincial capital into an "open costal city" (26), staying means losing one's masculinity. Therefore, the indebted woman is the spouse of a migrant, confined to the status of caregiver while her husband leaves to make his fortune in the United States. Yet paying for the man's airfare requires heavy female borrowing, meticulous repayment practices, and a flawless reputation. Legitimizing the man's success and respectability also requires much female devotion, with regular offerings to gods, asceticism, and modesty.

In the suburbs of Dakar in Senegal, indebted women are active lenders, including to their own husbands, since they have their own budget and cash (Buggenhagen 2012; Guérin 2006, 2008). Due to specific family norms that define the family unit around the mother and children, women have historically been entitled to a "separate purse," allowing them some financial (and sexual) autonomy (Guérin 2008, 62). The country has been in chronic crisis since the 1980s, with successive structural adjustment plans, currency devaluations, and state privatizations in the 1990s and trade liberalization since 1997. This has led women to have increasing financial responsibilities. They partially cover the failure of men, who have been heavily affected by the crisis and failed migration projects, and who sometimes seek salvation in Islam. Thanks to the support of NGOs, which more or less substitute for the failing state, the indebted woman massively invests in women's reciprocal circuits to develop her own protection network. She also discreetly finances her husband's or sons' religious investments. The indebted woman must constantly "guard against shame," a common expression that refers to the duty to both fulfill her obligations and pay her debts (Guérin 2006, 554; Buggenhagen 2012, 145–46).

Of course, there are cases where family intimacy successfully resists capitalist debt, and other forms of exchange ensure the material reproduction of families. In Cuba, which still partly functions as a state-run economy, time and the ability to wait for state subsidies constitute the backbone of women's (and elderly) domestic work (Destremau 2021). Remote village community life and agricultural self-production can protect women and families from the debt trap, maintaining some distance from urban lifestyles and central power, or outright rejecting them. This is also what Isabelle and her French colleagues observed in the 2010s in some remote Berber regions of Morocco (Morvant-Roux et al. 2014). Despite the active expansion of the financial industry, both men and women of the village rejected it and were wary of market debt, which they perceived as dangerous and intrusive and identified, rightly or wrongly, with a central state considered authoritarian and despotic (2014, 308).

These few cases from various regions around the world deserve much further discussion. But they allow us to outline both the similarity and diversity of the indebted woman as a figure. The common thread is to note, as we have throughout this book, that when social reproduction depends on a market and capitalist debt, it is a female prerogative. This in turn feeds and reinforces an ethic of responsibility, which is often exacerbated by moral denigration. Great variations then emerge, which must be taken into account in order to avoid what Saiag describes as an "essentialist" vision of debt (2020a, 2)—in this case, female debt.

The extent of women's obligations and moral denigration varies depending on patterns of kinship and sexuality, which themselves are linked to social, family, health, education, housing, and migration policies. The intensity of

financial predation depends on the extent of the financialization of social reproduction, and on the regulation and supervision of the credit market.

In France, debt remains limited due to strong banking regulation and
active public health and housing policies. The French indebted woman is
certainly better off than her Spanish or American counterpart, even more so
when it comes to women of color. But she is the one who deals with overindebtedness, and she is not spared from shame or guilt. In Spain and the United
States, indebted women are not only victims of unscrupulous bankers. They
also fall victim to active public discourse, measures, and policies to encourage access to private property as a symbol of social mobility and a successful,
happy, and respectable marriage, while prohibiting any personal bankruptcy
proceedings, in the name of morality and individual responsibility.

In Argentina, the indebted grandmother reflects the processes of the
"collateralization of social policies" (Lavinas 2017, 9; 2020) or "financialized
'deduction' system" (James 2017, 68). Cash transfers (in this case, pensions)
from the state that pensioners receive become collateral for lenders, meaning that the latter face fewer risks of nonrepayment. Thus, the state secures
the financial industry of the poor. Since women are the prime recipients of
cash transfer policies, they are also the prime targets of the financial industry. Far beyond Argentina, this has been observed in Mexico, Brazil, and
South Africa. By constructing mothers as "responsible" women, cash transfer
policies develop their creditworthiness, but they also actively construct the
figure of the obligated and indebted woman (Destremau and Georges 2017,
12). In India, as in Senegal, the making of the indebted woman comes about
through NGOs that are supported by public policies and relayed through
private companies.

We read little or nothing in the few ethnographies cited here about how
women use their bodies to build or sustain their creditworthiness. Both academic and activist literature is prolific on shocking cases of "'forced marriage,'
'trafficking' and 'sex trafficking'"—where the sale of women and girls can be
used to pay off debts (O'Connell Davidson 2015, 3; Lainez 2022). Our research
reveals something less dramatic and more ordinary, yet just as shocking in
its way—the everyday practice of substituting sex for money in an attempt to
settle debt. This is a valiant yet fruitless pursuit, as those debts remain ultimately unpayable. The scale of monetary debts and the intensity of patriarchal
control over women's bodies nourish this inextinguishable and unpayable
debt.

Are Tamil Dalit women unique in using their bodies as collateral and engaging in what we have termed sex-for-debt exchange? While to our knowledge, these ordinary, banal forms have not yet been documented elsewhere, that is not to say they do not exist. It took us eight years to identify them and to build the trust for women to talk about them. In a context marked by both men's ever-increasing control over the economy and debt as a condition of survival, it is easily conceivable that many other women from working classes and disadvantaged groups have no choice but to use their bodies to build or maintain their solvency.

Men's role should also be highlighted. Women's debt not only reflects and reinforces patriarchy but other forms of social differentiation such as class, caste, race, and place. The husband, partner, or son of the indebted woman is also bound by norms of masculinity that dictate the status of breadwinner, successful migrant, or accomplished religious man. Yet the indebted woman, by meeting the expenses that men fail to, and financing migration or religious expenses, strives to help preserve men's status. Of course, now as ever, men also have debts and obligations. And men's bodies regularly continue to be used to repay debts or pay for the faults of nonrepayment, through slavery, forced labor, corporal punishment, incarceration, or death. We have seen several examples in this book, in Tamil Nadu and elsewhere. And yet as we have regularly stressed throughout this book, there is something unique about women's debt: it is engraved in women's bodies and sexuality, and it is inseparable from their obligations as wives and mothers called on to sustain life.

Ultimately, capitalism, state policies, kinship, and sexuality intertwine to give rise to a specific demand for credit and particular forms of female creditworthiness and repayment ethics. Two driving factors appear to shape the gender of debt: the justification of a patriarchal social order and the creation of credit markets.

What Does the Future Hold?

If we bring kinship and marriage back to the heart of the analysis, it is difficult to endorse the idea that money and the market are the main vectors of violence and oppression against the indebted woman. The ever-increasing commodification of social reproduction is without a doubt a major contributor to this oppression. But to echo Fraser (2013), it would be wrong to presume that a return to an economy of the gift and reciprocity would be more emancipatory, or that the state could be the solution.

As we have seen, some indebted women successfully create microspaces for negotiation, care, and recognition outside the market and kinship group with their lovers or friends. These are only interstices, mostly devised to better endure their suffering by periodically freeing their bodies and their words from the patriarchal straitjacket and market discipline. These interstices reveal the indebted woman's deep aspirations, as she desperately seeks to exist as a subject of value and desire.

As Graeber has rightly observed, "We don't 'all' have to pay our debts. Only some of us do" (2011, 391). A case in point is the huge contrast between the Indian banking industry's colossal nonperforming assets, mainly issued to rich men, and its excellent microcredit repayment rates, which are mainly issued to poor women. This profound debt repayment inequality stems from the very definition of who is a creditor and who is a debtor, "who owes what to whom, and why?" (Shipton 2007, x). The mere fact that women are considered permanent debtors, simply by virtue of being born as women, justifies this patriarchal debt order.

Such a patriarchal order is far from inevitable. History is interspersed with the struggles of debtors against their creditors, resulting in regular debt write-offs when those debts posed too great a threat to the social order (Finley 1964, 235; Graeber 2011, 82, 390). Only the most recent of these struggles have documented the presence of women (Gerber, Moreda, and Sathyamala 2021). But women's apparent absence from past struggles may simply be historical oversight. Women are heavily involved in antidebt movements. In India, the pandemic and the ensuing lockdown exacerbated the pressure on women microcredit clients, and in 2021 various debt cancellation campaigns were organized in various parts of the country (Guérin, Joseph, and Venkatasubramanian 2021).

"We want to be alive, free and debt-free" (*vivas, libres y desendeudadas nos queremos*), is the slogan of an Argentine feminist movement that started in 2017 (Cavallero and Gago 2021). Women have been at the center of antidebt movements focused on mortgages, such as *El Barzón* in Mexico in the 1990s (Gerber, Moreda, and Sathyamala 2021) and the Platform for People Affected by Mortgages (*Plataforma de Afectados por la Hipoteca*) in Spain since 2010 (Ravelli 2022). They are also at the heart of the anti-microcredit movements that regularly emerged from the late 1990s, including in Pakistan, Andhra

Pradesh and Karnataka (South India), Morocco, and Bolivia (Guérin, Labie, and Servet 2015; N. Joseph 2013). In Sri Lanka in 2020, women microcredit clients adopted the slogan "Life and blood of our country, but we only have debt" (Wedagedara 2020), and debt is like "rubbing salt into a raw wound" (Ratnarajah 2020). In Morocco in 2014, with the support of the Committee for the Abolition of Illegitimate Debt, women organized the "International Microcredit Caravan," bringing together Moroccan women from different countries across Africa, South America, Europe, and Haiti.[1]

It is crucial to note, however, that these feminist movements rightly call for something other than debt cancellation. Cancellation can only temporarily, but not sustainably, resolve a massive imbalance between creditor and debtor. The structural conditions of the imbalance are what have to be addressed. Feminist movements primarily demand social policy measures to help women avoid getting into debt in the first place.

In some campaigns, women have also demanded a creditor status, on the basis that much of the population—men, dependents, and society as a whole—owes them a "care debt" (Carrasco et al. 2014, 49). In Greece in 2011, the "Women on the Move Against Debt and Austerity Measures" initiative aimed to coordinate European feminists to protest the "debt system," calling for audits of national and local public accounts, as well as audits of hospitals, social centers, schools, and other public institutions (Vanden Daelen 2017). In Belgium, the action committee "Here is the bill!" (*V'là la facture!*) was set up in 2015 to contend that the state is indebted not to the banks but to women who work for free due to deficient public services. Here it is indeed a reevaluation of "who owes what to whom" that is being demanded, and a recognition of the immense debt that the entire society owes to women (Federici 2018, 184). A further demand is to link women's monetary debt to state public debt, on the basis that these are "two links of the same chain" (Carton et al. 2022).

Women are indeed not the only ones who depend on the credit market. States do, too, since they are increasingly dependent on the financial markets for their own financing. In a welfare state, citizens are rights holders, which makes them the creditors of a social debt. When states finance themselves on the financial markets, they become dependent on private financial actors as another type of creditor. The austerity policies of contemporary states are the result of an arbitrage in favor of financial debt, to the detriment of social debt (Lemoine and Théret 2017; Bear 2015). When states allocate much of their budget to the repayment of their financial debts, this money is lost to healthcare, education, housing, and social protection policies—in other words, to their social debt.

Finally, these campaigns demand to reverse the stigma, shame, and guilt of indebtedness. As Argentine feminists Cavallero and Gago have argued, "Taking debt out of the closet is a political move against guilt" (2021, 4). In Spain, the first step in campaigning against subprime borrower evictions was to convince the debtors of their innocence and of the banks' guilt (Ravelli 2022).

It is also worth noting the current campaigns for financial citizenship (Wherry, Seefeldt, and Alvarez 2019). Its advocates see debt as neither good nor bad, and this is also what we have observed throughout this book. The idea of financial citizenship argues for financial inclusion that is nonexploitative but that at the same time provides dignity, respect, and belonging. As we have seen repeatedly, this is what the indebted woman is asking for.

All these struggles and campaigns are salutary. The indebted woman is a symptom of both the failures and the contradictions of capitalism and patriarchy. The challenge is daunting and the pushback immense. It is easy to understand why feminist antidebt campaigns are struggling to make themselves heard. It is to be hoped, however, that their repeated campaigns and international coordination efforts will eventually pay off. Researchers have an important responsibility to document and analyze the making of the indebted woman. This project offers a modest contribution. At the end of our own journey with the Tamil indebted woman, there is one thing we would like to emphasize: reevaluating who owes what to whom and reversing the debt stigma means taking into account the central feminist argument that has guided our reasoning—namely, the mutual interdependence of kinship, sexuality, and debt. Female guilt is at the root of the indebted woman. This guilt comes from the very definition of womanhood, defined as "the other," as necessarily inferior, and dispossessed of her individuality and sexuality because she is at the disposal of others and of her kinship group. Antidebt struggles and financial citizenship campaigns won't solve anything as long as they remain geared to kinship systems and patriarchy ideologies that deprive women of access to capital and control over their bodies and lock them into an ontological status of debtor and guilty party. The first step in that journey is to accept the mutual interdependence of sexuality, kinship, and debt. The lesson is one that we need to take to heart if we are to understand what debt is, what gender is, and to think of possibilities and conditions for ending women's unpayable debt.

Notes

Introduction

1. There are many definitions of financialization (Mader, Mertens, and Van der Zwan 2020). The one used here considers that financialization occurs when life-sustaining activities—what feminists call social reproduction—become dependent on financial markets (Federici 2018; Fraser 2017; Adkins and Dever 2016; Allon 2014; A. Roberts 2015). See also Kalb (2020), Mikuš and Rodrik (2021).

2. According to UNCTAD analyses based on International Monetary Fund (IMF) data, the global stock of debt in relation to gross domestic product (GDP) has almost returned to its preglobal financial crisis level (260 percent in 2017, as opposed to 240 percent at the onset of the global financial crisis and 140 percent in 1980). This growth has largely been driven by rising private debt, which has increased more than twelve-fold since 1980. It accounted for two-thirds of debt worldwide by 2017. Southern countries, where private debt has long been kept to relatively low levels, are following the same trend: as a share of global GDP, private debt rose from 79 percent in 2008 to 139 percent in 2017 (UNCTAD 2019b, 74–75). Data aggregated at the global level by the IMF do not distinguish the share of household debt in private debt (which also includes corporate debt). National data are available on IMF's website: https://www.imf.org/external/datamapper/HH_LS@GDD/SWE/AUS/CAN/DEU/USA/GBR.

3. In 2021 and 2022, the media regularly reported worrying data from central banks and the banking sector about the rise of household debt. The World Bank has also expressed concern (2022, 123).

4. See, for example, the Global Financial Stability Reports by the IMF (2019, 2022). See also the reports of UNCTAD (2019a, 2019b).

5. Detailed references will be given all along in this book.

6. See the website of the Committee for the Abolition of Illegitimate Debt, which documents ongoing feminist struggles against debt: https://www.cadtm.org/English.

See also Federici (2018), Cavallero and Gago (2021), and Bruneau and Vanden Daelen (2022). For India, see N. Joseph (2013); Dattasharma, Kamath, and Ramanathan (2016); Guérin, Joseph, and Venkatasubramanian (2021); and Picherit (2015).

7. For an overview and global evidence, see Doss et al. (2019). For a detailed analysis of how an egalitarian law can turn out to be fundamentally unequal in practice and to perpetuate significant capital inequalities between women and men, see the case of France (Bessière and Gollac 2020).

8. See, for example, Cozarenco and Szafarz (2018) and Agier and Szafarz (2013), who show from French and Brazilian data that women, under equal conditions, are discriminated against in terms of loan amounts compared to men. See also Garikipati (2008), who shows from Indian data that women derive little benefit from their borrowing to economic investment because they rarely own their means of production.

9. This will be a key argument of chapter 4. We will also note the analyses led by Isabelle and two economist colleagues on repayment rates among 350 microcredit organizations in seventy countries: all other things equal (i.e., controlling by various variables such as age, education, wealth, income, etc.), women repay better than men (D'Espallier, Guérin, and Mersland 2011).

10. For a literature review of the few available statistics on women's debt, see Reboul, Guérin, and Nordman (2021) and Reboul (2021).

11. See the range of studies on this topic from the pioneering work of Marcel Mauss (1993a) to recent conceptual extensions (Fourcade and Healy 2013; Gregory 1997; Hart and Ortiz 2014; Hours and Ahmed 2015; James 2015; Peebles 2010; Roitman 2003; Saiag 2020a; Shipton 2007; Servet 2012; Théret 2009; Villarreal 2004a).

12. Apart from James, see, for example, Chu (2010), Han (2012), Kar (2018), Saiag (2020b), and Schuster (2015).

13. See, for example, Benería (1979), Brenner and Laslett (1991), Fraser (2017), and Verschuur (2013).

14. See, for example, Dalla Costa and James (1972), Federici (2009), Bhattacharya (2017), and Verschuur (2013).

15. Among the vast literature on caste and Dalit/non-Dalit opposition, see, for example, Jodhka (2012), Jodhka and Manor (2017), and Mosse (2020).

16. Among many references, see, for example, Harriss-White and Heyer (2014), Harriss-White and Gooptu (2001), Jodhka and Manor (2017), and A. Shah et al. (2018).

17. See, for example, Malamoud (1980), Galey (1980), and Hardiman (2000).

18. As suggested by anthropologist David Mosse, "'caste' is not a transhistorical social category, but refers to any of a wide variety of phenomena including the identity of endogamous groups (*jati*) or clusters of them, a division of labour, a social classification, the attribution of inherent or cultural difference, a public representation of social rank, a network, a set of values, social judgements or discriminations (of people, spaces, markets, practices), an administrative or legal category, among others" (2020, 1227).

19. See, for example, Chandrasekhar and Ghosh (2018a) and Chandrasekhar (2022). Since 2016, there has been an Insolvency and Bankruptcy Code (IBC) that provides

remedies not only for companies but also for individuals. However, in 2022, the part concerning individuals has essentially not yet been enacted.

20. Among many works, see, for example, Mohanty (2005) and E. Shah (2012).

21. See Chandrasekhar and Ghosh (2018a).

22. Here we use the ninety-day default ratio. In the 2020–21 period alone, the Indian financial industry's debt forgiveness was roughly equivalent to the outstanding credit of the microcredit industry (about USD 30 billion). For data on debt cancellation during the COVID-19 pandemic, see Chandrasekhar (2022). For microcredit data (bad debt ratios and outstanding debt), see the Da-Dhan Network's quarterly reports on the microfinance sector: https://www.sa-dhan.net/quarterly-mf-report/. See also N. Joseph et al. (2022). Banking data on nonperforming assets are accessible on the Reserve Bank of India's website: https://rbi.org.in/Scripts/FsReports.aspx. See also Chandrasekhar and Ghosh (2018a).

23. Here we use Judith Heyer's (2015, 431) expression on the emergence of the dowry for non-Dalits in another region of Tamil Nadu.

24. Anthropologist Karin Kapadia (1996) already observed a similar phenomenon among non-Dalit lower castes in a neighboring region of Tamil Nadu.

25. See, for example, Uberoi (1995).

26. Isabelle had sketched out this argument with several colleagues (Guérin, Saussey, and Selim 2015).

27. We borrow the term "essence" from anthropologist Hadrien Saiag, used in the context of debt in general (2020a, 2).

28. For an overview, see, for example, Mazzucato (2018).

29. We have previously discussed Louise Tilly and Joan Scott's (1989) founding work on the co-constitution of the categories of woman, family, and work. Feminist research has consistently shown how these different categories have themselves been part of capitalist modes of accumulation in their diversity, often with the complicity or active support of the state. See Collier and Yanagisako (1987) and Yanagisako (2003), Bear et al. (2015). In a pioneering article on the "sex/gender system," Gayle Rubin introduces sexuality into this dynamic pattern (1975, 159). For India, see Agarwal (1994, chap. 3) and John and Nair (2000).

30. This is our translation.

31. By informal lending, we mean lending that is not regulated by the state and is rarely subject to a contract. We will discuss informal lenders in chapter 3.

32. Regarding the higher price of credit for the poor and other disadvantaged groups, see, for example, Fourcade and Healy (2013), Chena and Roig (2017), and Ducourant (2013).

Chapter 1

1. See, for example, Gudeman and Rivera (2007), Sigaud (2008), and Bourdieu et al. (2011, 40).

2. For India, see, for example, the work of N. Roberts (2016) and Schwecke (2021).

3. Over half the women in two of the Dalit neighborhoods that the team knew very well were involved in sex-for-debt exchanges. As these were only two villages, we cannot generalize further.

4. A fascinating study on non-Dalit women in the 1990s by anthropologist Frédéric Bourdier (2001) clearly found, including quantitatively, that extramarital sexual relations were a wide-scale phenomenon, irrespective of gender, class, or caste.

5. As we will see in chapter 2, the political will to eradicate informal debt is an obsession that dates from colonial times.

6. Financial inclusion is measured through the percentage of adults with a bank account, either at a financial institution or through a mobile money provider, as this is an increasingly common practice in the Global South. Mobile money was just beginning to emerge in rural Tamil Nadu late in 2022 as we were finalizing our manuscript.

7. Data for 2021 indicate that the uptrend has stalled (Demirgüç-Kunt et al., 2022, 16, 176).

8. For simplicity, all dollar conversions are based on the 2018 conversion rate.

9. For a similar argument, see Radhakrishnan (2022, 33).

10. The first survey (RUME) was coordinated by Isabelle Guérin, Marc Roesch, and G. Venkatasubramanian. The second and third surveys (NEEMSIS-1 2016–17 and NEEMSIS-2 2020–21) were coordinated by Christophe Jalil Nordman, G. Venkatasubramanian, and Isabelle Guérin. The third survey took place face to face with respondents between two lockdowns. The sample was stratified according to caste, ecotype systems (irrigated/dry), and proximity to the city. A panel survey was used—that is, the same families were interviewed over time, with each wave adding about 100 families to avoid aging of the sample. Permanent migration was low, and therefore the attrition rate (the number of respondents who cannot be traced) was relatively low (around 4 percent). All details (sampling, questionnaire, manual survey, descriptive statistics of the entire survey) can be found in Nordman et al. (2017, 2019, 2022) and are available on the NEEMSIS website: https://neemsis.hypotheses.org/ (accessed November 10, 2022).

11. This is in contrast to certain contexts where fathers and adult children come and go, and where young children may regularly be handed over to relatives.

12. For a similar argument in the European context, see Lazarus (2021).

13. We have developed this in more detail in Guérin et al. (2022).

14. Among the richest (top quartile) and the highest castes, it was not unusual for the husband to be the only borrower (27 percent and 22 percent, respectively). This was rarer among the poorest people and Dalits (14 percent and 17 percent, respectively). The average women's debt share was 60 percent higher in the poorest (first quartile in terms of assets) than the richest, and one-and-a-half times higher in Dalit households than in upper-caste households. In other words, compared to wealthier and non-Dalit women, poor and Dalit women are much more likely to be indebted, and for larger amounts in proportion to their income. For more details, see Reboul, Guérin, and Nordman (2021).

15. In an ethnography of a Chennai slum, anthropologist Nathaniel Roberts mentions cases of female suicide related to excessive debt (2016, 83).

Chapter 2

1. Note that indebtedness for family and religious ceremonies is nothing new (Gregory 1997, 224; Pouchepadass 1980). In South Arcot, however, it is clear that the amounts of debt compared to income have increased significantly over the past two decades.

2. GDP growth averaged 4.4 percent per year in the 1970s and 1980s. It reached 5.5 percent in the 1990s and early 2000s, and over 7 percent in the decade 2010–20.

3. According to World Bank (2021) indicators and estimates (a poor person is someone who lives on less than 1.90 international dollars per day), the rate of monetary poverty fell from 54.8 percent in 1983 to 21.23 percent in 2011. For impact of the COVID-19 pandemic on poverty and employment, see Center for Sustainable Development (2021).

4. As a reminder, Hindutva is a political ideology and movement seeking to establish the idea of a Hindu nation, race, and civilization. Norms of female purity and devotion are seen as instrumental to constructing a male-nationalist identity.

5. The share of tax revenue of the top 1 percent earners was 6 percent in 1983–84 compared to 22 percent in 2014–15. This trend is not specific to India, but the explosion in inequality was nevertheless much more marked than in China.

6. In 1961, there were 976 girls to 1,000 boys in the under-six age group. The gap then widened to 914 to 1,000 in 2011 (date of the last census). There are wide disparities between states (Marius 2016, 71). Tamil Nadu's ratio, though one of the highest, is also declining (Guilmoto et al. 2018).

7. "Dravidian" refers to a southern Indian linguistic and cultural community of people and languages, of which Telugu, Tamil, Malayalam, and Kannada are the most important. Tamil Nadu's two main Tamil political parties, the Dravida Munnetra Kazhagam (DMK, Dravidian Progressive Federation) and the All India Anna Dravida Munnetra Kazhagam (AIDMK, All India Dravidian Progressive Federation), are grounded in Dravidian identity.

8. South Arcot covers the present districts of Cuddalore, Kallakurichi, and Villupuram.

9. In South Arcot, Dalits are mainly of the Paraiyar caste (or *jati*, which is the most appropriate term for the innumerable subdivisions of the caste system). *Paraiyar* is the origin of the English term "pariah," and in Tamil Nadu it continues to designate anyone who is considered an outcast. For this reason this caste name is considered deeply offensive today. The term "Dalit" ("oppressed") was the outcome of a political project to unite all the castes of ex-untouchables across India. The bureaucratic term "Scheduled Caste" (or SC) is often used as a synonym for Dalit, while excluding Christian and Muslim Dalits. Non-Dalits in our study area usually refer to Dalits as the "colony people" but also sometimes as "Paraiyar," but this is by way of insulting them.

10. We have studied this in more detail in Guérin (2013).

11. Social policies primarily include subsidized food, the beginnings of which date back to World War II. Since 2006, social policies also include a rural employment program offering 100 days of work per year at minimum wage to rural families (NREGA). In both cases, Tamil Nadu has demonstrated relatively fair and effective implementation compared to the country average, with priority given to women. For a broad overview, see Kalaiyarasan and Vijayabaskar (2021). For detailed case studies, see Djurfeldt et al. (2008); Harriss, Jeyaranjan, and Nagaraj (2010, 2012); and Heyer (2012). For South Arcot, we describe these changes in more detail in Guérin, Venkatasubramanian, and Michiels (2014).

12. "Colony" is the local term used to refer to the hamlet where the Dalits live. It always stands at some distance apart from the non-Dalit settlement, which is regarded as the "main village" and is called the *ur*. Non-Dalits regard the term "colony" as a euphemism for *ceri* (or *cheri*), the term previously used for the Dalit hamlet. It is worth noting, however, that Dalits very rarely use the term "colony," which has come to have a derogatory connotation (just as *ceri* does). Both Dalits and non-Dalits use the term *ur* to talk about the village settlement where the non-Dalits live.

13. Castes (or *jatis*) are administratively classified for the purposes of quotas and affirmative action policies. Vanniyars are classified as Most Backward Castes (MBC).

14. These are all classified as Other Castes (OC).

15. For a detailed analysis in other parts of India, see Jeffrey (2010).

16. Note that in India as a whole, in late 2022, agriculture continues to grow in absolute terms. This is not the case here, where an increasing amount of land is being left uncultivated or converted into residential plots.

17. According to World Bank (2021) data, the women's labor force participation rate dropped from 31.7 percent in 1990 to 22 percent in 2019, placing India at the 210th rank worldwide out of 233 countries referenced.

18. For more details, see Guérin et al. (2020). With the pandemic, and according to our 2020–21 survey, conducted after the initial lockdown, women's employment rate recovered slightly due to the key role of subsistence agriculture in which they are specialized.

19. See, for example, the analyses of Agarwal (1994, 481), Basu (2005), Sheel (1999), and Srinivas (1984), who emphasize that marriage payments only make sense in specific historic circumstances and cannot be reduced to functionalist analyses. Beyond the case of India, see Comaroff (1980) and Narotzky (1995).

20. Since 2005, after long feminist struggles, the amended civil code has provided for daughters' equal access to joint family property, including agricultural property, for Hindu families. Over fifteen years later, implementation of the law is still a struggle and the proportion of landowning women remains virtually unchanged (14 percent according to the most recent agriculture census in 2015) (India Ministry of Agriculture, para. 4.1.3, 26).

21. In precolonial India in the late nineteenth and early twentieth centuries, a young law graduate could claim the decent dowry sum of 10,000 rupees (Srinivas 1984). In

comparison, in 1920, workers' monthly wages rarely exceeded INR 50 (Burnett-Hurst 1925).

22. In the early 2000s, highly educated professional groups such as doctors and IT engineers could easily obtain dowries of one to two million rupees, or up to five million (around USD 80,000; for the time, it was a huge sum) if the job was abroad, especially in the United States. Sometimes the parents of future brides directly covered part of the school fees (Xiang 2005).

23. Following the pioneering sociological reflections of M. N. Srinivas (1984), precise ethnographies in various parts of South India have confirmed this analysis, while highlighting local disparities. See, for example, Heyer (1992), Kapadia (1996), and Srinivasan (2005).

24. See, for example, Heyer (1992) and Harriss-White (2003, chap. 5).

25. One lakh is a unit of the Indian numbering system equal to one hundred thousand.

26. Sovereigns are the weight units of gold; one sovereign weighs about 8 grams.

27. In 2020, the subsidy for Dalits is 4.5 lakhs, from which one has to deduct at least INR 30,000 in bribes.

28. According to our data, 36 percent of Dalit households benefited, as opposed to 23 percent for Vanniyar households and 17.5 percent for upper-caste households.

29. Even with the financial diaries method over nine months, the total cost of Yoganathan's and his two wives' housing debt was difficult to calculate since they juggled, and continue to juggle, several dozen debts over many years. Estimating the interest cost of the overall debt at a point in time (April 2018) is telling, however.

30. Black gram is a local and ancient variety of bean that today has become rather devalued.

31. As we have shown elsewhere, the NREGA did slightly compensate for the fall in employment among Dalit women and serves as a safety net (Guérin et al. 2020). Annual earnings represent only a meager share of family income (around 5 percent on average), but a higher share of women's income (20 percent on average) (Guérin, Venkatasubramanian, and Michiels 2014).

32. All these routine obligations also imply expenses that are mostly borne by women, while village festivals are part of the family budget. With regard to festivals, it should be noted that often only men are allowed to perform in public during processions, while women take care of the food, the reception of the guests, and the singing.

33. Several recent ethnographies in contexts as diverse as Paraguay, Greece, Spain, Azerbaijan, and South Africa have shown how the growing grip of market debt and financialization are both shaped by and constitutive of shifting household boundaries, and gender and intergenerational responsibilities (James 2015; Schuster 2015; Hann and Kalb 2021; Mikuš and Rodrik 2021). When it comes to production, investment, consumption, residential choices, accessing, and using or repaying debt, households are either disintegrating or joining forces. A long-term ethnography such as the one proposed here shows that it is not only the boundaries of the distinct household unit

that are shifting but the set of rights and obligations of its members, linked by ties of consanguinity and marriage—that is, kinship.

Chapter 3

1. For Indian data, see Sa-Dhan (2020, xviii). For worldwide data, see Cull and Morduch (2017).

2. For a review of microcredit and gender, see Garikipati, Johnson, et al. (2017).

3. See, for example, Rankin (2002), A. Roberts (2015), Karim (2011), Roy (2010), Bateman (2010), and Mader (2015).

4. For its promoters, financial inclusion aims at "ensuring access to financial services and timely and adequate credit where needed by vulnerable groups such as weaker sections and low income groups at an affordable cost" (Rangarajan 2008, 1).

5. Many historical sources describe the extent of the indebtedness of the lower classes and castes in India, but they are silent on the role of women. See, for example, Gooptu (2001), Chandavarkar (2002), and Hardiman (2000).

6. For a full description of borrowing options, see chapter 2.

7. By 2019, for-profit microcredit organizations accounted for 87 percent of clients and 84 percent of the outstanding microcredit portfolio in India (Sa-Dhan 2019, xv).

8. We note that sexual domination sometimes led to resistance and revolts. These may have been driven by male Dalits, who felt deeply emasculated by the control exerted over their own wives. See, for example, Sharma (1978, 181). Resistance and revolts may also have been driven by Dalit women themselves, either by opposing sexual abuse or by asking for compensation. See, for example, Racine and Racine (1995, 68–69) and Breman (2007, 112–13).

9. According to our quantitative survey, Vanniyars and upper-caste people borrowed almost nothing from Dalits in 2016–17 (under 4 percent by volume for Vanniyars, less than 2 percent for upper-caste people; the data in number of loans are similar). It is of course likely that non-Dalit respondents underestimated the money owed to Dalits, but the triangulation of questions limits this risk.

10. See, for example, Harriss-White and Colatei (2004).

11. The loan volume data are slightly lower, but the trend is also upward. For more details, see (Guérin et al. 2022).

12. Note that some of these men do not hesitate to circumvent the norm by making advances and inviting her to their home when the house is empty. We return to this in chapter 5.

13. We extend in this section an argument outlined in a joint publication with Supriya Garikipati, Isabelle Agier, and Ariane Szafarz (Garikipati, Agier, et al. 2017).

14. Very similar observations have been made in other parts of India (Karunakaran 2017; Radhakrishnan 2022, chap. 4). Echoing Pushpurani's words, anthropologist Smitha Radhakrishnan uses the term "social work" to capture the multiple tasks required to run microcredit groups (2022, 100).

15. Similar findings have been made in Morocco (Morvant-Roux and Roesch 2015, 120). In Paraguay, enrolling and maintaining the loyalty of clients, and coping

with competition, is akin to true entrepreneurship, and it is primarily carried out by women who are just as vulnerable as their female clients (Schuster 2015, 57). In Mexico, loan officers are trained in psychology to better identify the feelings of their (mostly female) clients and maintain their loyalty (Hummel 2013).

16. This is explained in more detail in Guérin et al. (2021) and N. Joseph et al. (2022).

17. Note that women, and non-Dalit women in particular, have long been involved in the management of gold, but their responsibilities in pledging and repayment have increased significantly over the past two decades. We have detailed elsewhere the transformation of the possession, use, and meaning of gold, including its ritual and auspicious dimensions (Guérin, Venkatasubramanian, and Reboul 2023).

18. For the United States, see Appel, Whitley, and Kline (2019) and Wherry, Seefeldt, and Alvarez (2019). For Spain, see Palomera (2014a), Ravelli (2022), and Suarez (2022).

Chapter 4

1. The analyses of the financial diaries on which this chapter is based were conducted jointly with Elena Reboul as part of her doctoral thesis (Reboul et al. 2019).

2. As a reminder, they are a lower-class non-Dalit family and are overindebted as a result of massive expenditures on education, housing, health, and Yoganathan's obligations as a maternal uncle. They have three sons, the elder two of whom work at odd jobs, earning wages far below what they had hoped given their level of education. The eldest son, Kumaresan, had a love marriage without a dowry, thus compromising the expected return on his education.

3. As the previous chapter noted, Santosh's attempt to trace all of Pushpurani's financial flows with the financial diaries method failed, so the data we have are approximate. Santosh, however, was able to reconstruct the complex process of financing the renovation of her home, as discussed later in this chapter.

4. As a reminder, they are a lower-class Dalit family with three sons. They are also heavily in debt, but not as much as Devaki's household compared to their income, this mainly to pay for their sons' education.

5. On visualization of the complex networks of indebtedness in which women are embedded, see also Sibel Kusimba's original method of self-portraits (2021, chap. 6) and José Ossandón's (2017) use of balls of wool illustrating the entanglement of relationships. Concerning the juggling of debts in a neighboring Tamil region, see Carswell, De Neve, and Ponnarasu (2021).

6. Isabelle, with her colleagues Solène Morvant-Roux and Magdalena Villarreal, had conceptualized this notion of juggling in a collective volume dedicated to this question. We wrote:

> Juggling literally involves throwing, catching, and keeping several things in the air at once, demanding speed and dexterity, but also risk-taking. These three facets are excellent in evoking the nature of financial practices: people

combine multiple financial tools in the context of ongoing borrowing, repayment and reborrowing practices (one borrows from one place to repay elsewhere). . . . There is no doubt that juggling debt is a form of financial calculation that attempts to substitute cheap debts for expensive ones. Juggling with debt is also a matter of temporalities, as lenders impose different time scales. But social motivations also count. Juggling practices often reflect deliberate choices, strategies or tactics aimed at multiplying and diversifying social relationships, and strengthening or weakening the burden of dependency ties. (2013, 11–12)

See also Ossandón et al. (2022).

7. See, for example, Kar (2018), Schuster (2015), and Hayes (2017).

8. We have discussed this in detail elsewhere (Guérin and Venkatasubramanian 2022).

9. See the pioneer work of sociologist Ann Oakley (2018).

10. Similar observations have been made in Kenya (Kusimba 2018).

11. For a critical analysis of financial literacy, see Bylander (2021) and Lazarus (2020).

12. See also Wherry (2016).

Chapter 5

1. Among the extensive literature on the subject, see Laslett and Brenner (1989), Mies (1998), and Bhattacharya (2017).

2. For a broad overview, see Lainez (2022) and O'Connell Davidson (2015).

3. For a review, see Reboul (2021, 45).

4. See, for example, Cole (2004), and Broqua, Deschamps, and Kraus (2014).

5. This echoes many ethnographies on transactional sex which show that women, even in unequal playing fields, are able to tactically use their sexual resources to seduce and extract money, such as through learning specific sexual techniques, being able to feign love, or humiliate and steal from men. See, for example, Brennan (2004), Absi (2014), and Groes-Green (2013).

6. See, for example, Hamermesh and Biddle (1994) and Mears (2014).

7. Today, we know that microcredit can help existing entrepreneurs but very rarely transform poor people into entrepreneurs. See Cull and Morduch (2017). In rural Tamil Nadu, the impact of microcredit on entrepreneurship has been even more limited, since entrepreneurship is often akin to disguised wage employment. See Guérin, D'Espallier, and Venkatasubramanian (2015). See also Garikipati (2008) and Karunakaran (2017).

8. This argument was outlined in Guérin and Kumar (2017b).

9. This is our translation.

10. See, for example, Karim (2011) in Bangladesh and Rankin (2002) in Nepal.

11. As we have seen earlier, high-caste moneylenders refused, at least publicly, to let Pushpurani into their homes, making her negotiate at their doorstep. The lender we

are discussing here is from a non-Dalit low caste, so the prohibitions of untouchability are less rigorous.

Chapter 6

1. Anthropology has long suffered from the same bias (Jankowiak and Fischer 1992). In the words of Abu-Lughod, the fact that sentiments are "veiled" does not mean they are absent (2016).

2. Several fascinating ethnographies highlight this (Bernstein 2007; Brennan 2004; Constable 2010). For the Indian case, see also Puri (1999) and Srivastava (2007).

Chapter 7

1. Fine-grained ethnographies in Chennai, West Bengal, and Paraguay reveal similar processes, pointing out the "social productivity of debt" (Kar 2018, 88), describing debt as "a key social practice for *creating* solidarity among women" (N. Roberts 2016, 96), and which "reshapes how women create and sustain family ties" (Schuster 2015, 87). Various ethnographies conducted in Europe also show how debt and overindebtedness reconfigure kinship relationships, without necessarily destroying them and sometimes strengthening them (Hann and Kalb 2020; Mikuš and Rodrik 2021).

2. See, for example, Carole Stack's (1975) groundbreaking ethnography of a Black neighborhood in the United States or Parker Shipton's (2007) more recent one among the Luo in Kenya. For India, see, for example, Nathaniel Roberts's (2016) ethnography in a Chennai slum. In the Amerindian communities of Chiapas in Mexico, political economist Solène Morvant-Roux observes that debt, including in its capitalist forms, obeys a logic of the "collective management" of individual cash surpluses or any "useful" goods (2013, 179).

3. This is developed in more detail in Guérin, Venkatasubramanian, and Kumar (2020).

4. This has been observed in various Global South contexts including South Africa (James 2015, chap. 4), Kenya (Shipton 2010; Kusimba 2021, chap. 5), and Mexico (Morvant-Roux 2009). For a more global and conceptual view, see Peebles (2014).

5. In the last twenty years, there have been eight cyclones. Note that the most tragic, the tsunami of 2004, did not affect the region studied because the villages are not on the coast.

6. On November 8, 2016, India's prime minister, Narendra Modi, announced the impending, almost immediate demonetization of all 500- and 1,000-rupee banknotes (USD 8 and USD 16) and the introduction of a new series of 500- and 2,000-rupee banknotes (USD 8 and USD 32). The country's 1.3 billion population had until December 30 (less than two months) to exchange their notes at a bank or post office branch. The poor preparation and multiple technical disruptions led the country into chaos for over three months. By curtailing black money, broadening the fiscal base, and promoting a cashless economy, demonetization was supposed to encourage the formalization of the economy, which in turn was expected to benefit the poor. There is

ample evidence today of the dramatic impacts it has had on the poor and the complete failure of the fight against corruption (Chandrasekhar and Ghosh 2018b).

7. Roberts describes a very similar process in a Chennai slum (N. Roberts 2016, 96–97).

8. A similar process was observed in the early 2000s in a neighboring region of North Arcot in Tamil Nadu (Polzin 2016).

9. Chapter 2 gives estimates of dowry and marriage costs.

10. For similar observations in other contexts, see, for example, Morvant-Roux (2013).

11. "Achievement is graded and profiled. People move up and down in increments, recognized in small nuances by others, who then make claims, but claims that are adjusted quite precisely to the means" (Guyer 2004, 147).

12. Over almost twenty years of fieldwork, and after meeting hundreds of Dalit women, we encountered just two Dalit women who were large-scale lenders. The first was the wife of a labor broker for sugarcane harvesting. Like the wives of landowners in the past, she only loaned to her husband's workforce and used that debt to ensure the workers' loyalty. Lending is considered the duty of the employer, and thus legitimate. The second lender acted as a financial intermediary for government employees and local politicians, who were mostly non-Dalits, seeking to invest their surplus cash without having to manage direct transactions with Dalits, or suffering the headache of collecting the payments. Even though she charged interest—1 or 2 percent monthly on the 3 or 4 percent charged by her financiers—she framed her business as "help." Both women made a comfortable income out of it. The former lost a lot of money during the 2020 lockdown, as the sugarcane agribusiness was shut down for more than six months. The latter, however, gained a lot.

13. This is the case of Devaki and her cowife: although they are non-Dalit (Vanniyar), and their husband considers indebtedness to Dalits to be the height of infamy, they sometimes borrow from Dalit women. Crushed by debt, they have no choice.

14. Of course, collective effervescence is a well-known enlistment and propaganda technique, which has been widely used to enroll the poor, including women. This has been the case with many political parties, starting with the far right. In India, ultranationalist Hindu parties such as the BJP and the Shiv Sena have always been able to effectively mobilize women by offering them specific spaces for recognition and expression (Sen 2007). Until recently, far-right parties had little presence in Tamil Nadu because of historical resistance against Brahmanism and Hindutva (Pandian 2012). Other forms of propaganda come from the Pentecostal churches, targeting women in particular. Kapadia (2017) has written that female Dalit Pentecostal converts in Chennai, the capital of Tamil Nadu, are motivated more by the rejection of patriarchy than of caste discrimination. While patriarchal conservatism weighs more heavily on the bodies of Dalit women in urban settings, as they are much less free than in their home villages, Pentecostal prayers offer moments of liberation. The women sing, pray, clap, sway, and go into a trance or ecstasy. Far from the corporal vindication to which they

are now expected to conform, they regain verbal and corporal autonomy, even if this is, of course, relative, partial, and temporary.

15. The following are a few examples. One woman talks about how she is so fat that her husband can't find the right hole. The poor guy, she doesn't dare to say anything, he is so thin, she feels like she has a sheet of newspaper on her, she feels nothing. Another says that her husband stinks so much that she forces him to wash himself—"I'm a garbage can or what?" Another says she can't ask for that, and the only thing she can do is threaten him with a ladle when he gets too beastly. Another always gives her husband money to drink alcohol before having sex, which makes him more efficient and it goes by faster. Trying to outdo one another, many say they drink alcohol themselves. They argue about quantities. A little helps them to be more active themselves, and they can handle the husband's ardour better. A larger quantity allows them to bear the pain or disgust. Another one comes back to the question of condoms: It's good when you have sex once, but how do you manage when he comes four times, she asked.

16. See, for example, the proposals of British deputy commissioner Malcolm Darling (1925) in the colonial era, who was known for his commitment to the poor (compared to his colleagues). He wrote down his observations and suggestions, including to encourage savings and credit cooperatives. For concrete cooperative initiatives dating back to colonial times in Tamil Nadu, see, for example, Cederlöf (1997).

17. It should be noted that the concept has been developed first in non-English-speaking regions such as France, Brazil, South America, and Scandinavia. See, for example, Laville (2016), Hillenkamp and Laville (2013), and Andersen, Hulgård, and Laville (2022). The term "solidarity-based economy" is more often used: "économie solidaire" (French), "economia solidária" (Portuguese), economía solidaria (Spanish). The idea of "community economies," developed by J. K. Gibson-Graham (2005) and based on North American and Asian examples, shows many similarities with the idea of a human and solidarity economy.

18. In his ethnography of village debt in Chhattisgarh (central India), Gregory argues that debt is not "good" or "bad" per se, but depends on preexisting power relations between debtors and creditors (1997, 223). He is absolutely right, and this is what explains the impunity of Indian elites from repayment. Our exploration of the gender of debt invites us to go well beyond the power relations between debtors and creditors, and to take into account instead the set of rights and obligations in which debtors are embedded.

Chapter 8

1. See the documentary, "Caravane Internationale MC Ouarzazate 2014," *CADTM* (blog), July 18, 2014. https://www.cadtm.org/Caravane-Internationale-con tre-le-microcredit.

References

Absi, Pascale. 2014. "La Valeur de l'Argent dans les Maisons Closes de Bolivie" [The value of money in the brothels of Bolivia]. In *L'échange Économico-Sexuel*, edited by Christophe Broqua, Catherine Deschamps, and Cynthia Kraus, 61–89. Paris: Éditions EHESS.

Abu-Lughod, Lila. 1990. "The Romance of Resistance: Tracing Transformations of Power through Bedouin Women." *American Ethnologist* 17 (1): 41–55.

———. 2016. *Veiled Sentiments: Honor and Poetry in a Bedouin Society.* Oakland: University of California Press.

Adkins, Lisa, and Maryann Dever. 2016. "The Financialisation of Social Reproduction: Domestic Labour and Promissory Value." In *The Post-Fordist Sexual Contract*, edited by Lisa Adkins and Maryann Dever. London: Palgrave Macmillan.

Agarwal, Bina. 1994. *A Field of One's Own: Gender and Land Rights in South Asia.* Cambridge, MA: Cambridge University Press.

Agier, Isabelle, Isabelle Guérin, and Ariane Szafarz. 2012. "Child Gender and Parental Borrowing: Evidence from India." *Economics Letters* 115 (3): 363–65.

Agier, Isabelle, and Ariane Szafarz. 2013. "Microfinance and Gender: Is There a Glass Ceiling on Loan Size?" *World Development* 42: 165–81.

Allon, Fiona. 2014. "The Feminisation of Finance: Gender, Labour and the Limits of Inclusion." *Australian Feminist Studies* 29 (79): 12–30.

Anandhi, S., J. Jeyaranjan, and R. Krishnan. 2002. "Work, Caste and Competing Masculinities." *Economic and Political Weekly*, 7–8.

Anandhi, S., and Karin Kapadia. 2017. *Dalit Women: Vanguard of an Alternative Politics in India.* New York: Routledge.

Andersen, Linda Lundgaard, Lars Hulgård, and Jean-Louis Laville. 2022. "The Social and Solidarity Economy: Roots and Horizons." In *New Economies for Sustainability: Limits and Potentials for Possible Futures*, edited by Luise Li Langergaard, 71–81. Cham: Springer International.

Appadurai, Arjun. 1989. "Small-Scale Techniques and Large-Scale Objectives." In *Conversations between Economists and Anthropologists: Methodological Issues in Measuring Economic Change in Rural India*, edited by Pranab Bardhan, 250–82. New York: Oxford University Press.

Appel, Hannah, Sa Whitley, and Caitlin Kline. 2019. *The Power of Debt: Identity and Collective Action in the Age of Finance*. Los Angeles: UCLA Publications.

Badue, Ana Flavia, and Florbela Ribeiro. 2018. "Gendered Redistribution and Family Debt: The Ambiguities of a Cash Transfer Program in Brazil." *Economic Anthropology* 5 (2): 261–73.

Basu, Srimati, ed. 2005. *Dowry and Inheritance*. New Delhi: Kali for Women.

Basu, Srimati, and Lucinda Ramberg, eds. 2015. *Conjugality Unbound: Sexual Economics, State Regulation, and the Marital Form in India*. New Delhi: Women Unlimited.

Bateman, Milford. 2010. *Why Doesn't Microfinance Work? The Destructive Rise of Local Neoliberalism*. London: Zed Books.

Bear, Laura. 2015. *Navigating Austerity: Currents of Debt along a South Asian River*. Stanford: Stanford University Press.

Bear, Laura, Karen Ho, Anna Lowenhaupt Tsing, and Sylvia Yanagisako. 2015. "Gens: A Feminist Manifesto for the Study of Capitalism." *Fieldsights*, March 30, 2015. https://culanth.org/fieldsights/gens-a-feminist-manifesto-for-the-study-of-capitalism.

Beauvoir, Simone de. 1990. *Le Deuxième Sexe*. Vol. 2, *L'expérience Vécue* [The second sex. Vol. 2, Lived experience]. Paris: Gallimard.

Benería, Lourdes. 1979. "Reproduction, Production and the Sexual Division of Labour." *Cambridge Journal of Economics* 3 (3): 203–25.

Benería, Lourdes, Günseli Berik, and Maria S. Floro. 2015. *Gender, Development, and Globalization: Economics as If All People Mattered*. London: Routledge.

Bernstein, Elizabeth. 2007. *Temporarily Yours: Intimacy, Authenticity, and the Commerce of Sex*. Chicago: University of Chicago Press.

Bessière, Céline, and Sybille Gollac. 2020. *Le Genre Du Capital: Comment La Famille Reproduit Les Inégalités* [The gender of capital: How families perpetuate wealth inequalities]. Paris: La Découverte.

Bhattacharya, Tithi. 2017. *Social Reproduction Theory: Remapping Class, Recentering Oppression*. London: Pluto Press.

Bouquet, Emmanuelle, Éliane Ralison, Betty Wampfler, Isabelle Guérin, Solène Morvant-Roux, and Magdalena Villarreal. 2013. "Does Juggling Mean Struggling? Insights into the Financial Practices of Rural Households in Madagascar." In *Microfinance, Debt and Over-Indebtedness: Juggling with Money*, edited by Isabelle Guérin, Solène Morvant-Roux, and Magdalena Villarreal, 211–32. London: Routledge.

Bourdier, Frédéric. 2001. *Sexualité et Sociabilité En Inde Du Sud: Familles En Péril Au Temps Du Sida* [Sexuality and sociability in Southern-India: Endangerered families in the time of AIDS]. Paris: Karthala.

Bourdieu, Pierre. 1986. "L'illusion biographique" [The biographic illusion]. *Actes de la Recherche en Sciences Sociales* 62 (1): 69–72.

———. 2000. *Esquisse d'une Théorie de La Pratique: Précédé de Trois Études d'ethnologie Kabyle* [Outline of a theory of practice: Preceded by three studies in Kabyle ethnology]. Paris: Seuil.

———. 2013. "Comprendre" [Understanding]. In *La Misère Du Monde*, edited by Pierre Bourdieu, 903–25. Paris: Seuil.

Bourdieu, Pierre, Alain Darbel, Jean-Paul Rivet, and Claude Seibel. 2011. *Travail et Travailleurs En Algérie* [Labor and laborers in Algeria]. Paris: Raisons d'Agir.

Breman, Jan. 2007. *Labour Bondage in West India: From Past to Present*. New Delhi: Oxford University Press.

Brennan, Denise. 2004. *What's Love Got to Do with It? Transnational Desires and Sex Tourism in the Dominican Republic*. Durham: Duke University Press.

Brenner, Johanna, and Barbara Laslett. 1991. "Gender, Social Reproduction, and Women's Self-Organization: Considering the US Welfare State." *Gender & Society* 5 (3): 311–33.

Broqua, Christophe, Catherine Deschamps, and Cynthia Kraus, eds. 2014. *L'échange economico-sexuel* [The sexual-economic exchange]. Paris: Éditions EHESS.

Bruneau, Camille, and Christine Vanden Daelen. 2022. *Nos Vies Valent plus Que Leurs Crédits: Face Aux Dettes, Des Réponses Féministes* [Our lives are worth more than their credits: Feminist responses to debt]. Paris: Le passager clandestin.

Bryan, Dick, and Mike Rafferty. 2018. *Risking Together: How Finance Is Dominating Everyday Life in Australia*. Sydney: Sydney University Press.

Budig, Michelle, and Nancy Folbre. 2004. "Activity, Proximity or Responsibility? Measuring Parental Childcare Time." In *Family Time: The Social Organization of Care*, edited by Nancy Folbre and Michael Bittman, 51–68. New York: Routledge.

Buggenhagen, Beth A. 2012. *Muslim Families in Global Senegal: Money Takes Care of Shame*. Indianapolis: Indiana University Press.

Burawoy, Michael. 1998. "The Extended Case Method." *Sociological Theory* 16 (1): 4–33.

Burnett-Hurst, Alexander Robert. 1925. "Labour and Housing in Bombay. A Study in the Economic Conditions of the Wage Earning Classes in Bombay." London: P. S. King.

Bylander, Maryann. 2014. "Borrowing across Borders: Migration and Microcredit in Rural Cambodia." *Development and Change* 45 (2): 284–307.

———. 2021. "'If You Fall, Stand Up Again': The Moral Nature of Financial Literacy in the Global South." Development and Change 52 (1): 26–53.

Carrasco, Cristina, Carme Díaz Corral, Inés Marco Lafuente, Rosa Ortiz Monera, and Marina Sánchez Cid. 2014. "Expolio y Servidumbre: Apuntes Sobre La Llamada Deuda de Cuidados" [Spoliation and servitude: Note on care debt]. *Revista de Economía Crítica*, no. 18, 48–59.

Carsten, Janet, ed. 2000. *Cultures of Relatedness: New Approaches to the Study of Kinship*. Cambridge: Cambridge University Press.

Carswell, Grace, Geert De Neve, and Subramanian Ponnarasu. 2021. "Good Debts, Bad Debts: Microcredit and Managing Debt in Rural South India." *Journal of Agrarian Change* 21 (1): 122–42.

Carton, Anaïs, Beatriz Ortiz Martínez, Camille Bruneau, and Fatima Zahra El Beghiti. 2022. "Microcrédit et endettement public: Deux maillons d'un même système qui renforce les inégalités de genre" [Microcredit and public debt: Two cogs that reinforce gender inequality]. CADTM (blog), February 20, 2022. https://www.cadtm.org/Microcredit-et-endettement-public-deux-maillons-d-un-meme-systeme-qui-renforce.

Cavallero, Lucí, and Verónica Gago. 2021. *A Feminist Reading of Debt*. London: Pluto Press.

Cederlöf, Gunnel. 1997. *Bonds Lost: Subordination, Conflict and Mobilisation in Rural South India c. 1900–1970*. New Delhi: Manohar.

Center for Sustainable Development. 2021. "State of Working India 2021: One Year of Covid 19." Bengaluru: Azim Premji University.

Chakravartty, Paula, and Denise Ferreira da Silva. 2012. "Accumulation, Dispossession, and Debt: The Racial Logic of Global Capitalism—An Introduction." *American Quarterly* 64 (3): 361–85.

Chancel, Lucas, and Thomas Piketty. 2019. "Indian Income Inequality, 1922–2015: From British Raj to Billionaire Raj?" *Review of Income and Wealth* 65: S33–62.

Chandavarkar, Rajnarayan. 2002. *The Origins of Industrial Capitalism in India: Business Strategies and the Working Classes in Bombay, 1900–1940*. Cambridge, MA: Cambridge University Press.

Chandrasekhar, C. P. 2022. "The Renewed Fear of Bad Debt." *Economic and Political Weekly* 57 (3): 7–8.

Chandrasekhar, C. P., and Jayati Ghosh. 2018a. "The Banking Conundrum. Non-Performing Assets and Neo-Liberal Reform." *Economic and Political Weekly* 53 (13): 129–37.

———. 2018b. "The Financialization of Finance? Demonetization and the Dubious Push to Cashlessness in India." *Development and Change* 49 (2): 420–36.

Chatterjee, Heramba. 1971. *The Law of Debt in Ancient India*. Calcutta: Sanskrit College.

Chena, Pablo Ignacio, and Alexandre Roig. 2017. "L'exploitation financière des secteurs populaires argentins" [Financial exploitation in Argentinian laboring classes]. *Revue de la regulation: Capitalisme, institutions, pouvoirs*, no. 22 (December). https://doi.org/10.4000/regulation.12409.

Chu, Julie Y. 2010. *Cosmologies of Credit: Transnational Mobility and the Politics of Destination in China*. Durham: Duke University Press.

Cole, Jennifer. 2004. "Fresh Contact in Tamatave, Madagascar: Sex, Money, and Intergenerational Transformation." *American Ethnologist* 31 (4): 573–88.

Collier, Jane Fishburne, and Sylvia Junko Yanagisako. 1987. *Gender and Kinship: Essays toward a Unified Analysis*. Stanford: Stanford University Press.

Collins, Daryl, Jonathan Morduch, Stuart Rutherford, and Orlanda Ruthven. 2009. *Portfolios of the Poor: How the World's Poor Live on $2 a Day*. Princeton: Princeton University Press.

Comaroff, John L., ed. 1980. *The Meaning of Marriage Payments*. London: Academic Press.

Constable, Nicole. 2009. "The Commodification of Intimacy: Marriage, Sex, and Reproductive Labor." *Annual Review of Anthropology* 38: 49–64.

———, ed. 2010. *Cross-Border Marriages: Gender and Mobility in Transnational Asia*. Philadelphia: University of Pennsylvania Press.

Cottereau, Alain, and Mokhtar Mohatar Marzok. 2012. *Une Famille Andalouse: Ethnocomptabilité d'une Économie Invisible* [An Andalusian family: The ethoaccounting of an invisible economy]. Paris: Bouchene.

Cozarenco, Anastasia, and Ariane Szafarz. 2018. "Gender Biases in Bank Lending: Lessons from Microcredit in France." *Journal of Business Ethics* 147 (3): 631–50.

Crowston, Clare Haru. 2013. *Credit, Fashion, Sex: Economies of Regard in Old Regime France*. Durham: Duke University Press.

Cull, Robert, and Jonathan Morduch. 2017. *Microfinance and Economic Development*. Policy Research Working Paper 8252. Washington, DC: World Bank.

Dalla Costa, Mariarosa, and Selma James. 1972. *Women and the Subversion of the Community*. Bristol: Falling Wall Press.

Darling, Malcolm Lyall. 1925. *Punjab Peasant in Prosperity and Debt*. London: Humphrey Milford.

Das, Veena. 1995a. *Critical Events: An Anthropological Perspective on Contemporary India*. New Delhi: Oxford University Press.

———. 1995b. "Voice as Birth of Culture." *Ethnos* 60 (3–4): 159–79.

Dattasharma, Abhi, Rajalaxmi Kamath, and Smita Ramanathan. 2016. "The Burden of Microfinance Debt: Lessons from the Ramanagaram Financial Diaries." *Development and Change* 47 (1): 130–56.

Deleuze, Gilles, and Félix Guattari. 1983. *Anti-Oedipus: Capitalism and Schizophrenia*. Translated by Robert Hurley, Mark Seem, and Helen R. Lane. Minneapolis: Minneapolis University Press.

Demirgüç-Kunt, Asli, Leora Klapper, Dorothe Singer, and Saniya Ansar. 2022. *The Global Findex Database 2021. Financial Inclusion, Digital Payments, and Resilience in the Age of COVID-19*. Washington, DC: World Bank

Demirgüç-Kunt, Asli, Leora Klapper, Dorothe Singer, Saniya Ansar, and Jake Hess. 2018. *The Global Findex Database 2017: Measuring Financial Inclusion and the Fintech Revolution*. Washington, DC: World Bank.

Dermineur, Elise, ed. 2018. *Women and Credit in Pre-Industrial Europe*. Turnhout: Brepols.

D'Espallier, Bert, Isabelle Guérin, and Roy Mersland. 2011. "Women and Repayment in Microfinance: A Global Analysis." *World Development* 39 (5): 758–72.

Destremau, Blandine. 2021. *Vieillir Sous La Révolution Cubaine: Une Ethnographie* [Aging in the Cuban revolution: An ethnography]. Paris: Éditions de l'IHEAL.

Destremau, Blandine, and Isabel Georges, eds. 2017. *Le Care, Face Morale Du Capitalisme: Assistance et Police Des Familles En Amérique Latine* [Care, the moral face of capitalism: Assistance and policing of families in Latin America]. Bruxelles: Peter Lang.

Djurfeldt, Göran, Venkatesh Athreya, N. Jayakumar, Staffan Lindberg, A. Rajagopal, and R. Vidyasagar. 2008. "Agrarian Change and Social Mobility in Tamil Nadu." *Economic and Political Weekly* 43 (45): 50–61.

Doss, Cheryl R., Carmen Diana Deere, Abena D. Oduro, Hema Swaminathan, Zachary Catanzarite, and J. Y. Suchitra. 2019. "Gendered Paths to Asset Accumulation? Markets, Savings, and Credit in Developing Countries." *Feminist Economics* 25 (2): 36–66.

Dreze, Jean. 1990. "Poverty in India and the IRDP Delusion." *Economic and Political Weekly* 25 (39): A95–104.

Ducourant, Hélène. 2013. "Why Do the Poor Pay More for Their Credit? A French Case Study." In *Microfinance, Debt and Over-Indebtedness: Juggling with Money*, edited by Isabelle Guérin, Solène Morvant-Roux, and Magdalena Villarreal, 86–102. London: Routledge.

Durkheim, Émile. 1912. *Les Formes Élémentaires de La Vie Religieuse: Le Système Totémique En Australie* [The elementary forms of religious life: Totemism in Australia]. Paris: Alcan.

Elson, Diane. 1993. "Gender-Aware Analysis and Development Economics." *Journal of International Development* 5 (2): 237–47.

Elyachar, Julia. 2006. *Markets of Dispossession: NGOs, Economic Development, and the State in Cairo*. Durham: Duke University Press.

Faier, Lieba. 2007. "Filipina Migrants in Rural Japan and Their Professions of Love." *American Ethnologist* 34 (1): 148–62.

Federici, Silvia. 2009. *Caliban and the Witch*. 3rd ed. Brooklyn, NY: Autonomedia.

———. 2013. "Commoning against Debt." *Tidal: Occupy Theory, Occupy Strategy*, no. 4, 20.

———. 2018. "Women, Money and Debt: Notes for a Feminist Reappropriation Movement." *Australian Feminist Studies* 33 (96): 178–86.

Feltran, Gabriel. 2020. *Entangled City: Crime as Urban Fabric in São Paulo*. Manchester: Manchester University Press.

Finley, Moses I. 1964. "Between Slavery and Freedom." *Comparative Studies in Society and History* 6 (3): 233–49.

Folbre, Nancy. 1991. "The Unproductive Housewife: Her Evolution in Nineteenth-Century Economic Thought." *Signs* 16 (3): 463–84.

———. 2006. "Measuring Care: Gender, Empowerment, and the Care Economy." *Journal of Human Development* 7 (2): 183–99.

Fontaine, Laurence. 2008. *L'économie Morale: Pauvreté, Crédit et Confiance Dans l'Europe Pré-industrielle* [The moral economy: Poverty, credit, and trust in early modern Europe]. Paris: Editions Gallimard.

Foucault, Michel. 2004. *Philosophie. Anthologie* [Philosophie. Anthology]. Paris: Gallimard.

Fourcade, Marion, and Kieran Healy. 2007. "Moral Views of Market Society." *Annual Review of Sociolology* 33: 285–311.

———. 2013. "Classification Situations: Life-Chances in the Neoliberal Era." *Accounting, Organizations and Society* 38 (8): 559–72.

François, Camille. 2018. "Faire Payer Les Femmes: Le Sexe Du Recouvrement Des Dettes de Loyer" [Making women pay: The gender of housing rental debt recovery]. In *Le Monde Privé Des Femmes: Genre et Habitat Dans La Société Française*, edited by Anne Lambert, Pascale Dietrich-Ragon, and Catherine Bonvalet, 37–56. Paris: INED Editions.

Fraser, Nancy. 2013. "A Triple Movement?" *New Left Review*, no. 81, 119–32.

———. 2017. "Crisis of Care? On the Social-Reproductive Contradictions of Contemporary Capitalism." In *Social Reproduction Theory*, edited by Tithi Bhattacharya, 21–36. London: Pluto Press.

Fuller, Christopher John. 2004. *The Camphor Flame: Popular Hinduism and Society in India*. Princeton: Princeton University Press.

Galey, Jean-Claude. 1980. "Le Créancier, Le Roi, La Mort: Essai Sur Les Relations de Dépendances Au Tehri-Garhwal (Himalaya Indien)" [The lender, the king, and death: Essay on relations of dependancy in Tehri-Garwhal (Indian Himalaya)]. *Purusartha Sciences Sociales En Asie Du Sud Paris*, no. 4, 93–163.

Garikipati, Supriya. 2008. "The Impact of Lending to Women on Household Vulnerability and Women's Empowerment: Evidence from India." *World Development* 36 (12): 2620–42.

Garikipati, Supriya, Isabelle Agier, Isabelle Guérin, and Ariane Szafarz. 2017. "The Cost of Empowerment: Multiple Sources of Women's Debt in Rural India." *Journal of Development Studies* 53 (5): 700–722.

Garikipati, Supriya, Susan Johnson, Isabelle Guérin, and Ariane Szafarz. 2017. "Microfinance and Gender: Issues, Challenges and The Road Ahead." *Journal of Development Studies* 53 (5): 641–48.

Gerber, Julien-François, Tsegaye Moreda, and C. Sathyamala. 2021. "The Awkward Struggle: A Global Overview of Social Conflicts against Private Debts." *Journal of Rural Studies* 86: 651–62.

Gibson-Graham, J. K. 2005. "Surplus Possibilities: Postdevelopment and Community Economies." *Singapore Journal of Tropical Geography* 26 (1): 4–26.

Gonzalez, Felipe. 2015. "Where Are the Consumers? 'Real Households' and the Financialization of Consumption." *Cultural Studies* 29 (5–6): 781–806.

Goode, Jackie. 2012. "Brothers Are Doing It for Themselves? Men's Experiences of Getting Into and Getting Out of Debt." *Journal of Socio-Economics* 41 (3): 327–35.

Gooptu, Nandini. 2001. *The Politics of the Urban Poor in Early Twentieth-Century India*. Cambridge: Cambridge University Press.

Gorringe, Hugo. 2017. "Liberation Panthers and Pantheresses? Gender and Dalit Party Politics in South India." In *Dalit Women Vanguard of an Alternative Politics in India*, edited by S. Anandhi and Karin Kapadia, 131–57. New York: Routledge.

Graeber, David. 2011. *Debt: The First 5,000 Years*. Brooklyn, NY: Melville House.

Greene, Joshua C., and Solène Morvant-Roux. 2020. "Social Reproduction, Ecological Dispossession and Dependency: Life Beside the Río Santiago in Mexico." *Development and Change* 51 (6): 1481–1510.

Gregory, Chris A. 1997. *Savage Money: The Anthropology and Politics of Commodity Exchange*. Amsterdam: Arwood Academic.

———. 2012. "On Money Debt and Morality: Some Reflections on the Contribution of Economic Anthropology." *Social Anthropology* 20 (4): 380–96.

Groes-Green, Christian. 2013. "'To Put Men in a Bottle': Eroticism, Kinship, Female Power, and Transactional Sex in Maputo, Mozambique." *American Ethnologist* 40 (1): 102–17.

Gudeman, Stephen, and Alberto Rivera. 2007. *Conversations in Colombia: The Domestic Economy in Life and Text*. Cambridge: Cambridge University Press.

Guérin, Isabelle. 2003. *Femmes et Économie Solidaire* [Women and solidarity economy]. Paris: La Découverte.

———. 2006. "Women and Money: Lessons from Senegal." *Development and Change* 37 (3): 549–70.

———. 2008. "L'argent des Femmes Pauvres: Entre Survie Quotidienne, Obligations Familiales et Normes Sociales." [Poor women's money: Between daily survival, family obligations, and social norms]. *Revue Française de Socioéconomie*, no. 2, 59–78.

———. 2013. "Bonded Labour, Agrarian Changes and Capitalism: Emerging Patterns in South India." *Journal of Agrarian Change* 13 (3): 405–23.

Guérin, Isabelle, Bert D'Espallier, and G. Venkatasubramanian. 2015. "The Social Regulation of Markets: Why Microcredit Fails to Promote Jobs in Rural South India." *Development and Change* 46 (6): 1277–1301.

Guérin, Isabelle, Vincent Guermond, Nithya Joseph, Nithya Natarajan, and G. Venkatasubramanian. 2021. "COVID-19 and the Unequalizing Infrastructures of Financial Inclusion in Tamil Nadu." *Development and Change* 52 (4): 927–51.

Guérin, Isabelle, Nithya Joseph, and G. Venkatasubramanian. 2021. "How Indian Financial Infrastructure Failed during the Pandemic." *The Wire*, June 23, 2021. https://m.thewire.in/byline/isabelle-guerin-nithya-joseph-and-g-venkatasubrama.

Guérin, Isabelle, and Santosh Kumar. 2017a. "Market, Freedom and the Illusions of Microcredit: Patronage, Caste, Class and Patriarchy in Rural South India." *Journal of Development Studies* 53 (5): 741–54.

———. 2017b. "Microcredit Self-Help Groups and Dalit Women: Overcoming or Essentializing Caste Difference?" In *Dalit Women: Vanguard of an Alternative Politics in India*, edited by S. Anandhi and Karin Kapadia, 158–86. New Delhi: Routledge India.

Guérin, Isabelle, Marc Labie, and Jean-Michel Servet, eds. 2015. *The Crises of Micro-credit*. London: Zed Books.

Guérin, Isabelle, Youna Lanos, Sébastien Michiels, Christophe Jalil Nordman, and Govindan Venkatasubramanian. 2017. "Insights on Demonetisation from Rural Tamil Nadu." *Economic and Political Weekly* 52 (52): 45.

Guérin, Isabelle, Solène Morvant-Roux, and Magdalena Villarreal, eds. 2013. *Microfinance, Debt and Over-Indebtedness: Juggling with Money*. London: Routledge.

Guérin, Isabelle, Arnaud Natal, Sébastien Michiels, Christophe Jalil Nordman, and G. Venkatasubramanian. 2022. "Surviving Debt and Survival Debt in Times of Lockdown." *Economic and Political Weekly* 57 (1): 41–49.

Guérin, Isabelle, Christophe Nordman, Sébastien Michiels, Elena Reboul, and G. Venkatasubramanian. 2020. "There Has Been No Silent Revolution: A Decade of Empowerment for Women in Rural Tamil Nadu." In *Advances in Gender Research: Critical Insight from Asia, Africa and Latin America*, edited by Marta Barbara Ochman and Araceli Ortega-Díaz, 183–200. Bingley, UK: Emerald.

Guérin, Isabelle, Magalie Saussey, and Monique Selim. 2015. "Indebtedness and Women's Material, Monetary, and Imaginary Debts in the Era of Globalized Gender." In *An Anthropological Economy of Debt*, edited by Bernard Hours and Pépita Ould-Ahmed, 161–80. London: Routledge.

Guérin, Isabelle, and G. Venkatasubramanian. 2022. "The Socio-Economy of Debt: Revisiting Debt Bondage in Times of Financialization." *Geoforum* 137 (December): 174–84.

Guérin, Isabelle, G. Venkatasubramanian, and Santosh Kumar. 2020. "Rethinking Saving: Indian Ceremonial Gifts as Relational and Reproductive Saving." *Journal of Cultural Economy* 13 (4): 387–401.

Guérin, Isabelle, G. Venkatasubramanian, and Sébastien Michiels. 2014. "Labour in Contemporary South India." In *Indian Capitalism in Development*, edited by Barbara Harriss-White and Judith Heyer, 118–35. London: Routledge.

Guérin, Isabelle, G. Venkatasubramanian, and Elena Reboul. 2023. "The Political and Moral Economies of Gold as Money in Rural Tamil Nadu." In *Gold in India: Commodity, Culture, and Economic Circuits*, edited by Anindita Chakrabarti and Barbara Harriss-White. Cambridge: Cambridge University Press.

Guilmoto, Christophe Z., Nandita Saikia, Vandana Tamrakar, and Jayanta Kumar Bora. 2018. "Excess Under-5 Female Mortality across India: A Spatial Analysis Using 2011 Census Data." *The Lancet Global Health* 6 (6): E650–58.

Guyer, Jane I. 2004. *Marginal Gains: Monetary Transactions in Atlantic Africa*. Chicago: University of Chicago Press.

Hamermesh, Daniel S., and Jeff E. Biddle. 1994. "Beauty and the Labor Market." *American Economic Review* 84 (5): 1174–94.

Han, Clara. 2012. *Life in Debt: Times of Care and Violence in Neoliberal Chile*. Berkeley: University of California Press.

Hann, Chris, and Don Kalb, eds. 2020. *Financialization: Relational Approaches*. New York: Berghahn.

Harcourt, Wendy. 2009. *Body Politics in Development: Critical Debates in Gender and Development*. London: Zed Books.

Hardiman, David. 2000. *Feeding the Baniya: Peasants and Usurers in Western India*. Oxford: Oxford University Press.

Harriss, John, J. Jeyaranjan, and K. Nagaraj. 2010. "Land, Labour and Caste Politics in Rural Tamil Nadu in the 20th Century: Iruvelpattu (1916–2008)." *Economic and Political Weekly*, 47–61.

———. 2012. "Rural Urbanism in Tamil Nadu. Notes on a 'Slater Village': Gangaikondan, 1916–2012." *Review of Agrarian Studies* 2 (2): 29–59.

Harriss-White, Barbara. 2003. *India Working: Essays on Society and Economy*. Cambridge: Cambridge University Press.

———. 2020. "The Modi Sarkar's Project for India's Informal Economy." *The Wire*, May 20, 2020. https://thewire.in/political-economy/the-modi-sarkars-project-for-indias-informal-economy.

Harriss-White, Barbara, and Diego Colatei. 2004. "Rural Credit and the Collateral Question." In *Rural India Facing the 21st Century: Essays on Long Term Change and Recent Development Policy*, edited by Barbara Harriss-White and S. Janakarajan, 252–83. London: Anthem Press.

Harriss-White, Barbara, and Nandini Gooptu. 2001. "Mapping India's World of Unorganized Labour." *Socialist Register* 37: 89–118.

Harriss-White, Barbara, and Judith Heyer, eds. 2014. *Indian Capitalism in Development*. London: Routledge.

Harriss-White, Barbara, and Lucia Michelutti. 2019. *The Wild East: Criminal Political Economies in South Asia*. London: UCL Press.

Hart, Keith, Jean-Louis Laville, and Antonio David Cattani, eds. 2010. *The Human Economy: A Citizen's Guide*. Cambridge, MA: Polity Press.

Hart, Keith, and Horacio Ortiz. 2014. "The Anthropology of Money and Finance: Between Ethnography and World History." *Annual Review of Anthropology* 43: 465–82.

Hayes, Lauren A. 2017. "The Hidden Labor of Repayment: Women, Credit, and Strategies of Microenterprise in Northern Honduras." *Economic Anthropology* 4 (1): 22–36.

Heyer, Judith. 1992. "The Role of Dowries and Daughters' Marriages in the Accumulation and Distribution of Capital in a South Indian Community." *Journal of International Development* 4 (4): 419–36.

———. 2012. "Labour Standards and Social Policy: A South Indian Case Study." *Global Labour Journal* 3 (1): 91–117.

———. 2015. "Dalit Women Becoming 'Housewives': Lessons from the Tiruppur Region, 1981–82 to 2008–09." In *Dalits in Neoliberal India: Mobility or Marginalisation*, edited by Clarinda Still, 228–55. New Delhi: Routledge India.

Hilger, Anne, and Christophe Nordman. 2020. "The Determinants of Trust: Evidence from Rural South India." IZA Discussion Paper No. 13150, Institute of Labor Economics, April 2020.

Hillenkamp, Isabelle, and Jean-Louis Laville, eds. 2013. *Socioéconomie et Démocratie: L'actualité de Karl Polanyi* [Socioeconomics and democracy: The current case of Karl Polanyi]. Paris: Erès.

Hirsch, Jennifer. 2003. *A Courtship after Marriage: Sexuality and Love in Mexican Transnational Families*. Berkeley: University of California Press.

Hirway, Indira, and Sunny Jose. 2011. "Understanding Women's Work Using Time-Use Statistics: The Case of India." *Feminist Economics* 17 (4): 67–92.

Hoang, Kimberly Kay. 2015. *Dealing in Desire: Asian Ascendancy, Western Decline, and the Hidden Currencies of Global Sex Work*. Berkeley: University of California Press.

Hochschild, Arlie R. 2012. *The Managed Heart: Commercialization of Human Feeling*. 3rd ed. Berkeley: University of California Press.

Hoodfar, Homa. 1997. *Between Marriage and the Market: Intimate Politics and Survival in Cairo*. Berkeley: University of California Press.

Hours, Bernard, and Pepita Ould Ahmed. 2015. *An Anthropological Economy of Debt*. London: Routledge.

Hummel, Agatha. 2013. "The Commercialization of Microcredits and Local Consumerism: Examples of Over-Indebtedness from Indigenous Mexico." In *Microfinance, Debt and Over-Indebtedness: Juggling with Money*, edited by Isabelle Guérin, Solène Morvant-Roux, and Magdalena Villarreal, 253–71. London: Routledge.

Hyman, Louis. 2011. *Debtor Nation: The History of America in Red Ink*. Princeton: Princeton University Press.

Illouz, Eva. 1998. *Consuming the Romantic Utopia: Love and the Cultural Contradictions of Capitalism*. Berkeley: University of California Press.

——. 2019. *The End of Love: A Sociology of Negative Relations*. New York: Oxford University Press.

ILO (International Labor Organization). 2020. "Global Wage Report 2020–2021: Wages and Minimum Wages in the Time of COVID-19." Geneva: International Labor Organization.

IMF (International Monetary Fund). 2019. "Global Financial Stability Report: Vulnerabilities in a Maturing Credit Cycle." Washington, DC: International Monetary Fund.

——. 2022. "Global Financial Stability Report." Washington, DC: International Monetary Fund.

India Ministry of Agriculture. 2020. "All India Report on Agriculture Census 2015–16." Accessed June 3, 2021. http://agcensus.nic.in/document/agcen1516/ac_1516_report_final-220221.pdf.

Jaffrelot, Christophe. 2021. *Modi's India: Hindu Nationalism and the Rise of Ethnic Democracy*. Princeton: Princeton University Press.

James, Deborah. 2015. *Money from Nothing: Indebtedness and Aspiration in South Africa*. Stanford: Stanford University Press.

——. 2017. "Deductions and Counter-Deductions in South Africa." *Journal of Ethnographic Theory* 7 (3): 281–304.

———. 2021. "Life and Debt: A View from the South." *Economy and Society* 50 (1): 36–56.

Jankowiak, William R., and Edward F. Fischer. 1992. "A Cross-Cultural Perspective on Romantic Love." *Ethnology* 31 (2): 149–55.

Jeffrey, Craig. 2010. *Timepass: Youth, Class, and the Politics of Waiting in India*. Stanford: Stanford University Press.

Jodhka, Surinder S. 2012. *Caste*. Oxford: Oxford University Press.

Jodhka, Surinder S., and James Manor, eds. 2017. *Caste in Contemporary India*. 2nd ed. London: Routledge India.

John, Mary E., and Janaki Nair, eds. 2000. *A Question of Silence: The Sexual Economies of Modern India*. London: Zed Books.

Jolly, Susie, Andrea Cornwall, and Kate Hawkins, eds. 2013. *Women, Sexuality and the Political Power of Pleasure*. London: Zed Books.

Joseph, Miranda. 2014. *Debt to Society: Accounting for Life under Capitalism*. Minneapolis: University of Minnesota Press.

Joseph, Nithya. 2013. "Mortgaging Used Saree-Skirts, Spear-Heading Resistance: Narratives from the Microfinance Repayment Standoff in Ramanagaram, India, 2008–2010." In *Microfinance, Debt and Over-Indebtedness: Juggling with Money*, edited by Isabelle Guérin, Solène Morvant-Roux, and Magdalena Villarreal, 272–94. London: Routledge.

———. 2015. "'And Our Ears Have Been Empty since Then'—Gold Ownership and Changing Work Vulnerability in the Informal Silk Reeling Economy of Post-Liberalisation South India." *IMTFI* (blog), August 10, 2015. https://blog.imtfi.uci.edu/2015/08/and-our-ears-have-been-empty-since-then.html.

Joseph, Nithya, G. Venkatasubramanian, Isabelle Guérin, Sébastien Michiels, Nithya Natarajan, Katherine Brickell and Vincent Guermond, 2022. "Shadow inclusion or financial citizenship? Microcredit in India during the Covid-19 pandemic." London: Royal Holloway, University of London.

Kabeer, Naila. 2016. "Gender Equality, Economic Growth, and Women's Agency: The 'Endless Variety' and 'Monotonous Similarity' of Patriarchal Constraints." *Feminist Economics* 22 (1): 295–321.

Kalaiyarasan, A., and M. Vijayabaskar. 2021. *The Dravidian Model: Interpreting the Political Economy of Tamil Nadu*. Cambridge: Cambridge University Press.

Kalb, Don. 2020. "Introduction: Transitions to What? On the Social Relations of Financialization in Anthropology and History." In *Financialization: Relational Approches*, edited by Chris Hann and Don Kalb, 1–42. New York: Berghahn.

Kamath, Rajalaxmi, and Nithya Joseph. 2023. "From Social Workers to Proxy-Creditors to Bank Tellers: Financialization in the Work of Microcredit Field Staff in a South Indian Town." In *Financializations of Development: Global Games and Local Experiments*, edited by Ève Chiapello, Anita Engels, and Eduardo Gonçalves Gresse. New York: Routledge.

Kāne, Pāṇḍuraṅga Vāmana. 2012. *History of Dharmaśāstra (Ancient and Mediæval Religious and Civil Law. Vol. III)*. Pune: Bhandarkar Oriental Research Institute.

Kapadia, Karin. 1996. *Siva and Her Sisters: Gender, Caste, and Class in Rural South India*. Delhi: Oxford University Press.

———. 2017. "Improper Politics: The Praxis of Subalterns in Chennai." In *Dalit Women: Vanguard of an Alternative Politics in India*, edited by Karin Kapadia and S. Anandhi, 305–34. New York: Routledge.

Kar, Sohini. 2018. *Financializing Poverty: Labor and Risk in Indian Microfinance*. Stanford: Stanford University Press.

Karim, Lamia. 2011. *Microfinance and Its Discontents: Women in Debt in Bangladesh*. Minneapolis: University of Minnesota Press.

Karlan, Dean, and Jonathan Zinman. 2008. "Lying about Borrowing." *Journal of the European Economic Association* 6 (2–3): 510–21.

Karunakaran, Kalpana. 2017. *Women, Microfinance and the State in Neo-Liberal India*. New Delhi: Routledge India.

Kumar, Sujeet. 2019. "India: Decades of Hostility against NGOs Have Worsened under Narendra Modi." *The Conversation*, May 1, 2019. http://theconversation .com/india-decades-of-hostility-against-ngos-have-worsened-under-narendra -modi-113300.

Kusimba, Sibel. 2018. "'It Is Easy for Women to Ask!': Gender and Digital Finance in Kenya." *Economic Anthropology* 5 (2): 247–60.

———. 2021. *Reimagining Money: Kenya in the Digital Finance Revolution*. Stanford: Stanford University Press.

Lainez, Nicolas. 2019. "Treading Water: Street Sex Workers Negotiating Frantic Presents and Speculative Futures in the Mekong Delta, Vietnam." *Time & Society* 28 (2): 804–27.

———. 2022. "Debt, Trafficking and Safe Migration: The Brokered Mobility of Vietnamese Sex Workers to Singapore." *Geoforum* 137 (December): 164–73.

Laslett, Barbara, and Johanna Brenner. 1989. "Gender and Social Reproduction: Historical Perspectives." *Annual Review of Sociology* 15 (1): 381–404.

Laville, Jean-Louis. 2016. *L'économie Sociale et Solidaire: Pratiques, Théories, Débats* [The social and solidarity economy: Practices, theories, and controversies]. Paris: Éditions Points.

Laville, Jean-Louis, and Antonio David Cattani, eds. 2006. *Dictionnaire de l'autre Économie* [Dictionary of the other economy]. Paris: Gallimard.

Lavinas, Lena. 2017. *The Takeover of Social Policy by Financialization: The Brazilian Paradox*. New York: Palgrave Macmillan.

———. 2020. "The Collateralization of Social Policy by Financial Markets in the Global South." In *The Routledge International Handbook of Financialization*, edited by Philip Mader, Daniel Mertens, and Natascha van der Zwan, 312–23. New York: Routledge.

Lazarus, Jeanne. 2020. "Financial Literacy Education: A Questionable Answer to the Financialization of Everyday Life." In *The Routledge International Handbook of Financialization*, edited by Philip Mader, Daniel Mertens, and Natascha van der Zwan, 390–99. New York: Routledge.

———. 2021. "L'argent des Femmes" [Women's money]. *Sensibilités* 9 (1): 60–71.

———. 2022. *Les Politiques de l'argent* [The politics of money]. Paris: Presses universitaires de France.

Lazzarato, Maurizio. 2012. *The Making of the Indebted Man: An Essay on the Neoliberal Condition*. Los Angeles: Semiotext(e).

LeBaron, Genevieve, and Adrienne Roberts. 2012. "Confining Social Insecurity: Neoliberalism and the Rise of the 21st Century Debtors' Prison." *Politics & Gender* 8 (1): 25–49.

Lemire, Beverly. 2011. "Budgeting for Everyday Life." *L'homme: Zeitschrift Für Feministische Geschichtswissenschaft* 22 (2): 11–27.

Lemire, Beverly, Gail Campbell, and Ruth Pearson, eds. 2001. *Women and Credit: Researching the Past, Refiguring the Future*. New York: Berg.

Lemoine, Benjamin, and Bruno Théret. 2017. "Les Assemblages de l'Etat de Finance. Hiérarchisation Des Dettes Publiques et Réversibilité Des Politiques Monétaires et Financières En France" [The assemblages of public debt: Reversibility of financial and monetary policies in France]. *Sociétés Politiques Comparées* 41: 171–214.

Le Play, Frédéric. 1855. *Les Ouvriers Européens: Etudes Sur Les Travaux, La Vie Domestique et Les Conditions Morales Des Ouvriers Européens* [European workers: Studies on the work, domestic life, and moral conditions of European workers]. Imprimerie Impériale.

Lerche, Jens. 2021. "The Farm Laws Struggle 2020–2021: Class-Caste Alliances and Bypassed Agrarian Transition in Neoliberal India." *The Journal of Peasant Studies* 48 (7): 1380–96.

Luzzi, Mariana, and Ariel Wilkis. 2018. "Financial Repertoires in the Making: Understanding the US Dollar's Popularization in Argentina." *Economic Sociology: The European Electronic Newsletter* 20 (1): 18–26.

Mader, Philip. 2015. *The Political Economy of Microfinance: Financializing Poverty*. Basingstoke: Palgrave Macmillan.

Mader, Philip. Daniel Mertens, and Natascha Van der Zwan. 2020. *The Routledge International Handbook of Financialization*. London: Routledge.

Mahmood, Saba. 2005. *Politics of Piety: The Islamic Revival and the Feminist Subject*. Princeton: Princeton University Press.

Malamoud, Charles. 1980. "Théologie de La Dette Dans Les Brāhamana" [Theology of debt in the Brāhamana]. *Purusartha*, no. 4, 39–62.

———. 1988. "Dette et Devoir Dans Le Vocabulaire Sanscrit et Dans La Pensée Brahmanique." [Debt and duty in Sanskrit vocabulary and Brahminical thought]. In *Lien de Vie, Noeud Mortel*, 187–205. Paris: Éditions EHESS.

Marius, Kamala. 2016. *Les Inégalités de Genre En Inde: Regard Au Prisme Des Études Postcoloniales* [Gender inequalities in India: A postcolonial perspective]. Paris: Karthala.

Maurer, Bill. 2006. "The Anthropology of Money." *Annual Review of Anthropology* 35: 15–36.

Mauss, Marcel. 1993a. "Essai Sur Le Don: Forme et Raison de l'échange Dans Les So-
cietés Archaiques (1923–24)" [The gift: Forms and functions of exchange in archaic
societies (1923–24)]. In *Sociologie et Anthropologie*, 143–279. Paris: Presses universitaires de France.

———. 1993b. "Les Techniques Du Corps" [Techniques of the bodies]. In *Sociologie
et Anthropologie*, edited by Marcel Mauss, 365–84. Paris: Presses universitaires de
France.

May, Martha. 1984. "The 'Good Managers': Married Working Class Women and
Family Budget Studies, 1895–1915." *Labor History* 25 (3): 351–72.

Mazzucato, Mariana. 2018. *The Value of Everything: Making and Taking in the Global
Economy*. New York: Public Affairs.

Mears, Ashley. 2014. "Aesthetic Labor for the Sociologies of Work, Gender, and
Beauty." *Sociology Compass* 8 (12): 1330–43.

Michelutti, Lucia, Ashraf Hoque, Nicolas Martin, David Picherit, Paul Rollier, Arild
E. Ruud, and Clarinda Still. 2018. *Mafia Raj: The Rule of Bosses in South Asia*. Stanford: Stanford University Press.

Mies, Maria. 1998. *Patriarchy and Accumulation on a World Scale: Women in the International Division of Labour*. London: Zed Books.

Mikuš, Marek, and Petra Rodrik. 2021. *Households and Financialization in Europe:
Mapping Variegated Patterns in Semi-Peripheries*. London: Routledge.

Mitra, Durba. 2020. *Indian Sex Life: Sexuality and the Colonial Origins of Modern
Social Thought*. Princeton: Princeton University Press.

Mohanty, Bibhuti B. 2005. "'We Are Like the Living Dead': Farmer Suicides in Maha-
rashtra, Western India." *Journal of Peasant Studies* 32 (2): 243–76.

Montgomerie, Johnna, and Daniela Tepe-Belfrage. 2017. "Caring for Debts: How the
Household Economy Exposes the Limits of Financialisation." *Critical Sociology* 43
(4–5): 653–68.

Morduch, Jonathan, and Rachel Schneider. 2017. *The Financial Diaries: How American Families Cope in a World of Uncertainty*. Princeton: Princeton University
Press.

Morgan, Mary S. 2011. "Seeking Parts, Looking for Wholes." In *Histories of Scientific
Observation*, edited by Lorraine Daston and Elizabeth Lunbeck, 303–25. Chicago:
University of Chicago Press.

Morvant-Roux, Solène. 2009. "Accès au Microcrédit et Continuité des Dy-
namiques d'endettement Au Mexique: Combiner Anthropologie Économique et
Économétrie" [Access to microcredit and continuity of debt dynamics in Mexico:
Combining economic anthropology with econometrics]. *Revue Tiers Monde*, no. 1,
109–30.

———. 2013. "International Migration and Over-Indebtedness in Rural Mexico." In
Microfinance, Debt and Over-Indebtedness: Juggling with Money, edited by Isa-
belle Guérin, Solène Morvant-Roux, and Magdalena Villarreal, 170–92. London:
Routledge.

Morvant-Roux, Solène, Isabelle Guérin, Marc Roesch, and Jean-Yves Moisseron. 2014. "Adding Value to Randomization with Qualitative Analysis: The Case of Microcredit in Rural Morocco." *World Development* 56: 302–12.

Morvant-Roux, Solène, and Marc Roesch. 2015. "The Social Credibility of Microcredit in Morocco after the Default Crisis." In *The Crises of Microcredit*, edited by Isabelle Guérin, Marc Labie, and Jean-Michel Servet, 113–30. London: Zed Books.

Mosse, David. 2020. "The Modernity of Caste and the Market Economy." *Modern Asian Studies* 54 (4): 1225–71.

Muldrew, Craig. 2001. "'Hard Food for Midas': Cash and Its Social Value in Early Modern England." *Past & Present*, no. 170, 78–120.

Nair, Tara S. 2005. "The Transforming World of Indian Microfinance." *Economic and Political Weekly*, 1695–98.

———. 2012. "Financing of Indian Microfinance: Evidence and Implications." *Economic and Political Weekly* 47 (25): 33–40.

———. 2020. "Precarious Livelihoods, Flourishing Finance, and the Delusion of Wellbeing: Women's Financialised Lives in Ahmedabad." In *Financialisation and Household Economies: An Interdisciplinary Inquiry in the Context of Select Indian States. Report of the Study Carried Out with ICSSR Project Grant under the Research Programme (2016–17)*, edited by Tara S. Nair. Ahmedabad: GIDR, 19–44.

Narayan, Kirin. 1993. "How Native Is a 'Native' Anthropologist?" *American Anthropologist* 95 (3): 671–86.

Narotzky, Susana. 1995. *Mujer, Mujeres, Género: Una Aproximación Crítica al Estudio de Las Mujeres En Las Ciencias Sociales* [Woman, women, gender: A critical approach to the study of women in the Social Sciences]. Madrid: Editorial CSIC-CSIC Press.

———. 2015. "The Payoff of Love and the Traffic of Favours: Social Capital, Reciprocity and the Collapse of Differentiated Value Realms in Flexible Capitalism." In *Flexible Capitalism: Exchange and Ambiguity at Work*, edited by Jens Kjaerulff, 268–310. Oxford: Berghahn.

Narotzky, Susana, and Niko Besnier. 2014. "Crisis, Value, and Hope: Rethinking the Economy: An Introduction to Supplement 9." *Current Anthropology* 55 (S9): S4–16.

Narring, Timothée. 2022a. "L'étreinte de La Dette: Une Ethnographie de l'endettement Des Milieux Populaires de Vitória, Au Sein et Au-Delà Des Favelas" [The grip of debt: An ethnography of indebtedness in working class Vitoria, within and beyond favelas]. PhD in Anthropology and Sociology, Université Paris Cité.

———. 2022b. "Les Fils Partent, Les Dettes Restent: Les Économies Morales de La Dette Dans Une Favela de Vitória (Espírito Santo, Brésil)" [Sons leave, debts remain: The moral economies of debt in a Favela of Vitória (Espírito Santo, Brazil)]. *Terrains & Travaux*, no. 2, 181–201.

Neiburg, Federico. 2006. "Inflation: Economists and Economic Cultures in Brazil and Argentina." *Comparative Studies in Society and History* 48 (3): 604–33.

Nelson, Julie A. 1993. "The Study of Choice or the Study of Provisioning? Gender and the Definition of Economics." In *Beyond Economic Man: Feminist Theory and*

Economics, edited by Marianne A. Ferber and Julie A. Nelson, 23–36. Chicago: University of Chicago Press.

Nietzsche, Friedrich. 2006. *On the Genealogy of Morals*. Translated by Carol Diethe. Edited by Keith Ansell-Pearson. Cambridge: Cambridge University Press.

Nordman, Christophe Jalil, Isabelle Guérin, Arnaud Natal, Sébastien Michiels, and Govindan Venkatasubramanian. 2019. "NEEMSIS Survey Report: A Full Statistical Picture of the Household and Individual Data." Pondicherry-Paris: French Institute of Pondicherry (IFP), Institut de Recherche pour le Développement (IRD).

———. 2022. "NEEMSIS Survey Report II: A Full Statistical Picture of the Household and Individual Data." Pondicherry-Paris: French Institute of Pondicherry (IFP), Institut de Recherche pour le Développement (IRD).

Nordman, Christophe Jalil, Isabelle Guérin, Govindan Venkatasubramanian, Sébastien Michiels, Youna Lanos, Santosh Kumar, Antony Raj, and Anne Hilger. 2017. "NEEMSIS Survey Manual (Technical Report). IRD, November." Pondicherry-Paris: French Institute of Pondicherry (IFP), Institut de Recherche pour le Développement (IRD).

NSSO (National Sample Survey Office). 2014. "Key Indicators of Debt and Investment in India for 2013." NSS 70th Round, NSS Key Indicators (70118.2). Ministry of Statistics and Program Implementation, Government of India.

Oakley, Ann. 2018. *The Sociology of Housework*. Chicago: Polity Press.

O'Connell Davidson, Julia. 2015. *Modern Slavery: The Margins of Freedom*. New York: Springer.

Oldenburg, Veena Talwar. 2002. *Dowry Murder: The Imperial Origins of a Cultural Crime*. New York: Oxford University Press.

Ossandón, José. 2017. "'My Story Has No Strings Attached': Credit Cards, Market Devices and a Stone Guest." In *Markets and the Arts of Attachment*, edited by Franck Cochoy, Joe Deville, and Liz McFall, 132–46. New York: Routledge.

Ossandón, José, Joe Deville, Jeanne Lazarus, and Mariana Luzzi. 2022. "Financial Oikonomization: The Financial Government and Administration of the Household." *Socio-Economic Review* 20 (3): 1473–1500.

Pairault, Thierry. 2004. "Femmes chinoises, patrimoine et cassette personnelle" [Chinese women, wealth, and personal funds]. *Outre-Terre* 6 (1): 289–98.

Palomera, Jaime. 2014a. "How Did Finance Capital Infiltrate the World of the Urban Poor? Homeownership and Social Fragmentation in a Spanish Neighborhood." *International Journal of Urban and Regional Research* 38 (1): 218–35.

———. 2014b. "Reciprocity, Commodification, and Poverty in the Era of Financialization." *Current Anthropology* 55 (S9): S105–15.

Pandian, M.S.S. 2012. "Being 'Hindu' and Being 'Secular': Tamil 'Secularism' and Caste Politics." *Economic and Political Weekly* 47 (31): 61–67.

Parry, Jonathan. 2012. "Suicide in a Central Indian Steel Town." *Contributions to Indian Sociology* 46 (1–2): 145–80.

———. 2014. "Sex, Bricks and Mortar: Constructing Class in a Central Indian Steel Town." *Modern Asian Studies* 48 (5): 1242–75.

Parvez, Fareen Z. 2020. "The Debt Economy in Urban India: From Bondage to Resistance in the Slums in Hyderabad." Weekly Seminar of the Institute for Advanced Studies, Social Sciences School, Princeton, NJ, March 2020.

Peebles, Gustav. 2010. "The Anthropology of Credit and Debt." *Annual Review of Anthropology* 39: 225–40.

———. 2014. "Rehabilitating the Hoard: The Social Dynamics of Unbanking in Africa and Beyond." *Africa* 84 (4): 595–613.

Perrin-Heredia, Ana. 2018. "La Gestion Du Budget: Un Pouvoir Paradoxal Pour Des Femmes de Classes Populaires" [Budget management: A paradoxical power for working class women]. In *Le Monde Privé Des Femmes: Genre et Habitat Dans La Société Française*, edited by Pascale Dietrich-Ragon, Catherine Bonvalet, and Anne Lambert, 193–212. Paris: INED Editions.

Perry, Donna. 2002. "Microcredit and Women Moneylenders: The Shifting Terrain of Credit in Rural Senegal." *Human Organization* 61 (1): 30–40.

Picherit, David. 2015. "When Microfinance Collapses: Development and Politics in Andhra Pradesh." In *The Crises of Microcredit*, edited by Isabelle Guérin, Marc Labie, and Jean-Michel Servet, 170–86. London: Zed Books.

———. 2018. "Rural Youth and Circulating Labour in South India: The Tortuous Paths towards Respect for Madigas." *Journal of Agrarian Change* 18 (1): 178–95.

Polanyi, Karl. 1977. *The Livelihood of Man*. New York: Academic Press.

———. 2001. *The Great Transformation: The Political and Economic Origins of Our Time*. Boston: Beacon Press.

Polzin, Christine. 2016. "Institutional Change in Informal Credit: Through the Urban–Rural Lens." In *Middle India and Urban-Rural Development: Four Decades of Change*, edited by Barbara Harriss-White, 229–50. New Delhi: Springer India.

Pouchepadass, Jacques. 1980. "L'endettement Paysan Dans Le Bihar-Colonial" [Peasant debt in colonial Bihar]. *Purusartha: Sciences Sociales En Asie Du Sud Paris* 4: 165–205.

Purewal, Navtej. 2018. "Sex Selective Abortion, Neoliberal Patriarchy and Structural Violence in India." *Feminist Review* 119 (1): 20–38.

Puri, Jyoti. 1999. *Women, Body, Desire in Post-Colonial India: Narratives of Gender and Sexuality*. London: Routledge.

Racine, Jean-Luc, and Josiane Racine. 1995. *Viramma, Une Vie de Paria: Le Rire Des Asservis* [Viramma: Life of an untouchable]. Paris: Plon.

Radhakrishnan, Smitha. 2022. *Making Women Pay: Microfinance in Urban India*. Durham: Duke University Press.

Ramberg, Lucinda. 2013. "Troubling Kinship: Sacred Marriage and Gender Configuration in South India." *American Ethnologist* 40 (4): 661–75.

Rangarajan, C. 2008. "Report of the Committee on Financial Inclusion." Mumbai: NABARD.

Rankin, Katherine N. 2002. "Social Capital, Microfinance, and the Politics of Development." *Feminist Economics* 8 (1): 1–24.

Rao, Nitya. 2012. "Male 'Providers' and Female 'Housewives': A Gendered Co-Performance in Rural North India." *Development and Change* 43 (5): 1025–48.

Ratnarajah, Nalini. 2020. "Feminisation of Micro Credit: 8th CADTM Asia Workshop 2020 in Colombo, Sri Lanka." *CADTM* (blog), February 20, 2020. http://www.cadtm.org/Feminisation-of-micro-credit.

Ravelli, Quentin. 2022. "Debt Struggles: How Financial Markets Gave Birth to a Working-Class Movement." *Socio-Economic Review*, 19 (2): 441–68.

Reboul, Elena. 2021. "Gender and Debt, Past and Present: Financing Social Reproduction." PhD in Economics, Université de Paris.

Reboul, Elena, Isabelle Guérin, and Christophe Jalil Nordman. 2021. "The Gender of Debt and Credit: Insights from Rural Tamil Nadu." *World Development* 142 (June): 105363.

Reboul, Elena, Isabelle Guérin, Antony Raj, and G. Venkatasubramanian. 2019. "Managing Economic Volatility: A Gender Perspective." Working Papers CEB 19-015, Universite Libre de Bruxelles.

Roberts, Adrienne. 2015. "Gender, Financial Deepening and the Production of Embodied Finance: Towards a Critical Feminist Analysis." *Global Society* 29 (1): 107–27.

Roberts, Adrienne, and Ghazal Zulfiqar. 2019. "Social Reproduction, Finance and the Gendered Dimensions of Pawnbroking." *Capital & Class* 43 (4): 581–97.

Roberts, Nathaniel. 2016. *To Be Cared For: The Power of Conversion and Foreignness of Belonging in an Indian Slum*. Oakland: University of California Press.

Roitman, Janet L. 2003. "Unsanctioned Wealth; or, The Productivity of Debt in Northern Cameroon." *Public Culture* 15 (2): 211–37.

Roy, Ananya. 2010. *Poverty Capital: Microfinance and the Making of Development*. New York: Routledge.

Rubin, Gayle. 1975. "The Traffic in Women." In *Toward an Anthropology of Women*, edited by Rayna R. Reiter, 157–210. New York: Monthly Review Press.

Rubin, Lillian. 1976. *Worlds of Pain: A Life in the Working-Class Family*. New York: Basic Books.

Sacks, Karen. 1979. *Sisters and Wives: The Past and Future of Sexual Equality*. Chicago: University of Illinois Press.

Sa-Dhan. 2010. "The Bharat Microfinance Report 2010." New Delhi: Sa-Dhan.

———. 2019. "The Bharat Microfinance Report 2019." New Delhi: Sa-Dhan.

———. 2020. "The Bharat Microfinance Report 2020." New Delhi: Sa-Dhan.

Saiag, Hadrien. 2020a. "Consumer Credit and Debt." In *Oxford Research Encyclopedia of Anthropology*. Oxford University Press, October 27, 2020; online ed. https://doi.org/10.1093/acrefore/9780190854584.013.227.

———. 2020b. "Financialization from the Margins: Notes on the Incorporation of Argentina's Subproletariat into Consumer Credit (2009–2015)." *Focaal: Journal of Global and Historical Anthropology* 87 (2020): 16–32.

Schijman, Emilia. 2019. *À Qui Appartient Le Droit? Ethnographier Une Économie de Pauvreté* [Who does the law belong to? Ethnographing an economy of poverty]. Paris: Maison des Sciences de l'Homme.

Schmitz, Amy J. 2014. "Females on the Fringe: Considering Gender in Payday Lending Policy." *Chicago-Kent Law Review* 89: 65–112.

Schuster, Caroline. 2015. *Social Collateral: Women and Microfinance in Paraguay's Smuggling Economy*. Stanford: Stanford University Press.

Schwecke, Sebastian. 2021. *Debt, Trust, and Reputation: Extra-Legal Finance in Northern India*. New Delhi: Cambridge University Press.

Scott, Joan Wallach. 1988. *Gender and the Politics of History*. New York: Columbia University Press.

Selim, Monique. 2021. "Médiations dans l'enquête anthropologique: Couples épistémologiques, alliés méthodologiques" [Mediations in anthropological investigation: Epistemological couples, methodological allies]. *Journal des anthropologues*, no. 166–167, 147–61.

Sen, Atreyee. 2007. *Shiv Sena Women: Violence and Communalism in a Bombay Slum*. Indianapolis: Indiana University Press.

Servet, Jean-Michel. 2007. "Le Principe de Réciprocité Chez Karl Polanyi: Contribution à Une Définition de l'économie Solidaire" [The reciprocity principle at Karl Polanyi: Contribution to a definition of solidarity economy]. *Revue Tiers Monde*, no. 2, 255–73.

———. 2012. *Les Monnaies Du Lien* [Monies and social bonds]. Lyon: Presses universitaires de Lyon.

Servet, Jean-Michel, and Hadrien Saiag. 2013. "Household Over-Indebtedness in Northern and Southern Countries: A Macro-Perspective." In *Microfinance, Debt and Over-Indebtedness: Juggling with Money*, edited by Isabelle Guérin, Solène Morvant-Roux, and Magdalena Villarreal, 44–65. London: Routledge.

Shah, Alpa, Jens Lerche, Richard Axelby, Delel Benbabaali, Brendan Donegan, Jayaseelan Raj, and Vikramaditya Thakur. 2018. *Ground Down by Growth: Tribe, Caste, Class, and Inequality in Twenty-First Century India*. London: Pluto Press.

Shah, Esha. 2012. "'A Life Wasted Making Dust': Affective Histories of Dearth, Death, Debt and Farmers' Suicides in India." *The Journal of Peasant Studies* 39 (5): 1159–79.

Shah, Svati P. 2014. *Street Corner Secrets*. Durham: Duke University Press.

Sharma, Miriam. 1978. *The Politics of Inequality: Competition and Control in an Indian Village*. Honolulu: University Press of Hawaii.

Shaw, James E. 2018. "Women, Credit and Dowry in Early Modern Italy." In *Women and Credit in Pre-Industrial Europe*, edited by Elise Dermineur, 173–202. Turnhout: Brepols.

Sheel, Ranjana. 1999. *The Political Economy of Dowry. Institutionalisation and Expansion in North-India*. New Delhi: Manohar.

Shipton, Parker MacDonald. 2007. *The Nature of Entrustment: Intimacy, Exchange, and the Sacred in Africa*. New Haven: Yale University Press.

———. 2010. *Credit between Cultures: Farmers, Financiers, and Misunderstanding in Africa*. New Haven: Yale University Press.

Sigaud, Lygia. 2008. "A Collective Ethnographer: Fieldwork Experience in the Brazilian Northeast." *Social Science Information* 47 (1): 71–97.

Skeggs, Beverley. 1997. *Formations of Class and Gender: Becoming Respectable*. Thousand Oaks: Sage.

Soederberg, Susanne. 2014. *Debtfare States and the Poverty Industry: Money, Discipline and the Surplus Population*. New York: Routledge.

Srinivas, Mysore Narasimhachar. 1984. *Some Reflections on Dowry*. New Delhi: Centre for Women's Development Studies.

Srinivasan, Sharada. 2005. "Daughters or Dowries? The Changing Nature of Dowry." *World Development* 33 (4): 593–615.

Srivastava, Sanjay. 2007. *Passionate Modernity: Sexuality, Class, and Consumption in India*. New Delhi: Routledge India.

Stack, Carol B. 1975. *All Our Kin: Strategies for Survival in a Black Community*. New York: Basic Books.

Still, Clarinda. 2015. *The Imperatives of Honour: Dalit Women and Patriarchy in South India*. New Delhi: Social Science Press.

Strathern, Marilyn. 1988. *The Gender of the Gift: Problems with Women and Problems with Society in Melanesia*. Berkeley: University of California Press.

Suarez, Maka. 2022. "'The Best Investment of Your Life': Mortgage Lending and Transnational Care among Ecuadorian Migrant Women in Barcelona." *Ethnos* 87 (1): 133–51.

Tabet, Paola. 1991. "I'm the Meat, I'm the Knife." *Feminist Issues* 11 (1): 3–21.

———. 2005. *La Grande Arnaque: Sexualité Des Femmes et Échange Économico-Sexuel* [The big scam: Women's sexuality and sexual-economic exchange]. Paris: Editions L'Harmattan.

———. 2012. "Through the Looking-Glass: Sexual-Economic Exchange." In *Chic, Chèque, Choc*, edited by Françoise Grange Omokaro and Fenneke Reysoo, 39–51. Geneva: Graduate Institute Publications.

Tebbutt, Melanie. 1983. *Making Ends Meet: Pawnbroking and Working-Class Credit*. New York: St. Martin's Press.

Théret, Bruno. 2009. "Monnaie et Dettes de Vie" [Money and life debts]. *L'Homme*, no. 190, 153–79.

Thorne, Deborah. 2010. "Extreme Financial Strain: Emergent Chores, Gender Inequality and Emotional Distress." *Journal of Family and Economic Issues* 31 (2): 185–97.

Thurston, Chloe N. 2018. *At the Boundaries of Homeownership: Credit, Discrimination, and the American State*. Cambridge: Cambridge University Press.

Tilly, Louise A., and Joan W. Scott. 1989. *Women, Work and Family*. London: Routledge.

Tronto, Joan C. 1993. *Moral Boundaries: A Political Argument for an Ethic of Care*. New York: Routledge.

Tseëlon, Efrat. 1995. *The Masque of Femininity: The Presentation of Woman in Everyday Life*. London: Sage.

Tsing, Anna Lowenhaupt. 2011. *Friction: An Ethnography of Global Connection*. Princeton: Princeton University Press.

Uberoi, Patricia. 1993. *Family, Kinship and Marriage in India*. New Delhi: Oxford University Press.

———. 1995. "Problems with Patriarchy: Conceptual Issues in Anthropology and Feminism." *Sociological Bulletin* 44 (2): 195–221.

UNCTAD (United Nations Conference on Trade and Development). 2019a. "Current Challenges to Developing Country Debt Sustainability." Geneva: United Nations.

———. 2019b. "Trade and Development Report 2019: Financing a Global Green New Deal." Geneva: United Nations.

Vanden Daelen, Christine. 2017. "Les Femmes d'Europe Face à l'austérité et à La Dette Publique" [European women faced with austerity and public debt]. *CADTM* (blog), February 2, 2017. http://www.cadtm.org/Les-femmes-d-Europe-face-a-l.

Verschuur, Christine. 2013. "Reproduction Sociale et *Care* comme Échange Économico-Affectif: L'articulation des Rapports Sociaux dans l'Économie Domestique et Globalisée" [Social reproduction and care as emotional-economic exchange: The articulation of power relations in the domestic and globalized economy]. In *Genre, Migrations et Globalisation de La Reproduction Sociale*, edited by Christine Vershuur and Christine Catarino, 23–36. Geneva: Graduate Institute Publications, L'Harmattan.

Vickery, Clair. 1977. "The Time-Poor: A New Look at Poverty." *Journal of Human Resources*, 27–48.

Vijayabaskar, M. 2015. "Youth Politics in TN: Evidence from a Youth Survey." Unpublished document.

———. 2017. "The Agrarian Question amidst Populist Welfare." *Economic and Political Weekly* 52 (46): 67–72.

Villarreal, Magdalena. 2004a. *Antropología de La Deuda: Crédito, Ahorro, Fiado y Prestado En Las Finanzas Cotidianas* [The anthropology of debt: Credit, savings, borrowings, and loans in the everyday finances]. Mexico: CIESAS, Porrúa y la Cámara de Diputados.

———. 2004b. "Striving to Make Capital Do 'Economic Things' for the Impoverished: On the Issue of Capitalization in Rural Microenterprises." In *Development Intervention: Actor and Activity Perspectives*, edited by T. Kontinen, 67–81. Helsinki: Center for Activity Theory and Developmental Work Research (CATDWR), Institute for Development Studies (IDS), and University of Helsinki.

———. 2014. "Regimes of Value in Mexican Household Financial Practices." *Current Anthropology* 55 (S9): S30–39.

Wacquant, Loïc J. D. 1995. "Pugs at Work: Bodily Capital and Bodily Labour among Professional Boxers." *Body & Society* 1 (1): 65–93.

Waring, Marylin. 1999. *Counting for Nothing: What Men Value and What Women Are Worth*. 2nd ed. Toronto: University of Toronto Press.

Wedagedara, Amali. 2020. "Life and Blood of Our Country, But We Only Have Debt!" *CADTM* (blog), March 5, 2020. http://www.cadtm.org/Life-and-Blood-of-our-country-but-we-only-have-debt.

Weiner, Annette B. 1976. *Women of Value, Men of Renown: New Perspectives in Trobriand Exchange*. Austin: University of Texas Press.

Wherry, Frederick F. 2016. "Relational Accounting: A Cultural Approach." *American Journal of Cultural Sociology* 4 (2): 131–56.

Wherry, Frederick F., Kristin S. Seefeldt, and Anthony S. Alvarez. 2019. *Credit Where It's Due: Rethinking Financial Citizenship*. New York: Russell Sage Foundation.

Wilkis, Ariel. 2018. *The Moral Power of Money. Morality and Economy in the Life of the Poor*. Stanford: Stanford University Press.

World Bank. 2022. "World Development Report 2022: Finance for an Equitable Recovery." Washington, DC: International Bank for Reconstruction and Development/ World Bank.

———. 2021. "Labor Force Participation Rate, Female (% of Female Population Ages 15+) (Modeled ILO Estimate)—India (1990–2021)." The World Bank Group. Accessed November 10, 2022. https://data.worldbank.org/indicator/SL.TLF.CACT. FE.ZS?locations=IN.

Xiang, Biao. 2005. "Gender, Dowry and the Migration System of Indian Information Technology Professionals." *Indian Journal of Gender Studies* 12 (2–3): 357–80.

Yanagisako, Sylvia Junko. 2003. *Producing Culture and Capital: Family Firms in Italy*. Princeton: Princeton University Press.

Yates, Frances A. 1999. *Selected Works*. Vol. III, *The Art of Memory*. New York: Routledge.

Zaloom, Caitlin. 2019. *Indebted: How Families Make College Work at Any Cost*. Princeton: Princeton University Press.

Zelizer, Viviana A. 1994. *The Social Meaning of Money*. New York: Basic Books.

———. 2005. *The Purchase of Intimacy*. Princeton: Princeton University Press.

———. 2013. *Economic Lives: How Culture Shapes the Economy*. Princeton: Princeton University Press.

Zinman, Jonathan. 2009. "Where Is the Missing Credit Card Debt? Clues and Implications." *Review of Income and Wealth* 55 (2): 249–65.

Index

CULTURE AND ECONOMIC LIFE

Global Borderlands: Fantasy, Violence, and Empire in Subic Bay, Philippines
Victoria Reyes
2019

The Costs of Connection: How Data Is Colonizing Human Life and Appropriating It for Capitalism
Nick Couldry and Ulises A. Mejias
2019

The Moral Power of Money: Morality and Economy in the Life of the Poor
Ariel Wilkis
2018

The Work of Art: Value in Creative Careers
Alison Gerber
2017

Behind the Laughs: Community and Inequality in Comedy
Michael P. Jeffries
2017

Freedom from Work: Embracing Financial Self-Help in the United States and Argentina
Daniel Fridman
2016

Printed in the USA
CPSIA information can be obtained
at www.ICGtesting.com
JSHW082046030823
45874JS00003B/4